Y0-CAS-965

The World's Children and Their Companion Animals

Developmental and Educational Significance of the Child/Pet Bond

Mary Renck Jalongo
Editor

A C E I

Association for Childhood Education International
17904 Georgia Ave., Ste. 215, Olney, MD 20832
800-423-3563 • www.acei.org

Cover Photo:
Novina Marie Maroney and Jon Paul Kraisinger,
with Buddy
Photographer:
Christina Maroney

Anne W. Bauer, ACEI Editor
Bruce Herzig, ACEI Editor
Deborah Jordan Kravitz, Production Editor

Copyright © 2004, Association for Childhood Education International
17904 Georgia Ave., Ste. 215, Olney, MD 20832

Library of Congress Cataloging-in-Publication Data
The world's children and their companion animals : developmental and
educational significance of the child/pet bond / Mary Renck Jalongo,
editor.
        p. cm.
Includes bibliographical references.
    ISBN 0-87173-162-2 (pbk.)
    1. Children and animals. I. Jalongo, Mary Renck.

    BF723.A45W67 2004
    155.4'18--dc22

                                                        2003020938

Table of Contents

Foreword

Stars in a Child's Universe

Michael J. Rosen

In the 15 seconds it takes to stroll past the previously empty room adjacent to ours at the little inn where we're vacationing, I overhear a man's highly animated voice: *"There he is, no, over here! Look, oops, oops, oops, here he is, right here! No, come look here. Oh there he went . . . no, wait, here he is! Lookathimlookathimlookathim—did you see him, Rena? No? Look here, not at me, over here. See? See him? No? Now he's gone. Say 'bye, Mr. Lizard, bye'—oh, wait, is that him? Is he back? Lookitlookitlook. . . ."*

I conclude two things: first, one of the island's pencil-size lizards has ventured into the room and is darting among this family's beach possessions, and second, we now have a toddler occupying the room next door.

Saint Bartholomew is a small rocky Caribbean island where most everyone is French or an American who took French with Mademoiselle Someone-or-another in junior high. The island offers two things: food and sun (seriously, there is almost no shade that isn't inside a restaurant). It also offers nothing for young children.

Half an hour later, as I finish breakfast, a young couple with a toddler (my new neighbors?) join me on the inn's otherwise vacant terrace. After we exchange groggy *"bonjours,"* I try to continue reading.

The parents discuss what their daughter can possibly eat from the *petit dejeuner* menu. Coffee? Hot chocolate? Croissants? Baguettes? The father orders in French, with the exception of asking if the kitchen has anything like "oatmeal"—a word whose translation escapes me as well. After several minutes and what appeared to have been a successful communication, a cereal bowl of hot milk is set before their daughter. While there's no shrieking, the fussing continues.

Rena says "wa-wa." She says "no." Repeatedly. She probably speaks a good deal more than this, but it's early and she hasn't had—*isn't going to have*—her oatmeal. Now she is chanting in perfect French, *"guava, guava, guava . . .,"* the other juice the server offered after *jus d'orange.* (Is there a word more suited to a toddler's powers of articulation?)

"What should we do today?" Mother redirects. "Swimming at the beach? How about that, Rena?"

"Doggie."

Mother replies: "Hmm . . . maybe we'll see a doggie at the beach, but maybe not, no—"

"Doggie," Rena repeats.

The father says, "No, honey, no doggies today. Maybe . . . pelicans—big birds to see?"

Rena repeats "doggie," as though she had come to this island for one thing and one thing only.

Finally the mother asks, "Is she thinking of that dog we saw when we checked in—at the office?"

The owner *does* have a yellow lab, I think to myself, who works the reception area where guests attempt to understand the French for "there's a $40 charge for losing a room key . . .," for "we're committed to conserving water, which means one beach towel should last you an entire week . . .," for how the honor bar works, the phones charges apply, the—it's a dizzying litany, even in English. And all the while, a dog basks on the cooler slate floor in the office doorway, conducting his own considerable business. (He hardly acknowledged *our* arrival. Being exuberant dog people we were miffed at first, but then pardoned the slight. It was hot, late, and we were only the umpteenth guest he'd welcomed this season.)

Rena's mother's voice rises again with excitement: "That big yellow dog from yesterday, honey? We'll see if he's downstairs later. At the office? Okay, maybe that nice lady brought him—"

"Zheeeno!" Rena squeals, as if demanding another kind of juice.

"Gee . . . ??" the father asks, hoping that she'll repeat a word (and thus a request he can fulfill).

Rena repeats the word again and again.

"What's a 'zheeno,' Rena?" the father asks.

"What about a bite of Mommy's yummy toast?" Mommy tears off a bit of croissant.

"Zheeenoooo!" Rena shrieks and pushes away the bread.

Finally, I can't pretend that I'm reading. "Gino," I whisper, leaning toward the parents, "is the name of the hotel's dog."

"You—you mean that lab? We didn't even meet—" the father breaks off his sentence and stares at his daughter as if just realizing he'd given birth to some prodigal Beastmaster.

"Did we even hear the dog's name?" the mother wonders. "Okay, honey, we'll see if Gino's here today. That nice Gino you saw. And then we'll swim at the beach and shop and have lunch at that place with the lobster tank. . . ."

⁂

Rena reminds me that animals are the stars under which we are born, the stars that shape and influence our lives, the stars we reach for. Yes, astrology may be one "sign" of all this, but here, on earth, the companion animals and the other creatures we encounter reawaken us to our own

place in the Animal Kingdom.

Children feel this natural kinship with animals, and it needs no guidance or urging. Whether it's their movements, peculiar physiognomies, unexpected actions, wide-eyed gazes, haplessness, beauty, or even scariness, animals preoccupy a child.

But let's take this idea further: children don't just identify with animals, don't just pretend to be animals with their play and in their dreams; children *are* animals. (Of course, adults are animals, too, but we obscure that fact with the camouflaging skills of rhetoric, deceit, bombast, bullying, and all the other deadly sins with which we burden our souls.) Children are still close to living in this world as animals; they negotiate our gerrymandering of Nature's own succession (what we call civilization or society) with the wariness, rashness, disorientation, abandon, and inquisitiveness of animals. (Some are wilder, some more domesticated, than others.)

But the primary, primal aspect is that children do not see the hierarchy or the dominion of humans in this Kingdom. Animals represent the seemingly infinite choices a child can imagine he or she might have been or might yet become, a wildness that stands at the border of the tame family circle.

⁂

Granted, the Animal Kingdom's vastness and variety is an unmistakable part of its mystery, but let's limit our focus to those companion animals or backyard creatures that are most accessible to children for our analysis:

Most animals are child-size, or at least closer to a child's stature than the luminaries of the adult world that tower over all that's out-of-reach.

They speak the same language, or at least they both utter their own, somewhat inscrutable sounds to order the muddled, bustling world into temporary comfort and satiety.

Animals fill their daily planners in much the same way young children do, with the id dictating the appointments: sleep, play, tussle with your siblings, chase that gleaming object, nap in the sun, whine, eat, drink, pee, and poop.

Indeed, both creatures share these innate desires, caring little for honor bars, exchange rates, dinner reservations, or replacement keys (unless they jingle). And at least around the households I know best, animals and children often yield to those same desires together, sharing the same bed for naps, the same food for snacks (the dog's having been dropped from the high chair or snitched from the unattended ice-cream cone), and the same ambiguously designated toys ("No, the squeaking, rubber hamburger is for the *puppy's* mouth, and you hold onto your little bunny pillow—she can't have that.").

And, perhaps most poignantly, both creatures are frequently unable to articulate their confusion or suffering, and this innocence confounds us in similar ways. We cannot assure animals or young children that some indefinite wait, disagreeable taste, or sudden pain will abate; that the doctor is *helping,* not hurting; or that the electrical cord and Grandpa's saw and hundreds of other things are all danger in one of its guises. Even as the children and companion animals in our lives mature and learn, our grown-up wisdom, our tendered words, are destined to fail them, often at the most unbearable moment.

I am always fascinated at the way children understand animals, which, oftentimes, means they do not; they give up trying and sense no further problem in this. This logic is no clearer to a child than why something dropped must fall instead of rise, why a raisin is really just a grape, or why you have to do things just *because*. ("Because," being the one law of nature we definitely understand.)

For 25 years, I have been sharing animal stories with children. Two particular books, *SPEAK! Children's Book Illustrators Brag About Their Dogs* and *Purr . . . Children's Book Illustrators Brag About Their Cats*, inspired a treasury of stories that I've collected. One popular book-related activity that teachers have used prior to my visiting their school is having the students compose letters from a pet's point of view. While I'm always honored to see hallways filled with drawings, snapshots, and letters, invariably I find myself saddened by many of the letters. (Not that I look for animals to pity! But our joys run in a pack, adding their common energy to other joys, while each sorrow lingers by itself. . . .) A typical "anthology" from the classroom will have snippets about adventures, silly tricks, little mishaps, yucky encounters, and so

forth—all the very winning, enthusiastic proofs of this devoted companionship—but so many letters allude to the sympathies more fully articulated in this 3rd-grader's letter from his dog:

> *Hi, my name is Dee Dee. The people that take care of me don't like to take care of me. They make me stay in the dog house all day. Do you know what I play with? A doll. A doll that's for a girl dog. I do not like the doll. I do not like to eat dog food. I do not like to lay in my dog house. I think I'm going to run away. Nobody will know where I'm at. If I ran away for a long time and came back they will love me. . . .*

For children who don't have a companion animal (and no one at Grandma's or the neighbors' to stand in), kids often choose a pet they'd *like* to have, writing letters from this imaginary companion. Oddly, whether the pretend speaker is a pony, lion, toucan, or boa constrictor, in these dreamed-up companionships, the subject of loneliness or neglect is never far from the surface. Here's a koala speaking:

> *I don't have anything to do while you are at school and everybody is gone from the house. What am I to do but eat and sleep. And another thing, you always have homework every day except Saturday and Sunday and then you are always gone on Saturday and Sunday. We never use our imagination like to go on adventures. When we watch TV I sit in your lap but you fall asleep on me. I want to do something together because if we don't then I am afraid I am going to leave and find another owner, please make up your mind and tell me that we can spend more time together. When you first got me you were so excited about me. You just would not put me down. You used to make . . . little sweetheart sweaters for me. But now you stopped doing all that stuff for me; it's like you put me out of your life. . . . Well even if you don't like me or love me I still love you, no matter what happens to us. Our friendship may go away but my love is still here for you at all times. It will never leave you at all.*

I have come to believe that what young children understand about animals is themselves, their own nature. Sure, kids insatiably devour cool trivia and curious details about cheetahs, dolphins, poisonous dart frogs, and any other creature they discover. From the companionship of their pets, however, I sense that children appreciate something more profound than just animal-care information and fun facts about their physiology.

Children have a superabundance of natural empathy, just as they do creativity. (What is it along the path of maturing—going from wild to tame?—that so often diminishes both?) And animals, who are *more* unknowing and *more* vulnerable than even children, almost universally elicit a child's greatest empathy. These letters, this ventriloquism, is the sound of a fledgling testing the water, of a neophyte sounding out the harsher ways of the world in an unself-conscious, unembarrassed manner. An animal's plight in this simpler, natural context offers words—or at least images—for a child's inarticulate feelings.

A child can watch how the adults of the world respond to a given animal—the kitten who's shredded the toilet paper roll again, the dog who jumps on everyone who comes to the door—and theorize about the generosity or patience or justice that awaits his or her own mischief or misjudgment. An animal can show a child where the limits seem to be.

But beyond serving as the child's emissary into the puzzling society of the house, neighborhood, school, and beyond, a pet is often a child's peer, bedfellow, counselor, den mate, ever-prepared teammate, conspirator, guardian, surrogate nightlight, sidekick. Even a stranger's pet, like Gino, or an "anonymous" lizard, has the capacity to captivate—*and free*—a child's attention and imagination. In the many contributions that follow, each scholar, teacher, and writer shares further insights into the richness and rapture that animals welcome into the increasingly complicated lives of children.

Michael J. Rosen is the author of numerous children's books including an award-winning collection of stories for older children, *The Heart Is Big Enough: Five Stories*, as well as editor of numerous books about the human/companion animal bond, including: *Dog People: What We Love About Our Dogs—Writers and Artists on Canine Companionship; Horse People: Writers and Artists on the Horses They Love; Speak! Children's Book Illustrators Brag About Their Dogs* (and a matching volume on cats, *Purr . . . Children's Book Illustrators Brag About Their Cats*); and *The Dog Department: James Thurber on Hounds, Scotties, and Talking Poodles.* Michael is involved in a wide array of charitable works. A frequent visitor in classrooms, he has used the royalties from various books to fund a granting program, The Company of Animals, that supports humane efforts throughout the county. He also has created children's books and cookbooks whose proceeds benefit Share Our Strength's efforts to end childhood hunger (www.strength.org).

8

Introduction

The Special Significance of Companion Animals in Children's Lives

—Catherine Peter
USA

Mary Renck Jalongo
with Marsha R. Robbins and Reade Paterno

A bulletin board in a suburban school displays drawings and writings that depict kindergartners' delight in their classroom pet, a rabbit that is trained to use a litter box and stay within the confines of the classroom.

A group of 3rd-graders marvel at the unusual pets of their E-pals, including a jellyfish owned by a girl from Japan and the two parrots of a boy from Costa Rica.

As part of their study of advertising, students at an urban high school design posters of homeless cats and dogs that will be on display in local businesses; they also create a calendar featuring photos of former shelter animals that will be used as a fundraiser.

In each of these school scenarios, companion animals have been the impetus for expanding children's knowledge, developing their skills, inspiring their creativity, fostering humane treatment of animals, and promoting prosocial behavior. This book is about all of these things. It is about the developmental and educational significance of the child/companion animal bond.

To begin, we allow a child to lead us. A 9-year-old boy named Reade Paterno will introduce the multi-dimensional topic of the child/companion bond, for it is stories like the one that follows that offer the most compelling argument for a more thoughtful and serious study of how the human animal's ties to nonhuman animals affect a child's life.

Getting Habibi
Reade Paterno, 3rd Grade
International School of Brussels

Dogs are my favorite animals. I wanted one so badly! One day I heard my Mom and Dad talking in the other room. I put my ear next to the door so I could hear them. I was able to hear just a little bit. I could hear some words—"buy" and "dog." I hoped that what I heard was true so much! So I opened the door and this is what they were whispering: "We will buy a dog from somebody." I ran in and asked, "Where are we getting the dog?"

My parents told me that the secretary from school had a dog that had just had babies. That night I wrote a letter to the secretary. The next morning I walked into the secretary's office and handed her the letter. She read it carefully and said, "I will think about it and call you to let you know."

That night I couldn't sleep. I tossed and turned, but could not sleep. I kept thinking about a new puppy. I finally fell asleep.

The next morning I woke up because I heard something ringing. I quickly picked up the telephone and said, "Hello," and asked who was calling. It was the school secretary and she said that I could have one of the new little puppies.

I had no clue how to choose a puppy, so the next day I went to the library and checked out a book on dogs. It was called: How To Choose Your Puppy. *Perfect! I read the book, but I still didn't have much of an idea how I was going to choose. I decided to let the secretary choose for me.*

When I went to her house to meet the puppies, the secretary came up the stairs from the basement with the cutest puppy in her hands. I ran up to get a closer look. It was so cute that I just wanted to hug it! I asked if it was a he or a she. "It's a she," said the secretary. Then I asked if I could hold the puppy. She said, "Yes." I picked up the little dog as gently as I could. She was so chubby that you could barely see her little puppy dog face. When we left my Mom paid for the dog, but we couldn't take her home yet because she was too young.

When I was in the car and we were driving home, I felt really sad. "Mom," I asked, "when do we get to bring her home?" My Mom answered, "We will get her in a couple of weeks."

I was really excited thinking about the day the little puppy would come to live with us. The second we got home I went straight outside and started building her kennel. As the days went by I got more and more anxious to see her again. Finally, when it was the night before she would come to live with us, I couldn't sleep at all. Maybe it was because my brother had his light on or maybe it was because I was about to get a new member of the family. I think it was because I was finally about to get my dog. At last, I fell asleep.

When I woke up the next morning, I put my clothes on quickly and went straight to breakfast. When I went to school I went straight to the school office to see the secretary. When I walked into the room, she had the puppy in her hands. I reached up for the puppy and the secretary whispered, "Be gentle. She's asleep."

As I walked out of the office with the puppy in my arms, I was practically running. As soon as I was outside the building, I took as many photos of her as the camera would let me. We decided to name her Habibi, which means "sweetheart" in Arabic.

As the days went by, Habibi and I made up a new game. It's called doggy football. If I get the touchdown without Habibi tackling me, I get a point. But if she holds onto the ball for 10 seconds, she wins. We still play this game to this very day.

As Reade's story illustrates, the bond between children and their companion animals shapes childhood, for Habibi clearly has made a place for herself in Reade's daily life and will be an important part of his childhood memories. The 3rd-grader's relationship with his companion animal also has educational significance, for he writes a letter to the secretary to get the puppy, chooses this story as his best piece of writing, and lavishes attention on the writing until it adequately captures his feelings. Habibi's story also spans several developmental domains as Reade conducts research at the library (cognitive), gets to know the secretary at his new school (social), thrills at the prospect of bringing the puppy home (emotional), photographs his new puppy (aesthetic), and plays games outdoors with her (physical).

Practical lessons are also evident in the story. Reade must wait before separating the puppy from her mother and must rein in his impulse to tightly hug a tiny, sleeping puppy. Additionally, most adults appreciated and understood the relationship between Reade and Habibi; thus, it is a basis for an intergenerational meeting of the minds. This single experience, captured and preserved by Reade's story, helps to illustrate why a book about the child/companion animal bond is well-suited for the Association for Childhood Education International, an organization dedicated to child development and education.

Rationale for the Book

My anecdotal impression is that, taken as a group, educators tend to be rather friendly toward companion animals. Even if we do not completely share a child's enthusiasm for an animal (such as the garter snake in a jar that one of my 1st-graders brought to school), we cannot, out of respect for children, dismiss their delight, wonderment, and attachments to animals—any more than we could trample on a child's treasured toy. And animals are much more than toys because they are alive and, as my nephew wisely observed when he was in 4th grade, "a living thing is just more important." So, even if we are not animal enthusiasts to begin with, those who spend their days in the company of children often become attached to companion animals, or at least learn to adjust to them. In fact, one could argue that such actions as providing a classroom pet for children, allowing a specially trained therapy animal to visit children in the hospital, and tolerating the inevitable inconveniences associated with a family pet are expressions of caring, not just for the animal but also for the child. As we support the child/companion animal bond, there are at least four reasons to more closely examine it from an educational perspective.

First, *for the majority of children and families, companion animals are an integral part of their lives.* Why should all contemporary educators— not only science teachers—be interested in the bonds that children form with companion animals?

Perhaps the most obvious reason is that companion animals play an increasingly significant role in the lives of many children and families. Companion animals are, by definition, a part of everyday life. Today, over 50 percent of Western households are home to at least one pet (Podberscek, Paul, & Serpell, 2000). Many contemporary children spend more time in the company of a companion animal than with any other living creature (Rud & Beck, 2000). Americans, according to one survey, spend nearly 95 percent of their time indoors (Goodall & Bekoff, 2002). When Tracy, a "latchkey" child, arrives at her family's New York City apartment, it is their two cats, Tiny and Tiger, who are always there to welcome her, who will curl up with her as she studies or works at the computer, and who contribute to her sense of home. When the family was involved in the September 11th tragedy, all of them considered their cats' survival to be a sign of hope that renewed their determination to rebuild their lives. Surely, anything that has such importance for children and families merits the attention of educators.

Another way in which animals are integral to the lives of children is that, more often than not, companion animals are part of the family (Cohen, 2002). Most parents and families do not need to be convinced of a pet's importance to a child; they

Photo courtesy of Darrell Combs

TJ and Hotshot the turtle.

intuitively grasp the significance of these relationships. One mother shared a story about her son, Jefferson, who was brain-injured at birth. Through a group called Canine Assistants, Jefferson was paired with Jett, a lab mix shelter dog who had recovered from the life-threatening parvovirus. From the very first meeting between dog and boy, they were affectionate toward one another. Jefferson's mother attributed this response to the fact that "each had a difficult time staying in the world, each through no fault of his own" (Bickerstaff, 1997, p. 58). In the weeks that followed, Jett was trained to be a service dog and became Jefferson's constant companion.

> *When Jefferson goes for physical therapy, Jett comes along and works with the other children. When they do their exercises, they get to shake hands with Jett or hug him as a reward. Sometimes, when their exercises are painful or difficult, he will lick their tears. . . . Jett's greatest contribution is the way he helps to remove the stigma of Jefferson's disability. People see that Jett loves Jefferson dearly. Other kids are more interested in Jett and the way he will shake hands or retrieve than they are in the fact that Jefferson is creeping on his hands and knees instead of walking. You would have to see Jett and Jefferson together at Boy Scouts to realize how this works.*
> *Every day Jett helps Jefferson cope with the loneliness of being different. (Bickerstaff, 1997, p. 60)*

While I was working on this project, I found that the mere mention of pets and therapy animals was enough to evoke stories—family stories about funny, brave, and loyal animals; contrasting examples of the way various animals are treated in other countries, cultures, or particular families; sad stories about the loss of a pet; horrifying stories about mistreatment of animals; and inspiring stories about remarkable animals. Because companion animals are so much a part of the family life fabric, they can connect the home with other social contexts, just as Jett became a bridge between Jefferson's home and schools, hospitals, the animal shelter, the Canine Assistants personnel, and the Boy Scouts.

Second, *companion animals are part of the construction of childhood and autobiographical memory.* Many of us would agree with Podberscek, Paul, and Serpell's (2000) assertion that "We are who we are as much because of our relationships with nonhuman animals as because of the human ones, and we do ourselves a great disservice—and probably great harm—by denying or ignoring this" (p. 2). Childhood is a period of life that is qualitatively different from that of adulthood, a time during which the adult's capacity to identify with the child is crucial. Pet keeping is often a pivotal point for this adult/child identification. If adults can identify with the child's longing for a pet, affection for a pet, or earnest desire to save one, it can build a bridge of intergenerational understanding.

Heather, an 8-year-old girl, owns a beagle/basset hound mix named Bud. This dog surely must be one of the most ungainly creatures on earth. He has the thick tail, big head, and long ears of a basset hound, with the skinny legs and small torso of a beagle. Bud could be used by the American Kennel Club as a disturbing example of what can go awry when breeds mix; he looks that bad. To Heather, however, that dog composed of mismatched parts is a canine marvel. Heather prefers Bud over any other dog, even the best in show at Westminster; Bud appears to be equally devoted to Heather, never leaving her side, watching her every move. We could be coldly logical about their relationship and argue that Bud sees Heather as the alpha wolf and pays such attention to her because he is on the alert for some food to be tossed his way. But his devotion is more than that. And we might think that if something should happen to Bud, we could comfort Heather with the prospect of getting another dog. But Heather would find little comfort in the hollow and often hurtful remark, "Don't worry, you can get another dog."

If we really identify with a child and plumb the depths of the child's attachment, we would set aside our adult notion of a pet's worth being contingent on its price tag or pedigrees. We would exclude physical attractiveness as a measure of a pet's value. We would never give away or mistreat a child's pet. And we certainly would never imply that pets are interchangeable and can be easily replaced. In retrospective studies in which adults were asked to recall their childhoods, bonds with companion animals frequently were a major theme in autobiographical memory (Wells & Hepper, 1997). Other species can leave indelible marks on children's minds. Anyone who cares about children should endeavor to make those enduring memories positive ones.

Third, *the child/companion animal bond can support children's development and motivate them to learn.* From the beginning of recorded history, in ancient Greece, Rome, and Egypt, children have been encouraged to nurture animals as a way of preparing them to be more caring in their interpersonal interactions as someone's child, sibling, peer, or parent. Grier's (1999) analysis suggests that casting children in the role of pet keeper was an invention of the Victorian era, a time when society was concerned with preventing cruelty and

violence. Pet keeping was regarded as way to counteract such tendencies, partly because it made children responsible for a dependent creature and partly because the animals themselves embodied positive characteristics, such as loyalty and affection. Historically speaking, long before animal-assisted therapy was popular, enlightened professionals from various fields who worked with children included animals in their practice. Maria Montessori, the Italian pioneer of early childhood education, created a curriculum near the turn into the 20th century in which the care of small animals figured prominently. Montessori explained her philosophy and innovative practices this way: "Education is acquired not by listening to words but by experiences" (Shute, 2002, p. 74). The vignette below helps to illustrate how companion animals can be part of that experience.

FUZZY and John
Marsha R. Robbins

John came into our classroom when he was 8 years old. Although he had a learning disability, John had been doing fine in a private school until he experienced a family tragedy. After the incident, John had "shut down" completely in his school performance. The small school had tried to be patient, but still John refused to speak, to pick up a pencil, or even to use the bathroom like a normal 8-year-old. Finally, in desperation, John's parents agreed to have him attend a class in the public school with teachers who were trained in special education.

John was small for his age, and completely overwhelmed by the other students in my class, who tended to be violent. By contrast, John just withdrew further when the fistfights erupted over the slightest issue. Although he was not involved in the violence, he did not engage in the learning activities, either. John was an observer.

I knew he understood what was being presented in the lessons, because he attended to what I was doing and would chuckle to himself whenever I made a joke. I also noticed how his gaze became riveted when the classroom hamsters were being handled. The solution was clear. John liked humor and he was fascinated by Fuzzy, a Russian dwarf hamster. Fuzzy was the smallest of the small, but he ran in his exercise wheel with the enthusiasm of a greyhound in the heat of a race.

I started out by holding the hamster and sitting next to John. I made silly jokes about Fuzzy pulling a wagon, or going to hamster obedience school to learn to do more than run in a wheel. Although John smiled and was fascinated by Fuzzy, he initially shook his head "no" when I asked if he would like to hold the little critter. Finally, one day when my humor really struck his funny bone, and there were quite a few students absent because of bad weather, he nodded and gently took the hamster in his hand. I could almost hear the conversation that he was having in his head while he was holding and gently stroking the two-inch rodent. John's eyes gentled and he tilted his head while his heart communicated with the little cuddler, using nary a word. The furry one relaxed and so did John. Finally, I had found the way to reach John—just let the hamster be the diplomatic mediator.

For several days I just let John hold the hamster whenever there were a few moments available. His face would light up when I made the offer. He would even get out of his seat to come across the room to get the hamster when the time for interaction arose. I could see that the more John handled

the hamster, the more he relaxed around me. Finally the day came when I could present an idea to my reticent student. If he could do a little work, then he could have a full 20 minutes to hold his furry little buddy, instead of the 3 or 4 minutes that we could steal from the daily routine. I made the offer and walked away. John still wasn't talking, but I knew he was considering my offer.

I went on to start the next lesson. We were doing our vocabulary words. The students copied them from the board into their journals, and then we went on to talk about the definitions of the words and use them in sentences to generalize the meanings and cement understanding. I listed the five words and had various students decode them as I added each to the list. When the last word was on the board and it was time for the children to write in their journals, GUESS who had a pencil in his hand? John wrote the words in his primary scrawl, and then silently walked to the front of the room to hand me his masterpiece. As I took it from him and praised his efforts, he turned and walked to the little blue and yellow cage, smiling broadly in anticipation of his 20-minute reward.

John went on to increase the amount of work that he completed to earn his time with Fuzzy, but he still never let his voice be heard at school. He smiled readily when I talked to him, and laughed quietly when I resorted to making funny remarks, but he would not utter a word. As the weeks went on, John's silence became a major obstacle to assessing his progress in reading. He also was a passive participant in each lesson, because his only response was a written one. I knew that John really liked and trusted me, but he still wouldn't talk.

Finally, a compelling argument to get John to talk presented itself. I had daily Communication Books that the students carried home to their parents to let them know what the homework was and what new things we were studying, as well as inform the parents about their child's participation in the day at school. John's mom included a short message in his Communication Book, saying that John had told her about the classroom hamster and she wanted to know where to get one for him. I grinned at John and said, "Would you like to take the hamster home to meet your family?"

I thought that my little John was going to jump out of his skin with excitement! His face broke into the smile of a lifetime as he nodded in agreement. "Okay!" I said. "Let's go call your mom and see what she says about it."

John literally bounced by my side as we walked to the phone in the teacher's room. I handed him the phone and asked him to dial. He never hesitated because we had practiced dialing their home phone numbers on a classroom phone. When I heard his mother answer I said, "Hey, John. Tell your mom what you want." He looked at me with huge eyes, shocked by the suggestion and flooded with indecision. I made sure my voice was loud enough for his mom to hear and then went on, "Hurry, or she will think it is a wrong number and hang up!"

It worked! He said, "Mom, Mrs. Robbins says I can bring Fuzzy home to show you what kind of hamster he is. Can I?" Those were the sweetest words ever spoken by that young man. I could hear the emotion in his mom's voice as we made plans for the hamster's ride to John's house. John walked happily back to the classroom with me and giggled as I chattered about the prospects of the evening's events at home, when his little buddy would meet his family. He didn't answer, but I knew the silence had been broken and that it was only a matter of time and patience until I would hear the boy's voice again. John was happy and proud because he had accomplished something that mattered to him. Fuzzy would hang out at John's house, and return to the classroom to reinforce John's progress. A rodent so small it fit into the palm of his hand gave John the safety and courage to speak. The important part was that Fuzzy also fit into his heart.

I met John's mom in the parking lot of a nearby grocery that day after school. She beamed as she took the cage from my hands. She thanked me for the miracle. She had no idea that it wasn't only me that enticed John to speak on the telephone that day at school. All of us—John, his mom, and his teacher— had a Fuzzy connection that built new lines of communication among us.

The bond between humans and nonhuman animals is a burgeoning area of study (Franklin & White, 2001). Contemporary writing for educators is replete with stories of practice in education and the allied professions that describe children's positive responses to animals, such as classroom pets (Rud & Beck, 2000), assistive therapy animals of school counselors (Burton, 1995), service dogs for children with special needs (Hart, Hart, & Bergin, 1987), dogs that visit in hospital and effectively reduce children's blood pressure and stress responses (Wells, 1998; Wilson & Turner, 1998), and more. From the early primers that taught letters of the alphabet using black ink drawings and phrases such as "c is for cat" to a Web site that enables children throughout the world to create virtual pets and environments at www.NeoPets.com, animals have long figured as motivational tools for children's learning. The need to develop compassion and prevent brutality is no less keenly felt today than it was during the Victorian era, and there is a growing body of research to suggest that cruelty to animals often is the precursor of violence against human beings (Raupp, 1999). Empirical support is growing for the commonly held view that the gentle care and nurture of animals in homes and classrooms can yield benefits for society, and that educators can play a special role in making companion animals available to children who might otherwise be deprived of such opportunities (Myers, 1998).

Fourth, *animals play a major role in the imagination, dreams, and hopes of childhood.* Whether children adore an animal or are terrified of it, the fact remains that animals are part of their fantasy lives.

Of course, not all of the imaginings about animals are pleasant. Two Venezuelan parents were expecting to be accepted into graduate programs in the United States. In an effort to build their 6- and 4-year-old daughters' English proficiency, their parents had been sharing picture books, written in English, with them. One of the stories was *The Three Bears.* When the parents received their acceptance letters from the university and told the two preschool daughters that they would be moving to the United States, both children burst into tears. After some discussion, it became apparent that the girls had formed the impression that the United States was plagued by bands of marauding bears that broke into people's houses and destroyed them!

Whether or not children's fears are well-founded, analysis suggests that animals predominate in the dreams of 3- to 7-year-old children (Foulkes, 1982). A survey conducted by naturalist Brenda Patterson (2000) found that children's dreams center on animals nearly 80 percent of the time, and adults' dreams still included animals; thus, human dreams originate from a place richly populated with other species. Furthermore, becoming an owner of a pet is a frequently mentioned wish among kindergartners (Chiu & Nevius, 1983). The specific animals that populate dreams tend to be those that are encountered in everyday life (Serpell, 2000). Jane Goodall (Goodall & Bekoff, 2002) reports that the overwhelming majority of children's responses to an activity that is part of her Roots & Shoots program include animals. The children write essays using the statement: "I have a dream that _____ and I am thankful for _____."

Animals feature prominently in the hopes and wishes of children (Chiu & Nevius, 1983). When children without pets were asked if they would like to own a companion animal, over 90 percent

"This is my cat They very pretty I like white cat better but white doesn't see well paper I color them But they still lovely and pretty"

Dreams of owning white cats by Ann Zhang.

said yes (Kidd & Kidd, 1985). Two drawings done by 8-year-old Ann Zhang, a Chinese student who moved to the United States, illustrate this yearning for a pet. She draws two white cats—not cats that she owns or would be permitted to own in her family's apartment, but pets that she dreams of owning. Because companion animals figure so prominently in children's imaginative lives, they are well represented in such forms of creative expression as children's art and writing (Hindley, 1999).

Twelve-year-old Burkely has grown up in a rural area and has been privileged to live in the company of animals throughout her life. Her fondness for the dogs, cats, and horses that populate her neighborhood are reflected in her activities, drawings, and writings. Using materials she found around the house, she designed a "Kitty Condo," a special play space for her cat, and an obstacle course at just the right level of challenge for her dachshund. Burkely's drawings and poems about horses clearly illustrate the reality of ownership as well as her imaginings; she labels each horse as "real" or "made-up."

For many of the world's children, pet keeping is inextricably linked with intense emotions that run the gamut, from the joy and pride of being a pet owner to the grief and loss when a pet is surrendered or dies. Everyday experience and observation would dictate that the young human animal's ties to other species often are major develop-

Real and made-up horses and poem by Burkely Twiest.

mental incidents, with lifelong implications. Companion animals should matter to educators, if for no other reason than that they matter so much to children.

Organization of the Book

Many fascinating questions about children and animals can be asked, including: How are children's bonds with companion animals similar to and different from those of adults? What does the way that a child treats companion animals reveal about that child as an individual, as a member of a family, as a member of a particular ethnic or cultural group, and about the dominant cultural context? Are interactions with companion animals during early childhood predictive of interactions with companion animals during later childhood or adulthood? Is there a connection between the way that children respond to animals and their relationships with other people? How might the human/companion animal bond affect children's development—physical, social, emotional, and cognitive? In this book, we address all these questions, and more.

The book is divided into three parts. In Part One, Children, Families, and Companion Animals, we begin in Chapter 1 with a discussion of the link between companion animals and child development written by the editor. Chapter 2, written by teacher educator Anne Creany, delves into gender differences in children's interactions with companion animals. Chapter 3 explores the companion animal in families, both those that are well-functioning and those that are violent and abusive. It is co-authored by the editor; Marjorie Stanek, a graduate student in sociology; and Beatrice A. Fennimore, a teacher educator.

Part Two, Companion Animals in Schools and Communities, branches out into the larger social and cultural contexts in which companion animals are found—schools, therapy situations, other cultures and countries, and in the drawings and writings of children from various parts of the world. It begins with Chapter 4, which offers practical advice about classroom pets and curriculum resources. The chapter is co-written by science educators Mark Twiest and Meghan Twiest, and by the editor. Chapter 5 focuses on animal-assisted

therapy. It is co-authored by the editor; Marsha Robbins, a special educator and animal-assisted therapy expert; Marjorie Stanek, a sociology graduate student; Nancy Patterson-Uhron, a nurse and equine-assisted therapy expert; and Dana M. Monroe, director of educational programs for autistic children. Chapter 6, written by teacher educator Jyotsna Pattnaik, examines companion animals from a multicultural and global perspective. The focus in Chapter 7 is on children's drawings and writings about their pets. It is written by literacy expert Trish Crawford and Moses Mutuku, a teacher educator who gathered children's drawings and writings from his homeland of Kenya, Chapter 7 examines how children portray their attachments with companion animals in story and illustration.

Part Three, Companion Animals in Print and in the Media, is offered as a helpful resource for educators and those in the allied professions dedicated to the care and education of children. It begins with Chapter 8, an examination of children's literature centered around several companion animal themes by children's services librarian Melissa Renck and the editor, with Jeffrey C. Brewster. Part Three concludes with a host of developmentally appropriate recommendations on computer software, Web sites, and online lesson plans by computer experts Susan W. Haugland and Elma A. Ruiz, with doctoral candidate Yi Gong (Chapter 9).

Conclusion

In many ways, writing this book about the bond between children and the animals they care for, and about, has been both a joy and a challenge. It has been a joy because, as authors, all of us are convinced of the topic's importance and because, throughout the project, it has been possible to identify more fully with children and appreciate their attachments to companion animals. Nevertheless, there were challenges associated with our project. Perhaps the most daunting, at times, was the interdisciplinary nature of the topic. Just type the words "children" AND "pets" OR "companion animals" as part of an online search and the list of articles that results will be culled from the fields of anthropology, nursing, sociology, education, psychology, science education, pediatric medicine, child development, special education, veterinary medicine, parenting, and many more. Furthermore, the research on companion animals is an emerging rather than a well-established field, and much of that research has not found its way into the educational literature. In many ways, the child/companion animal bond is, at least from a scholar's standpoint, backwards because the research has not yet "caught up" with insights acquired through direct observation of children interacting with companion animals in homes, schools, therapy programs, and other settings. In order to do justice to this important and timely topic, we had to weave together research findings from many fields; solicit the professional perspectives of practitioners in diverse settings; collect the comments, stories, and drawings of children from different countries; and review the available print and nonprint media focused on companion animals. Despite such obstacles, we were encouraged—in the original sense of that word, which means to be emboldened. This boldness was necessary because we are accustomed to having advanced degrees that specifically qualify us to write about a particular topic when no such credential for writing about the child/companion animal bond exists. Rather, it was the case that we taught ourselves what we needed to know in order to write authoritatively on a topic of significance to children and families as well as professionals.

The word "encourage," derived from the French, also means to take heart. In this sense of encouragement, children were the primary source. As authors, all of us had witnessed the transformative effect of companion animals on children in various contexts—in our professional practice, in our families and communities, and in our own lives as children. Our topic had powerful intuitive appeal. While dissertations and other major writing endeavors frequently elicit polite, puzzled stares from noneducators, this book on the child/companion animal bond seemed to instantly persuade others of its importance. Many people would mention a study that they had heard about through the mass media that affirmed the contributions of companion animals to human animals. Some would talk about their child's devotion to a pet, share a family snapshot, or volunteer their child to be interviewed. Others would reminisce about their childhood pets and the experiences, good and bad, that influenced their attitudes as adults.

As authors, we forged ahead, amazed by the depth and range of the responses that animals evoke from people and bolstered by the research from many different nations about interspecies connections. Finally, united by the belief that bonds with companion animals contribute immeasurably to children's development and education, we were able to assemble the materials and the chapters began to take shape. Through this process, *The World's Children and Their Companion Animals: Developmental and Educational Significance of the Child/Pet Bond* was transformed from an interesting idea into an ACEI book.

References

Bickerstaff, P. (1997). Jett. In E. Lufkin (Ed.), *Found dogs: Tales of strays who landed on their feet* (pp. 58-60). New York: Howell Book House/Simon & Schuster.

Burton, L. E. (1995). Using a dog in an elementary school counseling program. *Elementary School Guidance and Counseling, 29*(3), 236-240.

Chiu, J. P., & Nevius, J. R. (1983, January). *Wishes of white and Mexican American kindergarten children: An index of materialistic preferences.* Paper presented at the Annual Meeting of the Southwest Educational Research Association, Houston, TX.

Cohen, S. P. (2002). Can pets function as family members? *Western Journal of Nursing Research, 24*(6), 62.

Franklin, A., & White, R. (2001). Animals and modernity: Changing human-animal relations, 1949-98. *Journal of Sociology, 37*(3), 219-238.

Foulkes, D. (1982). *Children's dreams: Longitudinal studies.* New York: John Wiley & Sons.

Goodall, J., & Bekoff, M. (2002). *The ten trusts: What we must do to care for the animals we love.* New York: HarperCollins.

Grier, K. C. (1999). Childhood socialization and companion animals: United States, 1820-1870. *Society and Animals, 7*(2), 95-120.

Hart, L. A., Hart, B. L., & Bergin, B. (1987). Socializing effects of service dogs for people with disabilities. *Anthrozoos, 1*(1), 41-44 .

Hindley, M. P. (1999). Minding animals: The role of animals in children's mental development. In F. Dollins (Ed.), *Attitudes to animals: Views in animal welfare.* Cambridge, England: Cambridge University.

Kidd, A. H., & Kidd, R. M. (1985). Children's attitudes towards their pets. *Psychological Reports, 57,* 15-31.

Myers, O. E. (1998). *Children and animals.* Boulder, CO: Westview Press.

Patterson, B. (2000). *Build me an ark.* New York: Norton.

Podberscek, A. L., Paul, E. S., & Serpell, J. A. (Eds.). (2000). *Companion animals and us: Exploring the relationships between people and pets.* New York: Cambridge University Press.

Raupp, C. (1999). Treasuring, trashing, or terrorizing: Adult outcomes of childhood socialization about companion animals. *Society & Animals, 7*(2), 141-149.

Rud, A. G., & Beck, A. M. (2000). Kids and critters in class together. *Phi Delta Kappan, 82*(4), 313-315.

Serpell, J. A. (2000). Creatures of the unconscious: Companion animals as mediators. In A. L. Podberscek, E. S. Paul, & J. A. Serpell (Eds.), *Companion animals and us: Exploring the relationships between people and pets* (pp. 108-121). Cambridge, England: Cambridge University Press.

Shute, N. (2002, September). Madam Montessori. *Smithsonian, 33*(6), 70-74.

Vinal, W. G. (1930). Pets as the center of interest. *Childhood Education, 6*, 387-395.

Wells, M. J. (1998). The effects of pets on children's stress responses during medical procedures. *Dissertation Abstracts International, Section B: The Sciences and Engineering, 59*(6-B), 2689.

Wells, D. L., & Hepper, P. G. (1997). Pet ownership and adults' views on the use of animals. *Society & Animals, 5*(1), 45-63.

Wilson, C., & Turner, D. C. (Eds.). (1998). *Companion animals in human health.* Thousand Oaks, CA: Sage.

Chapter 1

Bonding With and Caring for Pets: Companion Animals and Child Development

Amy's dog scratching.

—*Amy Haigh*
England

Mary Renck Jalongo with
Mimi Brodsky Chenfeld and Marsha R. Robbins

In World War II during the bombings of London, children were evacuated from the city for their personal safety. Perhaps you have seen heart-rending documentary film footage of these children and their parents. One less well-known aspect of this tragic situation, which makes it all the more poignant, is that the children had to abandon their pets, leaving the animals behind to be, in most cases, euthanized. In *No Time To Wave Goodbye* (Wicks, 1988), Joan Chapman recalled that she was in anguish over the fate of her three pets:

> *Smut the cat, Joey the canary and a large tortoise we had had for 16 years . . . what were we to do with them? There was only one thing left and that was to have them put to sleep.*
>
> *I bravely put Smut into a box, the tortoise into a bag on my back and the cage in the other hand. I walked along the Hastings seafront to a vet's. I can tell you how much I hated Hitler.*
>
> *Putting my sad cargo down to have a rest and have a cry, I was aware of a soldier staring at me. He asked me what was wrong and when I told him he offered to help.*
>
> *Only the tortoise never did get to the vet's—instead we put him into the local park flower beds. But sadly we joined a long queue at the vet's. People were all forced to do the same. Sorrowfully we walked back empty-handed. (pp. 72-73)*

Children like Joan who were sent away to live with other families suffered such negative developmental consequences that, in hindsight, many Londoners wondered if it would not have been better to take the risk and stay together. We will never know how much the abrupt break in the child/companion animal bond may have contributed to the distress, depression, and developmental regression that were manifested in many of these children. But it is not difficult to imagine that a child's powerlessness to protect a beloved animal and being forced to take a helpless creature to its death must have affected many children deeply.

These devastating circumstances, precipitated by war, raise the most fundamental developmental questions. For example, would these children seek a companion animal replacement at the earliest opportunity? Might their adult lives be characterized by a particular devotion to family pets, warm encouragement of their children's requests to become pet keepers, and a commitment to protecting animal rights? Or, conversely, might some of these children harden their hearts and treat animals as disposable? The answers, no doubt, depend on many things, including: the strength of the bond the child had formed with the animal, the child's capacity for understanding the events, the strategies the individual child used to cope with the loss, the child's individual life and circumstances at that precise moment, and the amount and kind of support they received. Furthermore, the complex interaction of such variables would affect adult outcomes. In many ways, this single incident encapsulates the most important questions raised about developmental events during childhood: What was the effect? Will any of the benefits endure? Can any of the damage be reversed?

The chapter begins with a review of the literature on the child/companion animal bond and developmental sequence. The developmental area that has received the most attention in studies is social/emotional development, and so the third section reviews that research, including a special section on loss. The chapter concludes with recommendations for educators.

Research on the Developmental Significance of Companion Animals

Relationships between children and companion animals have a long history (Bodson, 2000; Colt, 1994; Menache, 2000); they create memories and bonds that endure throughout life (Beck, 1993) and reflect a complex closeness that, when assessed, often rivals the relationships with human beings (Cohen, 2002; Eckstein, 2000; Rud & Beck, 2000). Many fascinating questions about the human/companion animal bond can be asked, including: What is unique about the relationships that people have with their pets? What does pet keeping tell us about ourselves and our cultures? How might the ways that we interact with nonhuman animals be related to or predictive of interactions with people? How might the human/companion animal bond affect our physical and psychological well-being? (Podberscek, Paul, & Serpell, 2000). Pursuing answers to such questions requires a true interdisciplinary and international approach.

Today, adults take devotion to family pets for granted and assume that such relationships always existed; however, the notion of pet keeping as moral training for children only emerged between 1820 and 1870 in middle class America (Grier, 1999). In a popular painting of the era, called "The Choice," a mother holds several kittens on her lap and the children must decide which one is to live and which are to be drowned. Boys were

Photo courtesy of Shireen DeSouza

Tarun with his pet dachshund.

considered by Victorian-era adults to be developmentally prone to brutality and violence. Out of a concern for preventing cruelty in society, animals became a source for children's socialization.

Of course, the mere presence of a pet is not sufficient to yield a strong bond between a child and a companion animal. Children need instruction in appropriate ways to care for animals in the home (Olson, 1997). Four dimensions appear to influence the strength of the attachments formed between children and their pets: 1) interest in and affect toward the pet, 2) knowledge about the pet and its care, 3) time invested in and the particular activities directed toward the pet, and 4) behavioral responsiveness to the pet and its needs (Melson, 1990). Measures for evaluating and determining the strength of the bond exist for each of these dimensions, which Melson (1990) evaluates, based on reliability and validity issues, in her review.

Based on a series of studies conducted in France, family dogs respond differently to the scent of their child companions. In one study, 100 family dogs were presented with three different dolls—one dressed in the companion child's clothing, one dressed in another child's clothing, and another dressed in new, unworn clothing—and filmed for 5 minutes; the dogs sniffed the companion child's clothing longer and in different ways, leading the researchers to conclude that dogs use olfaction to interpret human behavior (Filiatre, Eckerlin, Millot, & Montagner, 1990). In a related study of 2- to 5-year-old children's spontaneous interactions with the family dog in the home environment, the researchers found that young children approached the family dog and initiated interaction with it twice as often as the dogs initiated contact with the child (Millot, Filiatre, Gagnon, & Eckerlin, 1988). In further studies, it was found that the age of the child is the strongest influence on the manner of child-dog interaction, that children use touch as the primary means of interacting, that 43 percent of children's behaviors are followed by observable changes in the dog's behavior, and that the child's behavior directs the olfactory behavior of the dog (Filiatre, Millot, Montagner, Eckerlin, & Gagnon, 1988).

How does developmental level affect children's responses to pets? A toddler, for example, may barely seem to notice the loss of a pet while a school-age child can be devastated by such a loss. In a British study of 374 children ranging in age from 8 to 15 years, children's descriptions of their pets changed with age (Morrow, 1998). The apparent strength of that relationship for older children led Morrow (1998) to conclude that, when considered from the child's perspective, pet care has a meaning far beyond that of rehearsal for adult activities; relationships with companion animals have value in their own right. There is one point on which several child development experts agree: being forced to give up an animal is a developmental event of major proportions (Melson, 2001; Raupp, 1999).

Melson (1998) reviewed the research on companion

Photos courtesy of David and Susan Miloser

Kimberly with beagle puppy; Amanda with rabbit and kitten.

animals in children's development using a theoretical framework that incorporated Erikson's developmental challenges (trust, autonomy, industry, identity) at the four levels of Bronfenbrenner's ecological model (microsystem, mesosystem, exosystem, and macrosystem). She concluded that the child/companion animal bond merits further study as a major developmental force. Figure 1.1 includes a general developmental sequence for these bonds and gives an example of each.

Pet Keeping and Children's Socioemotional Development

Socioemotional development has been the main focus of programs that bring children and companion animals together. Special educator Marsha Robbins describes the effect that taking responsibility for caring for baby rabbits had on children in her classroom.

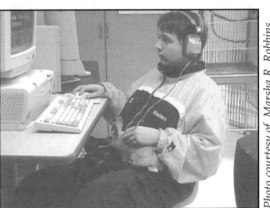

Zach and classroom rabbit named Flower.

Photo courtesy of Marsha R. Robbins

Rescue Rabbits
Marsha R. Robbins

Recently, our class received an emergency message from the director of the local animal shelter. They had so many rabbits that they couldn't house them all. Euthanasia would be the only solution—to be done that very day, in fact—if foster homes could not be found for the little bunnies. Panic filled our hearts. We asked the principal if we could foster a few of the rabbits in our classroom. With her approval, three of the six-week-old rabbits joined the three resident rabbits in our special education classroom. The children were charmed by the tiny creatures. They were experienced rabbit handlers because our classroom had been home to three mature rabbits since the beginning of the school year. The children were fascinated by the babies who could nestle into the palms of their hands, and they calmed themselves when handling the delicate babies. The charge to the students was that they could gentle the babies on their own time. We were to provide a service to the shelter. We would keep the bunnies alive and nurture their pet potential until they could be placed in a permanent home. In the meantime, we would teach the bunnies to use a litter box, walk on a leash, and be gentle when handled.

Within a week, the change in our classroom was amazing. The rabbits came to the front of the cage whenever a person approached. They knew how to use their litter box, and they would actually fall asleep in the students' laps. But the changes the teachers observed weren't only in the bunnies' behavior. There are children in our class who have a very hard time sitting still and attending to lessons. They have poor impulse control and interrupt lessons by tapping, squeaking the tables, or drawing on the furniture. Sometimes they find it difficult to still long enough to make it through a complete lesson, and so a behavior support plan is necessary.

One day I forgot to tell the students to put the bunnies back in their cages before I started teaching. I was going about the lesson when I realized that my students with ADHD were paying attention, not making a sound. As I looked to see if they were awake, I realized that they were cuddling the baby bunnies. They were totally focused on the lesson, just receiving the tactile input that they craved by absentmindedly stroking the bunnies as they listened. They could answer every question about the content of the lesson, and required no redirection. What a wonderful discovery!

It is now standard procedure in my classroom that when the children in my class start to get restless and find it hard to focus, they quietly get up and go get a baby bunny to hold. After they do, the students are back into the lesson in a heartbeat.

Baby rabbits are the most effective behavior intervention we have found in our work with the children in our class who have attentional difficulties. As soon as the bunnies find homes, we bring new baby ones to school and begin the training process all over again. The teachers like to refer to our classroom companion animals as "rescue rabbits," but I sometimes wonder who is rescuing whom!

Children's Responses
to Companion Animals

Care and responsibility for pets first must be demonstrated by the adults. From a developmental perspective, it is necessary for a child to grasp the nature of animal dependency in order to fulfill the role of caretaker. This ability to identify with an animal is what enables a child to accept responsibility for a companion animal.

Infants

Melanie, an 11-month-old, had learned to rocket around the house in a walker. While visiting her parents' friends who owned a mixed-breed border collie, Melanie rolled over the dog's paw, blocked it into the corner of the family room, and pulled a fistful of hair out of the dog's ear. Even with four adults sitting there, the incident happened so quickly that it was impossible to prevent. The dog yelped pitifully but, fortunately, it did not bite.

Inquisitive babies like Melanie who are mobile and exploring their environment are often a bad mix with animals. Even the friendliest, most well-trained, and laid-back animals may protect themselves from babies who want to grab tails, stick their fingers in eyes or noses, or grasp at fur. Animals need a "safe" area where they can get away from children who are so inclined. If an animal does retaliate, a young child may remain frightened of that animal for a lifetime. It is much better to wait until the child can be taught to treat the animal gently. Naturally, that will depend on the child's sensitivity, as well as on opportunities for closely supervised interactions with animals.

Toddlers

Kirstie the dog had caused 2-year-old Katie to cry on two separate occasions, both involving food. The first incident occurred when Katie was eating sticky candy and allowed the dog to lick her open hands. Unfortunately, the dog just kept going and ate the candy. The second incident occurred when Katie left an open box of cheese crackers out on the porch and returned to find Kirstie with her head inside the box.

Toddlers tend to expect animals to abide by the rules that are imposed upon them. Therefore, if grabbing food away is inappropriate behavior for them, they view an animal that does this as "bad." Part of preparing children as animal keepers is teaching them some basic expectations for animal behaviors.

Preschoolers

Jared, a preschooler who is usually quite animated, sits motionless on a playground swing, head down and shoulders slumped. When a frequent visitor to the child care center inquires about what happened, the teacher confides that the boy "stomped a cat." It seems that Jared was at a friend's house and began interacting with a cat in the same rough-and-tumble way that he used when playing with his large dog. When the friend's kitten began to sink its claws into Jared's leg and tried to bite, Jared panicked and could not shake the kitten off. He then jumped on the tiny kitten with his boots. The cat did not survive.

This traumatic situation was the unfortunate outcome of failing to orient Jared to feline behavior. The boy had no previous experience with cats and was frightened. Preschoolers need to learn how to adjust their style of interaction to the different companion animals they encounter. It cannot be assumed that young children know how to do this without adult coaching and supervision. Most preschoolers begin to understand that there are many things pets cannot do things for themselves, such as getting a drink. With experience, guided practice, and compassionate adult modeling of companion animals' care, most preschoolers start to appreciate that animals are dependent on people.

Figure 1.1

School-age Children

Ever since he first saw a potbellied pig on cable television's Animal Planet channel, 8-year-old Evan has been launching a major campaign to persuade his parents to allow him to get one. He scans the Internet, sends his beleaguered parents E-mails, and designs posters to post on the refrigerator door. Evan's efforts have gotten so intense that his exasperated mother has tried to convince her son to choose a different animal, while his father said the mere mention of the "p" word would make the "no" absolutely final! Evan's parents have given many reasons for their reluctance, but Evan seems to have a counterargument for each one.

As children enter the school years, their powers of persuasion increase due to their enhanced abilities in perspective taking and ability to generate logical counterarguments; interestingly, convincing a parent to buy a pet is often the task used to assess children's abilities to present persuasive arguments (Bartsch & London, 2000). The school years typically are the time when most children are considered to be sufficiently mature to identify with an animal's needs and accept some responsibility for its care. Usually, children can begin with some simple duties, such as pet grooming or filling the water bowl. Gradually, children can take on added responsibility for pet care, and can feed, walk, train, and clean up after pets. School-age children are also capable of striving to identify more closely with a particular animal (e.g., striving to understand underlying motives for behavior). Developmentally speaking, most school-age children give knowing looks and make comments that show they know something not only about the species but also about the individual characteristics of particular animals.

Early Adolescence

It is 8 a.m. on Saturday at a no-kill animal shelter when a teacher arrives with her middle school students and volunteers. The students have accepted a wide array of responsibilities at the shelter, including: recording an animal's history, bathing animals, cleaning cages, feeding and watering animals, updating information on the shelter's Web site, taking animals out of their cages for exercise or to meet potential adopters, and writing the success stories of pets with new homes. It is obvious from the students' demeanor that they are taking their jobs seriously and are proud of what they are achieving on behalf of these animals and the community.

Students who appear to be rather disinterested in academic pursuits will sometimes warm to the idea of doing something to help animals and put their skills to use for that goal. Many older children can assume an expanded range of duties for pets, including assisting during veterinary visits or pursuing advanced training options, such as dog obedience or agility training or horseback riding competition. Still, it cannot be assumed that all children of this age will treat animals with respect, so it is important to screen peers who will come into contact with companion animals, since deliberate cruelty toward animals is sometimes manifested at this age. Older children are also ready to deal with profound questions about why the same animal is revered in one society and considered to be a food source in another. Young adolescents also are ready to deal with social issues affecting human and nonhuman animals. Many cities, for instance, have ordinances against keeping farm animals. If a woman has two pet chickens that she loves dearly, is it a violation of her rights to force her to give them away? Other issues include: What should be done about feral dogs and cats? Is it cruel to selectively breed animals based on physical characteristics only? What about "puppy mills" and overbreeding to the extent that a popular breed begins to have genetic defects? What role should animal temperament play in deciding the worth of a companion animal? And so forth.

Figure 1.1
continued

Marsha Robbins' classroom experience illustrates how children's socioemotional growth can be affected by bonds with companion animals. An article published in the *Times Educational Supplement* (Spencer, 2000) reported that cats and dogs can be as important to children as parents or teachers. In a study of 5- to 13-year-old children's drawings, Kidd and Kidd (1995) hypothesized that physical proximity—the distances placed between the child, the pet, and other family members—could function as a measure of emotional distance, an idea that is generally accepted in psychological interpretations of children's art. Overall, children drew pets closer to themselves than family members, although, for younger children, the distance depicted between self and pets in drawings tended to be greater and a family member was placed between the self and pet more often. Older children tended to draw themselves in direct contact with companion animals (e.g., holding a kitten). The type of pet also had an influence on proximity to self in children's drawings, with cats, dogs, caged animals, and farm animals portrayed as closer to themselves than a fish, for example.

Apparently, the company of animals is a way for people to be alone without experiencing profound loneliness (Beck, 1999). Companion animals often function as sources of security. For 4- to 12-year-old latchkey children who were home alone and called a helpline (due to boredom), interviews with 90 self-care children revealed that, for all respondents, watching television was the most common activity while, for the children with pets, interacting with companion animals was the second most frequent coping strategy (Guerney, 1991). A study of preadolescent psychosocial development in 130 third- to sixth-graders led Van Houtte and Jarvis (1995) to conclude that the opportunity to own and care for animals had a particularly powerful influence on this age group and that it affected autonomy and self-esteem. In a study of 126 fifth-graders, children who were highly bonded to dogs had higher scores on self-esteem and empathy than children without pets (Bierer, 2001).

At the opposite end of the spectrum, a growing body of research suggests that a common behavior associated with children who have attachment disorder (ATD) is cruelty to pets and torture of small animals (Solot, 1997). In fact, this association between relationships with pets and people is so strong that animal cruelty is considered by many in the psychological community to be predictive of later violence toward human beings (Flynn, 2000) and, conversely, empathy for pets is associated with empathy for other children (Poresky, 1990). In a longitudinal study conducted in Scotland, twenty-seven 8- to 12-year-olds were evaluated when they had owned dogs for 1, 6, and 12 months. The researchers concluded that when dog-owning children were compared with controls, they had visited more with friends and engaged in more leisure activities at home with family (Paul & Serpell, 1996).

Another dimension of the child/companion animal bond has to do with loss. The death of a pet is often one of the child's first experiences when the skills for coping with a loss are necessary (Mack et al., 1991). Losing a beloved pet can be devastating for any child, but it may be especially difficult for the child with special needs whose service dog not only provides companionship but also a measure of greater independence. According to therapists and counselors, pet loss is a unique form of grief that merits the attention of everyone in the helping professions (Ross & Baron-Sorenson, 1998). Bekoff's (2002) synthesis of research, *Minding the Animals: Awareness, Emotions, and Heart*, serves as a powerful reminder that animals are not just living things; they are thinking and feeling creatures who deserve compassion and understanding from humans. Responsible ownership and care of pets elicits both positive and negative emotions from children. For example, fear of animals is the second most prevalent fear in children (Serpell, 2000). Surprisingly, fear of dogs, based on a study of college students and children, was not significantly more prevalent among those who had been attacked than among those who had never been attacked; the most powerful influence on dog-fearful children was repeated warnings from adults about dogs (Doogan & Thomas, 1992).

Recommendations for Professionals Who Work With Children

The following suggestions are a useful starting point in respecting the developmental significance of the child/companion animal bond.

1. Recognize That the Animal/Human Dynamic Has Changed in Modern Society

Just think for a moment how much attitudes toward animals have changed. In 1950s America if you went to the five-and-dime store, you could purchase a turtle and a shallow bowl, a parakeet and a small cage, or a goldfish in a bowl outfitted with a tiny fake castle. If you bought a pair of Buster Brown shoes at Easter time, you got a free chick that was dyed pink or purple—a practice that shortened their lifespan considerably. In most cases, the animals were crowded together, shipped under horrible conditions, poorly cared for at the store, and died rather quickly after they were taken home. Hardly anybody seemed to care. Attitudes toward animals in modern society are qualitatively different than in previous eras. In many societies, companion animals are credited with contributing to psychological well-being as they offer companionship to the lonely, security to the frightened, self-esteem to those who lack confidence, and opportunities for social interaction to those who are excluded (Gunter, 1999). Similarly, an Israeli study of adolescents' attitudes toward students with special needs found that typically developing children recommended domestic pets (right after computers, music, and sports) as a major way for children with disabilities to enhance their self-image and gain greater acceptance from peers (Brook & Galili, 2000).

2. Appreciate the Powerful Influence of Companion Animals on Children's Overall Development

Educators and other professionals who work with children should take care not to underestimate the consequences of disturbances in the emotional ties between children and companion animals. When parents divorce, a child can lose a beloved pet as well as contact with a parent—in fact, disputes over family pets are becoming so common that 12 law schools now offer courses in animal law (Salzman, 2000). Children who become homeless must surrender their companion animals and may be grieving the loss of a pet as much or more than the loss of a residence (Seifert & Stauffer, 2000). Raupp's (1999) retrospective study found that giving a pet away was a major developmental event that could harm children's future relationships with animals; 59 percent of the adults whose pets had been given away as children followed suit as adults and gave away their pets (or their child's pet). For adults whose pets had not been given away in childhood, the percentage was much lower—39 percent.

In consideration of how important animals are to children, educators should think carefully about how a classroom pet might help children cope when they are forced to abandon their companion animals. During the fall of Saigon in the waning days of the Vietnam War, the soldiers who were the handlers of the scouting, sentry, patrolling, and tracking dogs that had saved so many lives left behind their devoted companion animals to an uncertain fate when the U.S. government categorized the canine corps as "equipment" (Burnam, 2003). In interviews with and essays written by these veterans, it is clear that, even decades later, these soldiers are still heartbroken that they were powerless to save their loyal friends (Burnam, 1999; Morgan & Shaw, 1999). To think that children are any less affected by the surrender of their beloved animal companions is the height of adult insensitivity (Entin, 2001; Wilkins & Loughry, 2000).

3. Make Understanding the Child/Companion Animal Bond Part of Professional Preparation

Although the child-companion animal bond is an undeniably important topic, it has been neglected in the preparation of teachers and other professionals committed to the care of children. Serpell (2000) reports that, in a review of college-level textbooks on psychology and child development, not one of the major textbooks addresses the child/companion animal bond. Although there is observational evidence and a growing body of empirical evidence that companion animals, such as classroom pets kept by teachers (Rud & Beck, 2000), school counselors (Burton, 1995), or visiting nurses (Henshall, 2000), exert a positive influence on professional practice, the social sciences have largely neglected this topic in research, training, and advice to practitioners.

4. Treat the Loss of a Companion Animal As a Major Developmental Issue

When a child forms a bond of affection with a companion animal and that relationship is interrupted or destroyed, it leaves an indelible mark on the child's memory. Losing a pet should not be regarded as a form of loss that serves purely as practice for other, "real" losses later on. According to therapists and counselors, pet loss is a unique form of grief that merits the attention of everyone in the helping professions (Ross & Baron-Sorenson, 1998). Expert advice from veterinarians Carolyn Butler and Laurel Lagoni (1994) about helping children to cope with loss follows many of the same recommendations that are given for explaining loss of a loved one to a child, such as being honest with the child, encouraging involvement of children in ways that are commensurate with their understanding, avoiding euphemisms, making respectful arrangements for disposal or burial of the animal's body, and continuing to offer support and understanding as the child works through the grief process. A synthesis of professional advice and resources for helping children to cope with the loss of a beloved animal can be found in Figure 1.2.

5. Respect the Child's Choice of Companion Animal

Many of the best loved books about animals—such as *The Yearling* (Rawlings, 1988) and *White Fang* (London, 1994)—depict a child who is struggling against more powerful, and sometimes cruel, adults who do not share the child's compassion for the animal. Sensitive, caring adults put such attitudes aside and learn to appreciate a child's point of view on companion animals, as the following story from Mimi Brodsky Chenfeld illustrates.

Conversations With Sporty
Mimi Brodsky Chenfeld

In the midst of a lively Arizona-Ohio telephone call from our almost 8-year-old granddaughter, Chloe, she remembered that she forgot to tell me about Sporty.

"Do you want to talk to him, Grandma?"

"Of course!" (Remember, I'm Grandma!)

You know, when you're suddenly thrust into a conversation with a total stranger, you're often at a loss for words.

Chloe had warned me that he would be a little shy, so I kind of cut my monologue short.

"So, how's it going? What's happening? How are you?"

"He was really listening, Grandma. He got excited when he heard you."

We talk to Chloe a few times a week. Since that awkward first conversation with Sporty, we've had many chances to warm toward each other. Sporty isn't much of a talker, but Chloe reports that he is always eager to hear my messages. She constantly fills me in on his activities, habits, and meals.

"He gets a little hyper when you talk you him, Grandma!" Chloe giggles.

Last week, Chloe called bubbling with news.

"Guess what?"

"What?"

"Sporty moved into my room!"

"Cool!" I tried to match her enthusiasm.

"I stayed up all night watching him. I think he was happy to be in my room, so he hardly slept at all the whole night. He was watching me watch him!"

Today, when I was talking to Sporty, my next-door neighbor dropped in and sat down while I finished my conversation.

"Well, bye, buddy. Enjoy the day. Talk to you soon."

I hung up the phone and turned to my friend, who asked, "That sounded like such a sweet call. Who were you talking to?"

"Oh, that was Sporty, our granddaughter's pet fish."

Suggestions on Helping Children To Cope With the Loss of a Pet

- **Identify with the child's perspective.** Some children, particularly young children, may seem relatively unfazed by the loss of a pet because they do not understand that death is irreversible. Nevertheless, resist the urge to secretly "replace" a lost or dead pet without acknowledging the loss. If the child detects the impostor, it sends the message that living things can inexplicably disappear and be easily replaced. Other children may be devoted to a pet in ways that adults may not fully appreciate, particularly if the pet had the status of belonging to the child. Do not force a child to give up a pet simply because it has become inconvenient. This, too, teaches the child that living things are disposable and loyalty is not achievable.

- **Acknowledge losses directly.** Avoid euphemisms (e.g., the gerbil is sleeping) and explain (if you know) what occurred as well as why (e.g., "Sparky was very old and died because he was so sick that medicine could not help him"). If you are certain that the animal has died, do not pretend that it is just missing. If you truly do not know, make this clear, saying, for example, to an older child, "Babe got out under the fence. She may be lost, so we will keep searching for her in the neighborhood, at animal shelters, and online at Lost Paws (www.lostpaws.com). We will make posters and put them up all around here. But it is also possible that Babe may have been hurt or—and this would be the absolute worst—has died." Realize that circumstances surrounding the loss of a pet can extend feelings of grief. Accidental death can be more troubling and shocking than death due to illness, for example (Planchon, Templer, Stokes, & Keller, 2002).

- **Prepare for a variety of reactions.** Be prepared for responses ranging from relatively unconcerned to completely inconsolable. Expect to see different dimensions of the classic stages of grief, such as denial, as well as different stages of understanding in children of various ages. For example, preschool children frequently do not understand that death is permanent, attribute life to inanimate objects, engage in magical thinking, and may feel responsible for having caused an animal's death. Six- to 8-year-olds realize that death is permanent, but often do not see death as something that might touch their own lives. By age 9 and older, many children have more adult-like concepts about death being permanent, inevitable, and personal. Depending on their cognitive abilities, socioemotional maturity, and personal experiences with death, older children often can explain some of the basic processes that mark the cessation of life as well as describe some of the ways that human beings cope with such losses.

- **Provide choices for participation in grief rituals.** Offering choices during times of grief is very important. Observe the child's behavior and listen to the child's comments, questions, and concerns. Allow the child to participate to whatever extent he or she wishes. Children may or may not want to be involved in death-related ceremonies, for example. One child might want to assist in burying a dead animal, while another would be terribly upset by it. One child might cope with grief at the loss of a family pet by commemorating the pet in some way, such as constructing a photo album with captions about the pet, while another might be disturbed by this activity.

- **Follow the child's lead when deciding whether and when to acquire another pet.** Parents and teachers sometimes rush to replace the lost or dead pet with another one, but an immediate replacement can raise frightening questions in the child's mind about whether she

Figure 1.2

or he also might be so easily replaced. In general, it is best for children to initiate the process of acquiring a new animal companion. Make it clear that the new animal, whether it is the same species or a different one, does not replace the previous pet in memory or in affection.

- **Use carefully selected children's literature.** High-quality books can deepen children's understandings about the loss of companion animals as well as model ways of coping. When children's feelings of loss are intense, an indirect approach is often more appropriate; for example, reading about the trained gorilla's loss of her pet in *Koko's Kitten* (Patterson, 1987) rather than directly addressing the particular form of loss the child has experienced, such as in *The Accident* (Carrick, 1981), a story about a family dog that is killed by a car. Some other titles to consider include *Maggie and Silky and Joe* (Ehrlich, 1994), *Goodbye, Max* (Keller, 1987), *Better With Two* (Joosse, 1998), *The Tenth Good Thing About Barney* (Viorst, 1976), *Mustard* (Graeber, 1982), and *Whiskers, Once and Always* (Orgel, 1986). Look for books that are accurate, suited to the child's level of understanding, and explain death as a natural part of the life cycle.

Adapted from: Siebert, D., Drolet, J. C., & Fetro, J. V. (2003). *Helping children live with death and loss*. Carbondale, IL: Southern Illinois University Press.

Additional Resources:
Butler, C. L., & Lagoni, L. S. (1994). *The human-animal bond and grief*. Philadelphia: W. B. Saunders.
Dalpra-Berman, G. (2001). *Remembering pets: A book for children who have lost a special friend*. San Francisco: Robert D. Reed. (illus. by Barbara Hoss-Schneider).
James, J. W., Friedman, R., & Matthews, L. L. (2001). *When children grieve: For adults to help children deal with death, divorce, pet loss, and other losses*. New York: HarperCollins.
Mack, C., et al. (1991). *Separation and loss: A handbook for early childhood professionals*. Pittsburgh, PA: Generations Together Publications.
Nieburg, H. A., & Fischer, A. (1996). *Pet loss: A thoughtful guide for adults and children*. New York: HarperTrade.
Planchon, L. A., Templer, D. E., Stokes, S., & Keller, J. (2002). Death of a companion cat or dog and human bereavement: Psychosocial variables. *Society and Animals, 10*(1), 93-15.
Stephens, D. L., & Hill, R. P. (1996). The loss of animal companions: A humanistic and consumption perspective. *Society and Animals, 4*(2), 129-210.

Figure 1.2 (continued)

Conclusion

Children's bonds with companion animals are not pale imitations of the bonds with human beings; rather, these relationships are important in their own right, and they need to be understood and must be appreciated on their own terms (Raupp, 1999; Solot, 1997). Without question, children's ways of interacting with animals are shaped by the contexts in which they occur. Increasingly, experts from many fields are realizing that the child-animal bond also affects the course of children's development and shapes the kind of people that children will grow up to be (Melson, 2001). It is a basic principle of human development that early experience affects later experience in complex and profound ways, and a growing body of evidence suggests that bonds formed or broken with companion animals reverberate and resonate across the lifespan.

References

Bartsch, K., & London, K. (2000). Children's use of mental state information in selecting persuasive arguments. *Developmental Psychology, 36*(6), 352-365.
Beck, A. (1993). Pets foster kids' nurturing skills. *Futurist, 27*(1), 8-12.
Beck, A. (1999). Companion animals and their companions: Sharing a strategy for survival. *Bulletin of Science, Technology & Society, 19*(4), 285-289.
Bekoff, M. (2002). *Minding the animals: Awareness, emotions, and heart*. New York: Oxford University Press.
Bierer, R. E. (2001). The relationship between pet bonding, self-esteem, and empathy in preadolescents. *Dissertation Abstracts International Section B: The Sciences and Engineering, 61*(11-B), p. 6183.
Bodson, L. (2000). Motivations for pet-keeping in Ancient Greece and Rome: A preliminary survey. In A. L. Podberscek, E. S. Paul, & J. A. Serpell (Eds.). (2000). *Companion animals and us: Exploring the relationships between people and pets* (pp. 27-41). New York: Cambridge University Press.
Brook, U., & Galili, A. (2000). Knowledge and attitudes of high school pupils toward children with special

health care needs: An Israeli exploration. *Patient Education and Counseling, 40*(1), 5-10.

Burnam, J. C. (1999). *Dog tags of courage: The turmoil of war and the rewards of companionship.* New York: Lost Coast Press.

Burnam, J. C. (2003). *A soldier's best friend: The hidden history of canine units and their handlers.* New York: Carroll & Graf Publishers.

Burton, L. E. (1995). Using a dog in an elementary school counseling program. *Elementary School Guidance and Counseling, 29*(3), 236-240.

Butler, C. L., & Lagoni, L. S. (1994). *The human-animal bond and grief.* Philadelphia: W.B. Saunders.

Cohen, S. P. (2002). Can pets function as family members? *Western Journal of Nursing Research, 24*(6), 62-79.

Colt, G. H. (1994). Why we love dogs. *Life, 17*(10), 76-83.

Doogan, S., & Thomas, G.V. (1992). Origins of fear of dogs in adults and children: The role of conditioning processes and prior familiarity with dogs. *Behaviour Research and Therapy, 30*(4), 387-394.

Eckstein, D. (2000). The Pet Relationship Impact Inventory. *The Family Journal, 8*(2), 192-198.

Entin, A. D. (2001). Pets in the family. *Issues in Interdisciplinary Care, 3*(3), 219-222.

Filiatre, J., Eckerlin, A., Millot, J., & Montagner, H. (1990). An experimental analysis of olfactory cues in child-dog interaction. *Chemical Senses, 15*(6), 678-689.

Filiatre, J. C., Millot, J. L., Montagner, H., Eckerlin, A., & Gagnon, A. C. (1988). Advances in the study of the relationship between children and their pet dogs. *Anthrozoos, 2*(1), 22-32.

Flynn, C. P. (2000). Battered women and their animal companions: Symbolic interaction between human and nonhuman animals. *Society & Animals, 8*(2), 99-127.

Grier, K. C. (1999). Childhood socialization and companion animals: United States, 1820-1870. *Society and Animals, 7*(2), 95-120.

Guerney, L. F. (1991). A survey of self-supports and social supports of self-care children. *Elementary School Guidance and Counseling, 25*(4), 243-254.

Gunter, B. (1999). *Pets and people: The psychology of pet ownership.* London, England: Whurr Publishers.

Henshall, S. (2000). Paws for thought. *Nursing Times, 96*(31), 51.

Kidd, A. H., & Kidd, R. M. (1995). Children's drawings and attachment to pets. *Psychological Reports, 77*(1), 235-241.

Mack, C., et al. (1991). *Separation and loss: A handbook for early childhood professionals.* Pittsburgh, PA: Generations Together Publications.

Melson, G. F. (1990). Studying children's attachment to their pets: A conceptual and methodological review. *Anthrozoos, 4*(2), 91-99.

Melson, G. F. (1998). The role of companion animals in human development. In C. Wilson & D.C. Turner (Eds.), *Companion animals in human health* (pp. 219-236). Thousand Oaks, CA: Sage.

Melson, G. F. (2001). *Why the wild things are: Animals in the lives of children.* Cambridge, MA: Harvard University Press.

Menache, S. (2000). Hunting and attachment to dogs in the pre-modern period. In A. L. Podberscek, E. S. Paul, & J. A. Serpell (Eds.), *Companion animals and us: Exploring the relationships between people and pets* (pp. 42-60). New York: Cambridge University Press.

Millot, J. L., Filiatre, J. C., Gagnon, A. C., & Eckerlin, A. (1988). Children and their pet dogs: How they communicate. *Behavioural Processes, 17*(1), 1-15.

Morgan, P. B., & Shaw, P. B. (1999). *K-9 soldiers: Vietnam and after.* Central Point, OR: Hellgate Press.

Morrow, V. (1998). My animals and other family: Children's perspectives on their relationships with companion animals. *Anthrozoos, 11*(4), 218-226.

Olson, C. A. (1997). Home video instructional. *Billboard, 109,* 27, 81. Review of Dogs, Cats, and Kids. Pet Love Partnership, 30 min. $24.95.

Paul, E. S., & Serpell, J. A. (1996). Obtaining a new pet dog: Effects on middle childhood children and their families. *Applied Animal Behavior Science, 47*(1-2), 17-29.

Planchon, L. A., Templer, D. E., Stokes, S., & Keller, J. (2002). Death of a companion cat or dog and human bereavement: Psychosocial variables. *Society and Animals, 10*(1), 93-15.

Podberscek, A. L., Paul, E. S., & Serpell, J. A. (Eds.). (2000). *Companion animals and us: Exploring the relationships between people and pets.* New York: Cambridge University Press.

Poresky, R. H. (1990). The Young Children's Empathy Measure: Reliability, validity, and effects of companion animal bonding. *Psychological Reports, 66*(3), 931-936.

Raupp, C. (1999). Treasuring, trashing, or terrorizing: Adult outcomes of childhood socialization about companion animals. *Society & Animals, 7*(2), 141-149.

Ross, C. B., & Baron-Sorenson, J. (1998). *Pet loss and human emotion: Guiding clients through grief.* Philadelphia: Accelerated Development.

Rud, A. G., & Beck, A. M. (2000). Kids and critters in class together. *Phi Delta Kappan, 82*(4), 313-315.

Salzman, M. (2000). Pet trends. *Vital Speeches of the Day, 67*(5), 147-153.

Seifert, E., & Stauffer, C. (2000). *Homeless, not hopeless. An informational guide for school personnel: Understanding and educating homeless students.* St. Paul, MN: Saint Paul Public Schools. (ERIC Document Reproduction Service No. 450 178).

Serpell, J. A. (2000). Creatures of the unconscious: Companion animals as mediators. In A. L. Podberscek, E. S. Paul, & J. A. Serpell (Eds.), *Companion animals and us: Exploring the relationships between people and pets* (pp. 108-121). New York: Cambridge University Press.

Siebert, D., Drolet, J. C., & Fetro, J. V. (1993). *Are you sad too? Helping children deal with loss and death.* Scotts Valley, CA: ETR Associates.

Solot, D. (1997). Untangling the animal abuse web. *Society and Animals, 5*(3), 257-265.

Spencer, D. (2000). Pet rescue. *Times Educational Supplement, issue 4405,* 20.

Van Houtte, B. A., & Jarvis, P. A. (1995). The role of pets in preadolescent psychosocial development.

Journal of Applied Preadolescent Psychosocial Development, 16(3), 462-479.

Wicks, B. (1988). *No time to wave goodbye.* London: Bloomsbury Publishing/New York: St. Martin's Press.

Wilkins, P., & Loughry, A. (2000). How do we prepare our daughter for the death of a pet? *Parents, 75*(12), 28.

Children's Books

Carrick, C. (1981). *The accident.* Boston: Houghton Mifflin.

Ehrlich, A. (1994). *Maggie and Silky and Joe.* New York: Viking.

Graeber, C. (1982). *Mustard.* New York: Atheneum.

Joosse, B. (1998). *Better with two.* New York: HarperCollins.

Keller, H. (1987). *Goodbye, Max.* New York: William Morrow.

London, J. (1994). *White Fang.* New York: Baronet.

Orgel, D. (1986). *Whiskers, once and always.* New York: Viking/Penguin.

Patterson, F. (1987). *Koko's kitten.* New York: Scholastic.

Rawlings, M. K. (1988). *The yearling.* New York: Pocket Books.

Viorst, J. (1976). *The tenth good thing about Barney.* New York: Aladdin.

Chapter 2

Companion Animals in the Lives of Boys and Girls: Gendered Attitudes, Practices, and Preferences

Anne Drolett Creany

—*Amanda Urban*
Belgium

> *A man carries a euthanized pet tenderly to the grave he has prepared for this sad event. The tears in his eyes are not only for the faithful companion in his arms who lived to a ripe old age, but also for the young dog he lost when he was just 12, when another dog attacked his pet before his eyes. Then, as now, he freely expresses the emotions triggered by the loss of a beloved pet, and the precept that "big boys don't cry" is suspended.*

What factors cause boys or men who almost never cry to express unabashed sentiment about a pet? Do males and females have differing beliefs about the roles they should play in the care of companion animals and appropriate treatment of animals? Do boys and girls have the same preferences in companion animals, respond to their companion animals in the same way, and express the grief they feel in a similar fashion when a companion animal dies? This chapter will describe the differences in children's emotional sensitivity, examine the theoretical and empirical support for the benefits of companion animals in children's lives, address the factor of gender in children's attitudes toward and attachments to companion animals, explore children's gender-related species preferences and attitudes toward the care and use of animals, and consider further directions for research and classroom practice.

Emotional Sensitivity to Companion Animals

Certain aspects of personality appear to be gender-typed. Berk (2003) states that, from an early age, females are more emotionally sensitive than males. According to Berk, the basis for these differences is most likely a combination of biology and environmental influences. She notes that one line of thought proposes that girls are genetically predisposed to be more emotionally sensitive so that they will be prepared to act as caregivers. However, research does not verify girls' inherent nurturing inclinations. Fogel, Melson, Toda, and Mistry (1987) found that boys and girls younger than 5 years of age interact equally with babies, while boys' interest in babies declines by the age of 7. Where companion animals are concerned, however, boys have no qualms about displaying affection and care, even as they mature (Melson, 2001). Berk (2003) concludes that societal expectations are the likely source of gender differences in emotional sensitivity, and that parents encourage girls rather than boys to express their emotions and respond to others.

Benefits That Children Derive From Pet Ownership

Several theorists suggest that owning a companion animal offers numerous and varied advantages to both boys and girls. Levinson (1972) describes the advantages of pet ownership in relation to the developmental tasks of early childhood. Very young children receive tactile stimulation from touching a companion animal. Later, having an active companion animal to follow encourages children's crawling and muscle development, facilitates learning to walk, and provides a reason to practice walking. Levinson states that children who are attempting bowel and bladder control, and meet with parents' disappointment when they do not succeed, will profit from a pet's nonjudgmental stance. Later, in the preoperational period, children may angrily reject and send a companion animal away; when that companion animal does not abandon them, children will learn that wishes do not equal deeds and that an individual can be assertive without dire consequences.

Levinson (1972) also comments on the companion animal's ability to help a child

cope with separation anxiety. Leaving parents to attend school may cause a child anxiety. A companion animal that accompanies a child to school or faithfully awaits her return may ease the child's transition to this stage of life. Qihao, now a graduate student, recalls such an experience as a young child:

When I was 5 years old, my parents and I lived in Shanghai. Every weekend we took the bus to my grandparents' village. We got off the bus about five blocks from my grandparents' home and my grandfather's dog was always there waiting for us. When we left for the city again, the dog would accompany us to the bus stop. He always waited until we boarded the bus and sometimes he would *run after the bus when it left. I always wondered how he knew when it was time to meet us at the bus stop.*

Although Qihao was not separated from his parents, he did have to part from his grandparents, and the family dog helped him cope with that separation.

Other benefits provided by companion animals include friendship and love. Companion animals offer unconditional positive regard, and they love children even if they are messy (a greater likelihood of treats for the companion animal), struggle

Indian boys tending their goats.

Photo courtesy of Shireen DeSouza

in school, or fail to make the team. Companion animals also listen attentively to their owner's angry feelings, fears, triumphs, and disappointments (Bryant, 1990; Checchi, 1999; Melson, 2001). Thus, a boy who does not meet societal expectations for success still can be a hero in the eyes of a pet. Likewise, a girl who feels unlovely by social standards knows that she is adored by a faithful pet.

Companion animals provide another form of emotional support by providing children with feelings of security (Bryant, 1990; Checchi, 1999; Melson, 2001). Children's fear of a dark bedroom is allayed by the presence of a pet. In this respect, a pet can be especially helpful for boys, who are socialized to keep their fears to themselves. An animal can soothe a child's concerns/worries without exposing their fears.

Collins and McNicholas (1998) discuss the benefits of self-esteem and emotional support as part of the companion animal-child relationship. They suggest that these kinds of support from a companion animal may be more stable than the same type of support from humans. According to Collins and McNicholas, the very fact that companion animals are nonhuman provides the advantage of a relationship that is safe from the destructive effects of "weakness, emotion, or excessive demands" (p. 116). Fortunately, a pet's support is consistent even if an owner's behavior is unreliable. The authors state that additional benefits of companion animals include the sense of self-esteem that an owner derives from knowing a companion animal cares about and needs her, irrespective of the owner's status in her own or others' eyes. Animals offer their companionship even if the human owner lacks social skills; indeed, nonhuman animals sometimes provide a haven from the pressures of interactions with humans (Collins & McNicholas, 1998).

Companion animals provide children with an opportunity to nurture another being. Checchi (1999) notes that this benefit is especially valuable for boys; caring for a companion animal is a gender-neutral activity, while caring for babies or dolls is sex-typed as a female activity for children older than 5 in some societies. Melson (2001) concurs, noting that 7-year-old boys were as receptive as girls to the role of nurturing companion animals.

Companion animals also possess assets that are beneficial to both genders. Companion animals provide entertainment, comfort, and opportunities to learn and be creative, and they extend invitations for interactions with other youngsters (Checchi, 1999; Melson, 2001).

Empirical Support for Benefits Derived From Companion Animals

Research also supports the benefits derived from companion animals. McNicholas and Collins (2001) describe a study that examined the social networks of 22 children from the English Midlands. Seventeen of the 18 pet-owning children in the study included a family pet in their self-described social network. The authors conclude that children perceive cats and dogs as potential sources of comfort if they are ill, afraid, or in a situation that threatens their self-esteem.

In a larger study of companion animals' ability to help children cope with stress, 612 primary children from Slavonia, an area of Croatia deeply affected by the war, responded to a questionnaire that measured posttraumatic stress reactions (PTSR) and methods of coping with stress (Arambasic & Kerestes, 1998). This study compared three groups of children: those with no companion animals, those with a cat or dog, and those with companion animals other than a cat or dog. The results were somewhat conflicting: girls with companion animals other than a cat or dog had the highest level of PTSR, while boys without companion animals and girls with a cat or dog had the lowest levels of PTSR. The analysis of coping strategies showed that cat and dog owners express emotions, seek social support, and engage in problem solving to a greater extent than other groups. The authors concluded that children, especially girls, with a dog or cat have more differentiated coping strategies, which may reduce PTSR.

In another study, VanHoutte and Jarvis (1995) examined 130 third- through sixth-graders to determine the role of companion animals in their psychosocial development. The results indicated higher autonomy for pet owners in all grades, higher self-concept for 6th-grade pet owners, and higher self-esteem for 5th- and 6th-grade pet owners. VanHoutte and Jarvis speculate that companion animals may have the greatest impact as students approach adolescence. The authors suggest that owning a pet may be a way to foster autonomous behaviors such as responsibility and self-reliance. Additionally, since pet ownership correlated with higher self-concept and self-esteem for pre-adolescents, the authors propose that companion animals could serve as support for students who lack self-esteem and experience a greater than normal amount of stress.

Melson (1998) examined the effect of companion animals on the quality of life for children, which she describes as the "subjective symptoms, feelings, and well-being relevant to the child's ability to meet developmental challenges" (p. 222). She analyzed the findings of several research studies, concluding that many children turn to companion animals for comfort when they are sad, afraid, or upset. Melson also cites studies indicating that children identify companion animals as play partners, especially in middle childhood. She points to anecdotal evidence that suggests the presence of classroom pets increases students' learning about the animals or the subject matter; Melson acknowledges, however, that research is needed to verify this claim.

Despite all of the benefits associated with pet ownership, some costs exist as well. Children in grades 3 through 7 responded to questionnaires and identified both the advantages and costs of owning companion animals. Bryant (1990) reports that the costs include distress as a result of a companion animal's being given away or dying; worry about a companion animal's safety; dissatisfaction with a companion animal's needs, such as exercise; getting into trouble for failure to treat a companion animal appropriately; distress at not being permitted to care for the needs of a pet, such as when a companion animal cries to come inside; and unfair grief, or being held responsible for a pet's transgression. Bryant argues that since so many companion animals are abandoned or destroyed in the United States, adults should weigh the benefits of the child/pet bond against the costs that children experience because of pet ownership.

Boys' and Girls' Attachments to Companion Animals

Jordan is 5 years old and has grown up with her cat, Maestro. He stands guard at her bedroom door, curls up in her bedcovers at night, and seeks and submits to her attentions. In contrast, the cat is an annoyance to her 3-year-old brother, Zander. Maestro curls up inside the train track the preschooler has constructed and sometimes Zander must physically remove the cat. The youngest child in the family, Nolan, is a toddler who is walking well. He drops whatever he is doing or holding and follows Maestro, calling, "Kitty, kitty," if the cat crosses his line of vision.

The differences in these children's reactions to their companion animal mirror some of the research findings. Young children interact with their companion animals, girls are more likely to be cat owners, and some children become attached to their companion animals, while others reject them.

Kidd and Kidd (1987) examined the attachment behaviors and responses of 250 children to live companion animals versus a mechanical toy. The researchers visited the homes of pet owners in suburban San Francisco, bringing with them a mechanical toy dog that moved and barked, as well as a toy cat that meowed or purred when touched. Boys and girls between the ages of 6 months and 30 months were observed as they interacted with the toy pets and the companion animals in the home.

The researchers found that children's responses grew increasingly dissimilar with age and varied by gender. Kidd and Kidd (1987) report that 6- and 12-month-old boys exhibited a higher percentage of verbalizations and attachment behaviors, such as laughing or holding, following, or trying to follow their companion animals than did girls of the same age. At 18 months, girls showed more attachment behaviors to live companion animals than did boys and verbalized more often than boys did. Twenty-four-month-old girls also showed significantly more attachment behaviors to live companion animals than did boys; boys followed the companion animals more, but girls called them more often. Thirty-month-old girls continued to demonstrate a significantly higher percentage of attachment behaviors than did boys. Six-, 12-, and 18-month-old girls also showed more rejecting or pushing away behaviors toward their companion animals than did boys.

Kidd and Kidd (1987) explained these gender differences in terms of boys' and girls' different activity levels, socialization, and gender role training. The authors observe that boys are more active than girls are in the first year of life, and attribute the boys' greater attachment behaviors and verbalization to this trait. However, as girls are socialized, they become increasingly verbal. Similarly, parents, especially fathers, engage in more roughhousing with young boys and so young males may be accepting of a companion animal's physical advances, whereas girls ages 6-18 months pushed boisterous dogs away. However, by 24 months, both genders are capable of handling a companion animal and are familiar with, and accepting of, their companion animal's behaviors.

Kidd and Kidd's (1987) study also revealed that children 12-30 months of age showed a preference for the live pet over toys, a finding that they attributed to the animals' movement and reciprocal interaction with the child. The children also showed a preference for dogs over cats, most likely because the dogs approached the child and permitted contact more often than did cats. Dogs also elicited more smiles, laughing, and verbalizing than did cats.

In a study of older children's attachment to companion animals, Triebenbacher (1998) analyzed the responses of 385 students in grades 4-12 on the Companion Animal Bonding Scale (Poresky, Hendrix, Mosier, & Samuelson, 1987) and the New York Self-Esteem Scale/Rosenberg Self-Esteem Scale (Rosenberg, 1979). The results indicated that children with interactive companion animals, such as a cat or a dog, were significantly more attached to their companion animal than were students who had such companion animals as birds, rodents, reptiles, or horses. Triebenbacher also found that elementary school girls were significantly more attached to their companion animals than were boys. The author surmises that this finding may reflect gender role

socialization. Since girls are encouraged to be expressive and to connect with others, perhaps these connections apply to companion animals as well. Thirteen-year-old Alexandra's drawings of her dog Lilly reflect careful study of her companion animal's habits. Responses to different species of companion animals would affect the attachment process.

Vidovic, Stetic, and Bratko (1999) studied issues of attachment and the socioemotional traits of 826 pet-owning and non-pet-owning children in the 4th, 6th, and 8th grades in Zagreb, Croatia. The authors analyzed children's responses on questionnaires that measured their attachment to companion animals, as well as empathy, prosocial orientation, social anxiety, and perception of family climate. They found that girls had higher levels of attachment to their companion animals than did boys, girls were more empathic, girls were more prosocially oriented than were boys, and girls

Alexandra Creany's drawings of her dog Lilly.

perceived their family climate to be better than did boys. The research team commented that the degree of attachment with a companion animal evidently exerted a moderating effect on socioemotional traits, since less-bonded pet owners did not exhibit the higher empathy or prosocial behavior scores than did more attached owners.

Bulcroft (1990) also examined issues of attachment in a study of companion animals in the "average" family. With colleague Alexa Albert, Bulcroft conducted telephone interviews of 1,000 people, and followed up with interviews with 100 families representing different phases of family life, such as newlyweds, families with and without children, families in retirement, and widowed and never-married individuals. The researchers found that families with children were most likely to own companion animals, but those same families indicated the lowest levels of attachment to the pet. The highest levels of attachment were in households consisting of adults. Bulcroft speculates that adults without children may have more time to spend with companion animals or companion animals may serve as substitutes for children. In all stages of family life, the adult woman in the home is typically the primary caregiver for the pet although the adult males were more active in exercising the pet (Bulcroft, 1990).

In a similar study investigating attachment to companion animals and responsibility for their care, Kidd and Kidd (1990) surveyed the parents of 700 children from pet-owning and non-pet-owning homes in the San Francisco Bay area. The researchers sought to determine the relationship between children's activities with, interest in, and responsibility for companion animals, and parents' attachment toward companion animals and structure of the home. Parents responded to the Activities With Companion Animals scale, Interest in Companion Animals scale, and if they owned pets, they also responded to the Responsibility for Pet Care scale of the Melson Parent Questionnaire (cited in Kidd & Kidd, 1990). Parents' attachment scores were derived from the Pet Attitude Inventory for Pet Owners and for Nonpet Owners (Wilson, Netting, & New, 1987). Preschool children scored lower on the activity and interest

scales than did middle and high school children. In addition, grade school children scored higher than preschool or high school children did on responsibility for pet care. With respect to gender, girls scored higher than boys did on the interest scale; in households with companion animals, they scored higher on the responsibility measure. The researchers suggest that girls may be imitating their mother's behavior since the mother assumes the responsibility for companion animals in most families. They also propose that pet care may be viewed as a feminine pursuit, since it is akin to "mothering." This suggestion runs counter to Melson's (2001) description of nurturing a pet as a gender-neutral, not a "mommy," activity. Perhaps a distinction exists between nurturing and providing care since the former is more empathic and the latter resembles housekeeping chores.

Species Preferences and Gender

> *Brian, age 4, and Lauren, age 5, had the following conversation as they commuted to preschool:*
> *Lauren: I have 100 imaginary friends.*
> *Brian: I have 100 imaginary friends, too!*
> *Lauren: All of my 100 imaginary friends have a cat.*
> *Brian: Well, all of my 100 imaginary friends have a dog!*

Popular wisdom suggests that cats are "girl pets" and dogs are "boy pets." While research provides some support for this axiom, researchers acknowledge that the issue is complex and the answers are not clear-cut.

Covert, Whiren, Keith, and Nelson (1985) interviewed and administered questionnaires to 304 families in Michigan. The researchers found that 10- to 14-year-olds cared for a variety of animal species; however, dogs were highly represented, with 40 percent of the respondents listing dogs as their companion animals. Some species of animal were linked by gender. Girls were more likely than were boys to own a cat; boys were more often the owners of large animals, such as livestock or horses. This study also measured self-esteem and found that the self-esteem of animal owners was higher than that of non-animal owners, and that dog owners were shown to have higher self-esteem.

Poresky (1997) studied the effects of companion animals on young adults' self-concept. In this study, 394 young adults took the *Tennessee Self-Concept Scale* (Fitts, 1965) and the *Companion Animal Bonding Scale* (Poresky, Hendrix, Mosier, & Samuelson, 1987); the researcher wished to determine whether any effects can be associated with gender, type of companion animal, and bond with childhood pet. The demographics of the sample indicated that more females had cats (19 percent) than did males (10 percent), and that more males had dogs (55 percent) than did females (38 percent). The results of the study showed that boys who had dogs as companion animals and girls who had cats as companion animals had higher overall self-concept scores than did boys who had cats and girls who had dogs as childhood companion animals. Poresky explains that the boys and girls who had the more common pet for their gender had high self-concept scores, while the boys and

girls who had the less common pet for their gender had lower self-concept scores. He adds that it remains unclear whether children selected pets based on their personality, or if their personalities were shaped by their choice of pet in the context of social expectations for pet-gender-role expectations. Poresky further comments that these findings are not causal and may be affected by the small sample of young men who reported having cats as companion animals (n = 9).

Not all preferred companion animals are warm and cuddly. Laurent (2001) describes a type of companion animal that is popular in Japan—*mushi*, or insects. In the fall, Japanese children, especially boys, comb fields and pastures to collect insects that chirp or "sing" in autumn. References to mushi date back to 1685, when they were sold by vendors or in special stores. Today children can buy mushi in department stores or vending machines. Laurent (2001) explains that the tradition of collecting mushi nearly died out after World War II, but experienced a resurgence in the 1960s. Currently, Laurent states, the most popular

"This is a purcher of me and my cat Krissy. I love my cat very much, more than anythig be etsped my famliy and she is apart of my famliy and I would feel bad to loues her. Whenever I am on the couch Krissy jumps up on the couch and lay on me, but mom would not yell at her, she would just look up and jump off of my lap and on the floor and run."
by Mariah N. Benjamin

Mariah N. Benjamin with her cat Krissy.

Mariah's drawing of Krissy.

"Me and My Cat Krissey
I think my cat is special because along time ago, cats use to be used as a look out. I also like my cat because she behaved, and palys nicely. She loves me and I love her. I know that she is a girl because whenever you picked out a cat or a dog At The Animal Rescue league the vetiranean will tell you if it is a girl or a boy. My cat respects me and I respect her. And that is me and my cat Krissey that I love."
by Mariah N. Benjamin

Courtesy of Debra A. Gloster

mushi are stag and rhinoceros beetles, which can be observed in staged battles over a piece of fruit while their male owners cheer for their companion animals. According to Laurent (2001), Japanese children reap several benefits from participating in the collection of mushi: developing an appreciation for the seasons, interacting with nature and appreciating biodiversity, developing powers of observation and reflection, and becoming aware of life cycles.

Laurent (2001) further explains that an offshoot of the fascination for mushi is the appeal of virtual animals that mimic mushi. Like the mushi, many of these virtual animals metamorphose. Many of the popular Pokémon characters are based on the bodies of insects. Virtual pets also reveal some gendered attitudes. In an analysis of 512 interviews with children, Osborn (2000) found that girls, more so than boys, believed that their virtual pets needed attention. In addition, both boys and girls believed that female virtual pets were happier or sadder than male pets. Osborn concludes that these results indicate that children reconstruct their gender roles, rather than learn them from an adult's transmission.

Loss of a Pet

Collectors of mushi will see their companion animals die before the end of the year. Just as those collectors must face the reality of the life cycle so, too, will many pet owners. Researchers have examined how pet owners cope with the loss of a companion animal. Brown, Richards, and Wilson (1996) studied adolescents ages 12-17 to determine the strength of their bonding with companion animals, as well as their bereavement following the loss of a companion animal. The adolescents completed the *Companion Animal Bonding Scale* (Poresky, Hendrix,

Mosier, & Samuelson, 1987), the *Pet Attitude Scale* (Poresky, Hendrix, Mosier, 1988), and the *Texas Revised Inventory of Grief* (Fashingbauer, 1981). Results indicated that the degree of bonding (as measured by self-reports) is higher for girls than for boys; the more a subject was bonded to a pet, the more intense were feelings of grief when the pet died; and girls reported more intense feelings of bereavement than boys did. The authors note that the social pressure boys feel to minimize the expression of their feelings may confound the results of this study.

Attitudes About the Care and Treatment of Animals

Heath and Lori are siblings who live on a dairy farm that has been in their family for over a century. As part of their first 4-H project, each child selected a calf to train and show at the fair. Heath's calf was a Brown Swiss that he named Nugget; Lori's calf was a Guernsey that she named Princess Rose. When Nugget earned a ribbon, Heath stood by, smiling proudly; when Princess earned a blue ribbon at her very first fair, Lori threw her arms around Princess and kissed the calf despite the fact that her parents, particularly her mother, had cautioned her repeatedly about germs.

Heath and Lorelei Winsheimer with their prize-winning 4-H calves.

Photos courtesy of Eleanor Winsheimer

Gender-related findings also appear in studies of attitudes toward pets and the treatment of companion animals. Gage and Christensen (2001) examined essays written by students in grades 5, 8, 10, and 12 in response to a Minnesota newspaper's question: "In case of fire, what one possession would you save and why?" Of 1,265 essayists, 322 responded that they would save a pet. The authors analyzed those responses for frequency of patterns, identifying three idea categories: "guide," "I-me," and "eternal." The guide theme was rule-driven and reflected the topic of the essay—saving a valued possession. This theme was evident in the responses of both genders. The I-me theme was also frequently used by both genders, indicating an egocentric perspective on saving a companion animal. This perspective focused on the importance of the companion animal to the subject. In contrast, girls were far more likely than boys to use the eternal category. Girls' reasons for saving a companion animal focused on the companion animal and its inherent value and dependability, rather than focusing on the child's need for the companion animal (the I-me category).

Not all companion animals are so valued or receive consistent, loving treatment. Raupp (1999) examined frequently practiced behaviors that harm companion animals and factors that influence such behaviors. These practices include hitting companion animals and giving them away. The author claims that parental examples of subabusive treatment of animals are likely to influence grown children's treatment of companion animals. For example, if parents struck or gave away companion animals, children may be more likely to do the same as adults.

To test this proposition, Raupp (1999) conducted a study of 160 university students, to whom she administered a *Pet Abuse Potential Scale*. The results included several gender-related findings. Females reported stronger attachment to their companion animals than did the male subjects, especially if they viewed their mothers as being loving and kind to childhood companion animals. However, a father's dislike of childhood companion animals was associated with males who were less attached to companion animals and with

Indian girl feeding goats and kids.

Photo courtesy of Jyotsna Pattnaik

females who were more attached. Raupp explains this finding by speculating that sons may be more receptive to fathers' messages. The study also showed that males had a greater potential for abusing pets than females did, but subjects who reported giving away companion animals were less likely to abuse. Females who had not hit their companion animals perceived them as less burdensome, in contrast to males who had not hit companion animals, but saw their companion animals as very burdensome. This finding would seem to support the belief that females are comfortable in the role of caretaker.

In addition to assessing the attitudes of males and females toward companion animals, some studies examined gendered attitudes toward wild animals, attitudes that appeared to be affected by ownership of a companion animal. Kidd and Kidd (1997) conducted a study of adolescents ages 12-16 who worked as volunteers in a suburban wildlife museum in California. The authors found that female volunteers outnumbered male volunteers by a ratio of more than 2 to 1. In addition, females expressed a preference for working in the museum programs that were geared to young children, such as the petting circle of the pet library. Males, on the other hand, preferred conducting "walk throughs"—carrying or displaying larger animals to museum visitors. Both genders reported that their interest in wild animals began at an early age and was stimulated by family members, rather than by school experiences. Additionally, 95 percent of wildlife volunteers had companion animals at home, thus providing them with exposure to animals.

Wells and Hepper (1995) assessed the attitudes of rural and urban children in Northern Ireland about the use of animals. Their study included 650 children, ranging in age from 11-15 years, who responded to a questionnaire about issues related to animal use in ways that either 1) lead to their death, such as fox hunting or 2) do not lead to death, but can be considered exploitation (e.g., circuses, horseracing, or experimentation). Pet ownership was not considered as a factor in this study because so few subjects were non-pet owners that the analysis would be invalid. A significant effect by gender was found, however, with males expressing more agreement with the use of animals for hunting or exploitive purposes than females.

In a similar study, Bjerke, Odegardstuen, and Kaltenborn (1998) asked Norwegian students to respond to a questionnaire, using Kellert's (1996) attitude typology toward animals. The typology consists of the following categories:

• Humanistic (affection for individual animals)
• Moralistic (concern for the right and wrong treatment of animals)
• Utilitarian (concern for the material value of animals)
• Negativistic (avoidance of animals due to dislike or fear)
• Dominionistic (desire for mastery of animals, especially in sport)
• Naturalistic (interest in wildlife)
• Ecologistic (concern for the environment as a system).

Results indicated that Norwegian males scored higher than females on the naturalistic and utilitarian scales, and Norwegian females scored higher on moralistic scales. The authors drew comparisons between their study and that of Kellert and Westervelt's (1983) study, conducted in Connecticut, in which boys scored higher on dominionistic and ecologistic scales, and girls scored higher on humanistic and negativistic scales.

Bjerke, Odegardstuen, and Kaltenborn (1998) also referred to use of the same assessment instrument in Canada by Eagles and Muffit (1990), who found no gender differences on any of the typology scales. The authors conclude that the common finding in all three countries is that most respondents disagree with dominion and utilitarian statements, thus expressing their disapproval for a materialistic view of animals and opposing mastery and control of animals. In addition, all three studies reveal the strong affection children show for individual animals, especially companion animals, and a consensus that animals can be good friends.

Implications for Research and Education

From this brief review of the benefits of companion animals to children, what implications can be drawn for further research and classroom practice? Considering the benefits of companion animals for children, researchers would do well to document children's attitudes and preferences by using methods other than self-reporting. Self-reporting techniques are likely to be skewed by children's socialized beliefs about what constitutes a proper response. Thus, girls may be more willing to express their strong attachments to pets and grief at their deaths than boys, who are socialized to suppress their emotions. Observational studies, such as Kidd and Kidd's (1987), provide measures that are more objective and could serve as a model for additional research.

In addition, the link between self-esteem and ownership of a companion animal is certainly deserving of more research. To date, the results of such research is mixed; more studies may clarify this significant connection. Finally, more cross-national studies will illuminate attitudes of the world's children toward the care of animals, and indicate their readiness for instruction in this important issue.

Teachers and counselors would do well to capitalize on the strong bonds that exist between children and their companion animals. Providing children with opportunities to read and write about pets will forge important connections between school assignments and their home life.

Teachers and counselors certainly will appreciate the potential boost in self-esteem children may derive from acknowledgement of their companion animals in school. Furthermore, teachers and counselors should be sensitive to the depth of bereavement children may experience when a companion animal dies, and help them come to terms with such a loss.

Conclusion

Different societal expectations for male and female children are evident and/or appear at birth—at times, even prior to birth. Gender differences are evident in children's activities, emotional expression, patterns of social interaction, and beliefs about what is appropriate behavior for their gender. Gender also affects children's manner of interacting with companion animals in a curiously reciprocal way. Children's sensitivity to, preferences for, attachments with, and care and use of companion animals is not only shaped by gender but also serves as a way of breaking gender stereotypes.

Attitudes toward animals are shaped by gender when a boy rejects a cat as a "girl's pet," or a girl feels unconstrained about stating the strength of her attachment to her companion animal. Perhaps, children's preferences, attachments, and attitudes toward companion animals reflect the gender roles children bring to the human/pet relationship, rather than emanating from interactions between human and nonhuman animals.

Opportunities to interact with companion animals also may serve to challenge prevailing gender expectations in a society. By forming a bond with a companion animal, a male is able to care tenderly for a companion animal throughout its life and put aside the constriction that "big boys don't cry" when the companion animal dies. Males can challenge, without fear of censure, the gender stereotype of toughness and stoicism, choosing instead to be nurturant and compassionate. Ultimately, this ability to express feelings of tenderness with companion animals may help males express their feelings with human animals as well.

Bonds with companion animals can provide an opportunity for females to challenge the gender role status quo as well. The stereotypic gender expectations, such as acting nice and being pretty, can be set aside as girls experience unconditional positive regard from a companion animal that is unrelated to such social pressures.

Bonds with companion animals can challenge gender expectations in yet another way, as boys and girls learn to admire and respect one another's work ethic as animal shelter volunteers, skill in a dog obedience class, or loving care of a sick, abused, or injured nonhuman creature. Above all, boys and girls have a shared capacity to love and care for companion animals. Memories of these animals are treasures that will reside within boys and girls long after they bid farewell to their cherished friend. Perhaps most important of all, such memories can be carried into adulthood and become the foundation for becoming a more sensitive parent, worker, community member, and caretaker of the earth.

References

Arambasic, L., & Kerestes, G. (1998, September). *The role of pet ownership as a possible buffer variable in traumatic experience.* Paper presented at the 8th International Conference on Human-Animal Interactions, Prague, Czech Republic.

Berk, L. E. (2003). *Child development* (6th ed.). Boston: Allyn & Bacon.

Bjerke, T., Odegardstuen, T., & Kaltenborn, B. (1998). Attitudes toward animals among Norwegian adolescents. *Anthrozoos, 3*(2), 79-86.

Brown, B., Richards, H. C., & Wilson, C. A. (1996). Pet bonding and pet bereavement among adolescents. *Journal of Counseling and Development, 74,* 505-509.

Bryant, B. (1990). The richness of the child-pet relationship: A consideration of both benefits and costs of pets to children. *Anthrozoos, 3*(4), 253-261.

Bulcroft, K. (1990). Companion animals in the American family. *People, Animals, Environment, 8*(4), 13-14.

Checchi, M. J. (1999). *Are you the pet for me?* New York: St. Martin's Press.

Collins, G., & McNicholas, J. (1998). A theoretical basis for health benefits of pet ownership: Attachment versus psychological support. In C. Wilson & D. Turner (Eds.), *Companion animals in human health* (pp. 102-122). London: Sage.

Covert, A. M., Whiren, A. P., Keith, J., & Nelson, C. (1985). Companion animals, early adolescents, and families. *Marriage and Family Review, 8,* 95-105.

Eagles, P. F., & Muffit, S. (1990). An analysis of children's attitudes toward animals. *Journal of Environmental Education, 21,* 41-44.

Fashingbauer, T. R. (1981). *Texas Revised Inventory of Grief.*

Houston, TX: Honeycomb.

Fitts, W. H. (1965). *Tennessee Self-concept Scale.* Nashville, TN: Counselor Recording and Tests.

Fogel, A., Melson, G. F., Toda, S., & Mistry, T. (1987). Young children's responses to unfamiliar infants. *International Journal of Behavioral Development, 10,* 1071-1077.

Gage, M. G., & Christensen, D. (2001). Early adolescents' values about their pets. *Journal of Psychology, 12*(4), 417-425.

Kalisch, P., & Kalisch, B. (1984). Sex-role stereotyping of nurses and physicians on prime-time television. *Sex roles, 10,* 553-554.

Kellert, S. R. (1996). Attitudes toward animals: Age-related development among children. *Journal of Environmental Education, 16,* 29-39.

Kellert, S. R., & Westervelt, M. O. (1983). *Children's attitudes, knowledge, and behavior toward animals.* Washington, DC: Government Printing Office. (Government Printing Office report no. 024-010-00641-2).

Kidd, A. H., & Kidd, R. M. (1987). Reactions of infants and toddlers to live and toy animals. *Psychological Reports, 61,* 455-464.

Kidd, A. H., & Kidd, R. M. (1990). Factors in children's attitudes toward companion animals. *Psychological Reports, 66,* 775-786.

Kidd, A. H., & Kidd, R. M. (1997). Characteristics and motives of adolescent volunteers in wildlife education. *Psychological Reports, 80,* 747-753.

Laurent, E. (2001). Mushi. *Natural History, 110,* 70-76.

Levinson, B. (1972). *Companion animals and human development.* Springfield, IL: Charles C. Thomas.

Osborn, E. A. (2000). *Children's attribution of needs and feelings to virtual pets: Does gender matter?* Paper presented at the American Sociological Association. Abstract retrieved February 20, 2003, from the Sociological Abstracts database.

McNicholas, J., & Collins, C. (2001). Children's representations of companion animals in their social networks. *Child Care, Health and Development, 27*(3),

279-294.

Melson, G. F. (1998). The role of companion animals in human development. In C. Wilson & D. Turner (Eds.), *Companion animals in human health* (pp. 219-236). London: Sage Publications.

Melson, G. F. (2001). *Why the wild things are: Animals in the lives of children.* Cambridge, MA: Harvard University Press.

Poresky, R. H. (1997). Sex, childhood pets and young adults' self-concept scores. *Psychological Reports, 80*(2), 371-378.

Poresky, R. H., Hendrix, C., & Mosier, J. (1988). The companion animal semantic differential: Long and short form reliability and validity. *Educational and Psychological Measurement, 48,* 255-260.

Poresky, R. H., Hendrix, C., Mosier, J., & Samuelson, M. (1987). The Companion Animal Bonding Scales: Internal reliability and construct validity. *Psychological Reports, 60,* 743-746.

Raupp, C. (1999). Treasuring, trashing or terrorizing: Adult outcomes of childhood socialization about companion animals. *Society and Animals, 7*(2), 141-159.

Rosenberg, M. (1979). *Conceiving the self.* New York: Basic Books.

Triebenbacher, S. L. (1998). The relationship between attachment to companion animals and self-esteem: A developmental perspective. In C. Wilson & D. Turner (Eds.), *Companion animals in human health* (pp. 135-148). London: Sage.

Van Houte, B. A., & Jarvis, P. A. (1995). The role of pets in preadolescent psychosocial development. *Journal of Applied Developmental Psychology, 16,* 463-479.

Vidovic, V. V., Stetic, V. V., & Bratko, D. (1999). Pet ownership, type of pet, and socio-emotional development of school children. *Anthrozoos, 12*(4), 211-217.

· Wells, D. L., & Hepper, P. G. (1995). Attitudes to animal use in children. *Anthrozoos, 4*(3), 159-178.

Wilson, C. C., Netting, F. E., & New, J. C. (1987). The pet attitude inventory. *Anthrozoos, 1*(3), 76-84.

46

—Ana Velázquez
Spain

Chapter 3

Companion Animals at Home: What Children Learn From Families

Mary Renck Jalongo,
Marjorie L. Stanek,
and Beatrice S. Fennimore

When Mwongeli, a kindergarten child, moved from Kenya to Pennsylvania with her graduate student parents, the 5-year-old saw an unbelievable sight from her apartment window one Sunday morning. A woman was walking a small dog that was wearing a red raincoat and tiny boots! This was a dramatic departure from Mwongeli's prior experience with the fierce dogs that guarded property in Kenya. That docile, diminutive, well-dressed canine, her father said when delightedly sharing the story, "captivated her." After the initial sighting, on any early morning that Mwongeli was not already on her way to school she could be found sitting at the window, eagerly watching for the woman and her dog, curious to see which outfit the animal might be wearing that day. As soon as the pair came into view, Mwongeli would call out excitedly to her parents. Even though the kindergartner's parents and two older sisters looked forward to weekends that did not have to begin quite so early, they would humor her by gazing out the window, tired yet amused by her obvious fascination with the woman and her little dog.

From a child development perspective, a dog in clothing raises interesting questions about what is imaginary and seen only in picture books versus what is real and could be seen out in the world. The walking amalgamation of real and pretend represented by the snowy-haired lady and her matching dog no doubt tapped into Mwongeli's ability to recognize incongruity. From a cultural perspective, this animal that was extremely pampered, even by Western standards, served to underscore dramatic differences in the role of nonhuman animals in society as well as contrasting views of human beings' responsibility for animals' welfare. From a family perspective, the odd lady and dog, even at a distance on the pavement below, had an effect on this Kenyan family's routines, conversations, and relationships. Such influences are all the more powerful when the animal in question is not merely something to be observed from afar but a living creature that is taken into a child's mind, heart, and habitat. This chapter is about companion animals that are brought into homes, and about the positive and negative consequences of such decisions, both immediate and long range.

Cultural Influences on Bonds With Companion Animals

Although attitudes toward family pets are greatly affected by the way in which animals are treated in society generally, significant differences exist in the ways that relationships between humans and companion animals are perceived in cultural groups within a society (Podberscek, Paul, & Serpell, 2000). There is considerable diversity in "the extent to which we connect with animals through moral concern, empathy, dominion, or utility" (Raupp, 1999, p. 142).

In countries where inadequate food supplies exist for people, dogs are apt to be valued exclusively as workers; in an affluent society, by contrast, expensive purebred dogs who have no work duties can be valued as a status symbol. In the continent of Africa, where food is often scarce, "human-centered" animal welfare initiatives are more apt to be successful because they demonstrate clear benefits for people (McCrindle, 1998). The Heifer Project International, for example, is a nonprofit organization that strives to reduce world hunger by using donations to purchase food- and income-producing livestock (e.g., cattle, goats, lambs), giving them to people to raise, and educating the recipients in ways that can improve the situation for all of the species involved (www.heifer.org).

In Western cultures, according to a study conducted in the Netherlands, attitudes toward animals of all types are most often attributable to five variables: 1) geographic location, 2) degree of urbanization, 3) type of dwelling, 4) age of owners, and 5) size of household (Endenberg, Hart, & DeVries, 1990). The best illustration of these influences is what occurs when one or more of these variables changes. A 1999 survey of 871 households in Soweto, South Africa, revealed that interactions between humans and dogs changed as the area became more urbanized. Traditionally, dogs were expected to forage for food, and no controls were placed over their breeding. Once South Africans moved into the city, however, the researchers found that the number of dogs kept as family pets had risen to an average of .42 dogs per household (McCrindle, Gallant, Cornelius, & Schoeman, 1999). Likewise, in Northern Ireland, where dogs traditionally have been used for work (e.g., hunting, herding) and entertainment (e.g., racing, circuses, and fighting), researchers noted a shift in the way that families viewed dogs, moving away from manipulation toward companionship (Wells & Hepper, 1997). Their study of 422 adults revealed that 63 percent of families owned a pet, mostly dogs. In a New Zealand study based on a questionnaire of 312 parents of 8- to 12-year-olds, almost 90 percent of families owned at least one pet. "Dogs, cats, and/or birds live in 71% of households in Belgium, 63% in France, 61% in Italy, and 70% in Ireland" (Bekoff, 2002). According to Bekoff (2002), two surveys conducted during 1994 estimated that the United States is home to 235 million companion animals—including approximately 60 million cats; 57 million dogs; 12.3 million rabbits, guinea pigs, hamsters, gerbils, and hedgehogs; 12 million fish tanks; 3 million birds; 7.3 million reptiles; 7 million ferrets; and a variety of other creatures.

Overall, the best predictor of which households

will own pets is whether or not the parents owned pets themselves as children, according to a British study of 150 parents of 4- to 16-year-old children (Paul & Serpell, 1992). When American adults were sorted into the four groups of never-owned pets, always-owned pets, owned-in-childhood only, and owned-in-adulthood only, those in the owned-in-adulthood only group usually reported being persuaded by other family members, such as spouse or a child, to acquire a companion animal to which they later became very attached (Kidd & Kidd, 1997). Clearly, considerable variation exists in pet ownership across individuals, generations, and cultures.

Sometimes the opportunity to own pets involves a clash between social classes. Perry Ogden (1999a, 1999b), who photographs and interviews children and families living in low-income sections of Dublin, describes how owning a pony is frequently the child's fondest dream. The parents of many of these children are struggling financially or are unemployed, yet they regard the acquisition of these animals as a way to bring healing and excitement into their child's otherwise bleak existence, as well as a way to inculcate a sense of responsibility in the child. At one time, the children could rely on the city's patches of green to keep their ponies, and they would bring them to the center of the Dublin for a monthly horse fair. Now, however, the "emerald cowboys" who shine in Ogden's photo essays are not such a welcome sight to other residents of Dublin. Current stringent licensing laws threaten the "pony culture" and a tradition so dear to these families.

Availability of wished-for pets can become an economic issue even for families that are not low income. Britain's Royal Society for the Prevention of Cruelty to Animals reports that the cost of keeping a dog as a pet throughout its average lifespan of 12 years is, in U.S. dollars, approximately $12,100. In China, according to a report in *Business Weekly*, the average annual income is approximately 7,000 yuan. A dog license costs about 5,000 yuan (approximately US$600) and the annual registration fee costs another 2,000 yuan (Salzman, 2000). Health care for pets is another expense. American pet owners spend approximately $12 billion per year on veterinary care,

Courtesy of Natalie K. Conrad

My pets

Frank

Rusty

Ket

"I like all animals. I have three pets. I like all my pets but Franklin my turtle is the best, because he is mine. In the summer I take him outside to play. I have a dog his name is Rusty. I named him after my favorite racer. (Rusty Wallace). I have a cat her name is cricket. When she purrrrrs she sounds like a cricket. I love them all and they love me."
The end

"I have three pets a dog, bunny, and crab. Me and my dog Lady go outside together she pretects me. My bunny Lexy jumps around when I sing jump with the bunny hop with the bunny. My crab Crabby makes alot of noise."
The end

Joshua Maruska's drawing and story.   *Lindsey Phillips' drawing and story.*

according to the American Animal Hospital Association. Health insurance for family pets is commonplace in Sweden where 50 percent of pets are insured. In contrast, just 1 percent of Americans and 11 percent of British pet owners insure family pets. Clearly, the cost of owning particular companion animals in particular parts of the world can be prohibitive (Salzman, 2000).

A national survey published in Australia takes a very different approach to the expense of owning a companion animal. Based on the finding that dog and cat owners make fewer doctor visits and are less likely to be on medications, Headey (1999) estimates that pet ownership *saved* the country $98 million in the 1994-95 financial year.

Even after a family does make a financial commitment to pet keeping, the role of the pet has to be negotiated. In ancient Greece and Rome, keeping pets was a widely accepted practice that was frowned upon only when animals were treated as children (Bodson, 2000). By way of contrast, in the United States, home to approximately 53 million dogs and 61 million cats (Schoen, 2001) and 212 million other pets, with 60 percent of all households owning at least one pet, 7 out of 10 families view their companion animals as members of the family (Salzman, 2000). One explanation for the family member status afforded to companion animals has to do with the postmodern era. Postmodern times are characterized by insecurity: "Changes to aspects of social and cultural life are fragile and fugitive. As neighborhood, community, family, and friendship relations lose their normative and enduring qualities, companion animals increasingly are drawn in to those formerly exclusive human emotion spaces" (Franklin, Tranter, & White, 2001, p. 127).

Although people may not always think about a companion animal as a member of the family, it can be an integral part of their sense of place, home, and normalcy. Many people will go to great lengths to rescue a pet in life-threatening circumstances. A study of 397 California households that were part of an emergency evacuation during a flood found that only 20 percent of the families failed to take along their pets. Most pets that were left behind were dogs that lived outside or cats without cat carriers. More than 80 percent of the people who returned to the disaster site did so at personal risk to rescue a family pet (Heath, 2000; Heath, Kass, Beck, & Glickman, 2001).

"My Pets
My pets names are Simba and Trixie. Simba is a cat and Trixie is a dog. Simba thinks he's a dog. He drinks and eats from my dogs bowl. He talks to us, and he follows us around when he wants something. Trixie my other pet is thirteen. She is getting old, but Simba keeps her young! Simba chases Trixie around the house!

I am very happy to have Simba and Trixie."

by Alayna Tomaselli

Courtesy of Natalie K. Conrad

Variables Affecting the Choice of Companion Animals in Families

Some family pets are chosen carefully after much thought and research, while others show up on the doorstep. A father shared the following story about how a mistreated dog earned an honored place in his family:

> I heard a dog yelping outside, so I went in my backyard and saw my neighbor hitting his dog with a stick. I had seen him mistreat the animal before, but never like this. "If you're just going to beat that dog," I said, "you ought to give him away." My neighbor replied angrily, "Why don't you take him, then? He's a pain in the ass." I said, "I will if you don't want him," and the neighbor opened the gate and handed the rottweiler over to me. The first thing that I taught the dog was to stay inside our fence, mainly because I never wanted him to have a run-in with the neighbor again. That dog turned out to be the best animal I ever owned. Once, when my daughter was a toddler, she figured out how to open the gate and started to walk outside when my wife had taken her eyes off her for just a moment. The dog barked and grabbed onto my little girl's clothes to keep her from going out into the busy street. The dog is very gentle, but if anyone tries to come into the yard uninvited, his size and bark scares them off. I always feel like I have a protector around, especially if the kids are out there playing.

As this story illustrates, sometimes animals come into families in unexpected ways, or as strays. When such choices are more planned, however, variables that are commonly considered by families include the companion animal's cost, availability, care requirements, other family members' attitudes toward the animal, aspects of the environment, the animal's trainability, the pet's life expectancy, the child's emotional maturity, and any special needs of the child or other family members (Frith, 1982).

As many parents and families can attest, adults' and children's perspectives on pet ownership can be worlds apart. The adult thinks of the expense, inconvenience, property damage, and practical issues, such as what to do with the pet during vacations. The child dreams of unconditional acceptance from a devoted animal, happy hours spent in the pet's company, and the pride of being the official owner of the animal. Children frequently launch a campaign to own a particular animal, and consequently marshal all of the persuasive powers and resources at their disposal to convince adults to permit them to keep a pet. They might want one of the more common household pets, such as a dog or cat. Or, they may be interested in something less "warm and fuzzy," like a chameleon or a tarantula. Even when adults are not all that keen on getting a pet, they may sometimes acquiesce. Or, they may suggest a different animal that requires less maintenance, and try to persuade the child of that animal's positive attributes. They may ask the child to engage in a more thorough investigation of the choices as a way of postponing the decision.

Photo courtesy of Shireen DeSouza.

A father and son with the camel they trained.

Sometimes, adults extract promises from children about taking care of the pet that the child wants so desperately. If the adults accept from the outset that children are just learning about responsible pet care and that some failure in fulfilling such promises is inevitable, pet ownership can help "establish firm foundations for developing character based on respect, love, forgiveness, and altruism" (Schoen, 2001, p. 197). On the other hand, when an adult forces a child to give up a pet to "teach the child a lesson," children may adopt the attitude that animals are "disposable, like paper cups" (Hess, 1998). If a child is forced to surrender a family pet because the child failed to be a completely reliable caretaker for the pet, the real lesson learned is that "pets can be rejected when they are inconvenient" and that "living beings do not have any inherent value" (Hess, 1998, p. 206).

Familial attitudes toward animals often span generations. A review of the literature suggests not only that adults tend to keep the same kind of animals that were their companions during childhood (Serpell, 1999), but also that general attitudes toward animals—"treasuring, trashing, or terrorizing"—frequently are passed on from parent to child (Raupp, 1999). The three major influences on adults' attitudes toward companion animals are: 1) adults' experiences with companion animals when they were children, 2) the way in which animals are treated in society generally, and 3) the particular ways that relationships between human and nonhuman animals are perceived by cultural groups (Podberscek, Paul, & Serpell, 2000). Even if the dominant culture does not have a culture of pet keeping, variations exist within a cultural group and certain individuals may form a bond with a companion animal that is considered to be strange.

In spite of cultural differences, over 50 percent of Western households are home to at least one pet (Podberscek, Paul, & Serpell, 2000), and three-quarters of the children in the United States are more likely to grow up with a companion animal than with both parents (Melson, 2001). Often, family status is conferred upon a companion animal by one or more members of the family, perhaps out of the implicit belief that the animal possesses attributes worth emulating, such as loyalty or an even temperament (Beck, 1999). When an interspecies bond exists between a human and a companion animal, it frequently is more complex, intensely felt, and indelible than many people recognize. One research strategy for assessing the strength of the family-companion animal bond relies on drawings and the proximity of various family members to the child. Based on children's drawings in the *Family Life Space Diagram*, family members may perceive their relationship with the family dog to be as close as that with a human family member (Barker & Randolph, 1988).

Reasons for Pet Ownership in Families

When David and Jana first got married, they took in a stray tabby cat. A little while later, they got a black lab puppy. A relative remarked that they appeared to be "escalating" and wondered if a child might be next, to which Jana replied, "This is a test. If we can take care of a cat and a dog, we ought to be able to take care of a baby." The perspective of this young professional couple is

Matthew grows up with the family dog.

Photo courtesy of Sara Rutledge.

not unusual in the United States. Many people state, as this couple did, that pet keeping serves as a form of practice for parenting. Yet if pet keeping is merely a rehearsal, then pets would become obsolete when the new baby arrives. That seldom happens if the person/pet bond is strong and the animal remains even-tempered. Rather, most new parents tend to be very concerned that their pet might become "jealous" (notice the anthropomorphism here), and families are overjoyed when their companion animals co-exist peacefully with human offspring. Evidently, relationships with companion animals are valuable in their own right.

What reasons do parents and families offer for bringing their children together with companion animals? According to one study, the perceived advantages of pet ownership include such things as teaching the child responsibility and care, responding to the child's persistent requests for a pet, and providing children the opportunity to receive affection from their animal companions (Fifield & Forsyth, 1999). Many parents and families view the raising of animals as a way to help their children develop social competence, concern for the environment, and compassion for nonhuman creatures. Families who live in rural communities often encourage their children to participate in 4-H, an organization that is designed to educate children about raising livestock and learning the necessary skills to maintain the family farm or ranch. In some cases, such as on a dairy farm, these 4-H projects do become companion animals; hence, many ethical issues surround the animal's treatment.

Even when differences of opinion about which animals make suitable companions exist, most families already are convinced that animals play an important, positive role in family life. Animals serve many positive functions for their human counterparts, regardless of their age (Soave, 1998). Companion animals give their caretakers a sense that they are needed, and they develop a sense of responsibility in the caretaker. Companion animals free humans from loneliness because people can talk to them as a friend and companion, and animals reciprocate with trust and affection. In a 1999 survey by the American Animal Hospital Association (reported in

Salzman, 2000), 72 percent of married pet owners reported greeting their pets before their spouses when they arrive home and 34 percent said that talk about their pets is a major topic of conversation with friends and co-workers. About 65 percent of pet owners sing or dance for their pet, 63 percent celebrate the pet's birthday, 53 percent would take time off work to care for a sick pet, 52 percent prepare special meals for a pet, and 43 percent display a pet's photograph at work (Salzman, 2000). In a survey of former and current pet owners in the United States, more than half said that they would prefer a dog or cat companion to a human companion if they were stranded on a desert island (Salzman, 2000).

Companion animals educate their caregivers, as well as provide exercise and recreation. Many companion animals not only fill the role of helper and protector, but also provide a context for social interactions with other animal owners or animal lovers (Soave, 1998). In sad or uncertain times, companion animals provide a sense of security and support. Families frequently credit companion animals with reducing stress in their children's lives, helping children to gain friendship and love, and providing a basis for recreational activities (Covert, Whiren, Keith, & Nelson, 1985). Sadly, companion animals sometimes sacrifice their health or even give their lives for their owners by

Photo courtesy of Darrell Combs.

Daniel with his trained rabbit, Petra.

functioning as sentinels of unsafe environmental conditions. Historically, miners took birds into the shaft with them to serve as an early warning system of gas exposure. More recently, high blood lead concentrations in indoor pets was predictive of high levels of lead in the soil and in children (Berny, Cote, & Buck, 1995).

Obstacles to Bringing Companion Animals Into Families

Despite all of the perceived benefits of companion animals, parents and families also recognize that they can be a source of considerable anxiety, as children and families worry about their pets' safety, health, and emotional well-being. The major drawbacks of owning pets cited by families included the effort in finding suitable holiday care, the time and work involved in caring for pets, and the mess that animals can cause (Fifield & Forsyth, 1999).

Unfortunately, not all families are in a position to own or care for a companion animal. Allergies or illnesses may make it impossible to welcome or maintain a pet in a home, as may poverty, the parents' employment schedules, parental fear or dislike of animals, homelessness, or rules against animals in apartments or housing units. While the inability to get a pet may be disappointing or frustrating to a child and family, even more difficult are the circumstances in which beloved pets must be given up.

One couple had a cat for many years before the birth of their first child. When the child turned 4, he began to constantly sneeze and cough. A visit to the family pediatrician revealed an allergy that made it necessary to give the cat to a neighbor, much to the disappointment and sadness of the parents and child. The three children in another family longed to adopt a stray cat, but were warned by their father that his allergies might become uncontrollable. Although he took medication for the few months during which the cat lived in the home, his symptoms became too severe. The children and their mother took a sad journey to the local pet shelter, hoping that the cat they needed to give up might find better fortune with another family. A 12-year-old girl and her single mother had a beloved dog that had to be given away when the mother's AIDS weakened her to

the point where the dog could no longer be walked or cared for. The girl wept for days, and her sorrow was compounded by the knowledge that she too might need to find a different home if her mother's illness became terminal. In the United States at the turn of the century, it was estimated that 150,000 children would lose a mother, and thousands more a father, sibling, or other family member to AIDS (Geballe & Gruendel, 1998). These and many other children might be required to accept the fact that health conditions of a family member make the presence of animals in the home an impossibility.

Family pets are, in actuality, a luxury. Enough extra income needs to be available for food, shelter, veterinary needs, and other expenses. Animals often must be boarded when families go away, which can be a considerable expense. The home itself must be large enough to accommodate pets as well as people. And, of course, the family must have a home! It is estimated that 35.6 percent of the overall homeless population in the United States is made up of families, and that one in four of the homeless are children (Polakow, 1998). In 1995, the U.S. Department of Education estimated that 750,000 school-age children were homeless (Coalition for the Homeless, 1996). Clearly, a family in such financial straits could not possibly have a pet.

Other families live in apartments or public housing projects that do not allow animals. A professor visiting a public elementary school in an area characterized by high poverty was drawn to a display of "our best essays" in the front hallway. A beautifully written essay, written by a girl in the 4th grade, was illustrated with the portrayal of a weeping child (hearts surrounding her head) clutching a small dog. The essay told of a little dog she loved who one day disappeared. Her mother initially told her that the dog was at the vet. Ultimately, her father explained that they were not allowed to keep a dog in their housing project, and they had been forced to give it away. The child eloquently described her broken heart. While her father promised that she could have another dog if they were ever able to buy a house, it was that particular dog she had wanted so badly and now grieved for so deeply. There could be no doubt that this searing memory would stay with her for a lifetime.

Poverty, with all its devastating effects on the lives of children, most often makes family ownership of pets impossible. In any given year from 1987 to 1996, an estimated one in five of all children in the United States—some 12 to 14 million—lived in poverty. In fact, the United States has a higher rate of poverty than most other Western industrialized nations (Brooks-Gunn, Duncan, & Maritato, 1997). Children who do not have enough food to eat or clothes to wear, who cannot obtain regular medical and dental treatment, and whose communities are often characterized by violence and drug use, have problems far greater than the lack of pets in their lives. Yet, they are still children, and thus would benefit greatly from warm, close relationships with companion animals. Many children who experience poverty have single parents, or married parents, who struggle to hold two or more jobs yet are still unable to gain adequate income. Current changes in welfare legislation make it more likely that parents of children who are poor will be required to work many hours outside the home (Children's Defense Fund, 2001). Many children spend long hours alone after school and late into the evening, and many are responsible for younger siblings. When even the cost of child care is too prohibitive, money for the care of pets is obviously not available. Yet, sadly, the lonely hours many of these children experience would be greatly alleviated by the comforting presence of a family pet.

Some parents fear or dislike animals, and will not permit children to have pets in the home. Other parents, who may be cruel or emotionally unstable, may use pets to upset children. One adult woman still struggles with the memory from her childhood of her mother threatening to drown her cat. These threats would come when she forgot to feed her cat in the evening. Her mother also would toss the cat up into the air and out of the house for the night, even when the temperature was below freezing. The woman remembers hearing the cat cry outside, and worrying about it as she fell asleep. One college student, in response to the assignment of a written autobiography, wrote poignantly about the day on which her angry father, jealous of her mother's love for the family dog, suddenly gave the dog away to another family. She described crying and meeting the sad eyes of the dog, who jumped up into the back window to look at her, as the car of the adoptive family pulled away. As luck would have it, the dog bit someone in the car and was promptly returned to the home. Yet, so many years later, this student was pained by the sadness of the incident. These are instances in which families allow pets to live in the home, and yet through insensitivity or cruelty the pets are associated with painful experiences for the children.

Clearly, all the children affected by the sad circumstances discussed in this section are in need of comfort and care. As society advocates for their well-being and protection on social and economic fronts, part of that social care could be in the form of helping children who cannot have family pets to be involved, in healthy ways, in the lives of companion animals.

Abuse of Companion Animals in Families

Through systematic study, it has become increasingly clear that acts of violence against both children and animals have common origins and influences (Ascione, 1999, p. xvi). Since the 13th century, animal abuse and abuse of people have been linked; at times, both have been considered nameless and faceless property. Thomas Aquinas (1225-1274) contended that cruelty to animals would have a "brutalizing influence, which would dispose men to inflict cruelty on their fellow humans" (cited in Serpell, 1996, p. 105).

In 1874, Henry Bergh founded the American Society for the Prevention of Cruelty to Animals (ASPCA), an organization that forever changed people's attitudes toward the treatment of animals and children. Bergh was a true visionary and known for his kindness. He invented the concepts of the animal shelter, the clay pigeon to prevent the slaughter of so many birds during trap shooting, and even an ambulance for horses (6 years before the ambulance for humans was created). Social worker Etta Wheeler approached Bergh about the case of a Civil War orphan who had endured being beaten, burned, and cut with scissors by her foster mother of 7 years. Wheeler had unsuccessfully pursued every legal avenue to rescue the child from the abusive home. Would this man, noted for his compassion, help? Yes. The result was the first successfully prosecuted case of child abuse, based on animal cruelty laws. The court used a statute against animal cruelty to remove 8-year-old Mary Ellen Wilson from her foster parent's custody. The prosecution argued that Mary Ellen was a member of the animal kingdom, and thus was entitled to protections against abuse granted to animals (Regoli & Hewitt, 2003, p. 9). Following this highly publicized case, laws were enacted to protect abused children. To this day, the scissors that were used to inflict harm on Mary Ellen Wilson are on display at ASPCA headquarters as a reminder of the link between cruelty to helpless children and animals. (For more about the case, log on to http://home.swfla.rr.com/maryellenwilson/maryellen.html.)

The American Humane Association has had both child and animal protection divisions since its inception in the late 1800s (Hess, 1998). Today, First Strike, a special program of The Humane Society of the United States, is dedicated to further investigating the connection between abuse of children and animals. One hypothesis is that violence toward animals and children is interrelated, because both animal and child victims are vulnerable living creatures with a capacity for experiencing pain. The victim in either case also is capable of displaying outward signs of pain and hurt, and may die as a result of injuries (Regoli & Hewitt, 2003). Thus, it is important to understand both animal cruelty and child maltreatment in the hopes that we can prevent needless suffering and harm to the most vulnerable and defenseless members of our population. Abuse occurs when perpetrators misuse power and impose control on their victims. "Deeds of violence are performed largely by those who are trying to establish their self esteem, to defend their self image, and to demonstrate that they, too, are significant" (May, 1972, p. 23). Factors leading to violence against both animals and people are the same, as are the psychologically traumatic and damaging effects (Lacroix, 1999). Frank R. Ascione (1999), an expert on the subject of child and animal maltreatment

and domestic violence, has found that the cycle of violence in the home often begins with violence towards animals. Perhaps this is true because the basic power dynamic is similar. Abusers frequently perceive themselves as being relatively powerless to control a "difficult" animal or child, and they use cruelty as a way of establishing power (Sims, Chin, Eckman, Enck, & Abromaitis, 2001).

In many cases, animals are used as a means of control over both sexually abused children and victims of domestic violence (Ascione, Weber, & Wood, 1997). Dysfunctional environments, in which children witness violence being perpetrated against their companion animals, inflict greater harm and trauma on those within the household. "Abusers often threaten or actually injure or kill family pets to send a chilling message about what's in store for the child who tells about abuse" (Melson, 2001, p. 173). Many victims of domestic violence speak of trying to hide and protect their animals, often physically endangering themselves in the process (Arluke, 2000; Melson, 2001). In a study of 12 Wisconsin shelters conducted in 1994-95; three quarters of all the women and children interviewed reported that they had been threatened with the abuse of an animal. Many had been forced to witness the abuser hurting or killing an animal, often "for their benefit" (Melson, 2001, p. 174).

A study conducted by Michael Robin, a social worker from the University of Minnesota, investigated pet ownership among high school students who stayed out of trouble with the law and those who had a police record. He found that the rate of pet ownership among delinquent youth was comparable to that of other high school children. The variable on which the two groups differed was in the nurturance and protection of pets. At the time of the study, about 50 percent of the teenagers who had not been in trouble still had their companion animals, while fewer than 30 percent of those adolescents categorized as delinquents still had theirs. More than one-third of the teenagers who were troubled had lost their animal companions through some violent means. Often, the companion animal had been deliberately killed by a family member or other person in the community. The researchers concluded that this type of violent loss often characterized the lives of children with social and emotional behavior problems (reported in Beck & Katcher, 1996).

Another question raised in the research is whether ways of interacting with family pets are related in any way to patterns of interaction between and among family members. According to Yi Fu Tuan's (1984) theory of power, dominance coupled with affection will yield a pet, while dominance without affection will create a victim. Stewart (1993) hypothesized that insights into relationships with pets have implications for domestic violence therapy. In a study of 53 child-abusing families, the researchers found that 60 percent of these families also abused and neglected their pets (DeViney, Dickert, & Lockwood, 1983). Families that abused their pets tended to have younger pets, lower levels of veterinary care, and more family conflict over pet care than other families, leading the researchers to conclude that animal abuse may be an indicator of problems with human relationships in the family. Men who have a history of pet abuse are often violent toward family pets and family members (Weber, 1999), and 46.5 percent of male batterers, based on data gathered from women's shelter residents, used companion animals to control, hurt, and intimidate their spouses and children, usually by threatening to harm or give away the beloved animal companions (Flynn, 2000). At times, violent family members actually hurt or killed a family pet (Raupp, 1999). When 63 undergraduates were asked to participate in interviews that focused on different targets of family violence, 34 recalled joint discipline situations in which children were punished for what companion animals did, or vice versa. Some of these situations resulted in the pet being discarded or even killed. The majority of the interviewees found a connection between violence against children and violence against companion animals.

Today, the American Humane Association trains humane officers to recognize signs of abuse; in some states, it is mandatory for humane officers to report suspected abuse of animals, because the relationship between animal and child abuse is so strong (Hess, 1998).

Cruelty to Companion Animals Perpetrated by Children

As Andrew Vachss (1993) has observed, "We are tested and sometimes we fail. The maltreated child cries, 'I hurt.' Unheard or unheeded, that cry becomes prophecy" (p. 55). Children from dysfunctional and abusive households, as well as those afflicted with some sorts of behavioral disorders, sometimes engage in violent and cruel acts against animal companions. Many child victims of violence have a host of behavioral problems, including conduct disorder, which has been classified as a complex interplay of behavioral and psychological problems (Melson, 2001). The appearance of intentional animal abuse in children younger than age 7 was added to the list of symptoms for conduct disorder found in the Diagnostic and Statistical Manual of Mental Disorders in 1987, and is frequently the earliest manifestation of this disorder (Boat, 1999; Melson, 2001). Afflicted children are at a high risk for juvenile delinquency.

Animal abuse usually occurs as part of a "constellation of symptoms, including fighting, tantrums, truancy, vandalism, and fire setting" (Melson, 2001, p. 164). These delinquent acts cause many victims of conduct disorder to come under the supervision of the juvenile justice system, and may put them at risk for a lifelong propensity towards violence and aggression (Boat, 1999; Melson, 2001). Locating children who abuse animals may allow us to intervene earlier with those who are developing these tendencies before the violent behaviors escalate to victimization of their fellow citizens. Criminologists commonly report that animal abuse may be found in the developmental histories of between 25 and 67 percent of violent offenders (Regoli & Hewitt, 2003). Thus, we might use this red flag to identify at-risk youth before they become involved in the criminal justice system, or engage in increasingly violent behavior.

Disturbingly, more than half of the children questioned in the Wisconsin shelter study had perpetrated an abusive act on an animal themselves. This ratio has been supported in other similar inquiries (Ascione, 1999). Cases in which children repeat the abusive behaviors they witness are known as "abuse-reactive" (Loar, 1999). Abuse reactiveness suggests that exposure to animal cruelty in childhood may be associated with lower levels of empathy as well as later violence toward family members (Flynn, 2000). It seems almost counterintuitive that children traumatized by witnessing abuse of an animal would go on to perpetrate these same sorts of acts. Frank Ascione (1999) suggests that this replication of prior violence may occur for one of two reasons. In some cases, the child comes to identify with his or her aggressor, and thereby repeats the act. In others, through observational learning child victims come to believe that what they witness is "normal" treatment of animals. In both of these scenarios, "children carry out the abuse in an attempt to gain mastery over their own experience and to understand their parent's behavior" (Loar, 1999).

It is not the case, however, that children in every dysfunctional environment abuse their animal companions. In many cases, "children bombarded by violence seek solace in their pets, and are careful and solicitous of their well-being" (Melson, 2001, pp. 181-182). Child victims of abuse frequently endanger their own well-being to protect a beloved companion animal (Arluke, 2000; Melson, 2001). Often, children who have grown up in environments where animals are mistreated do not repeat the cycle of violence; rather, they become nurturers and protectors of their animal friends. Interestingly, Nebbe's (1997) dissertation study of 101 adults who were abused as children found that children who managed to form a strong human/animal bond did not perpetuate the abuse by abusing children or animals as adults, while those who formed no such attachments to pets did report participating in abuse as victims themselves or as abusers of children or animals. Although this is an apparent contradiction, it reveals an important point. Family violence may predispose certain children to the mistreatment of animals, but this tendency towards violence is dependent upon the individual child (Boat, 1999; Melson, 2001).

There is general agreement that children's perceptions of animals, ranging from treasuring to throwing away to mistreating, are colored by their home environment and family structure (Melson, 2001). We also can expect that a child's bond with companion animals will be shaped by the child's natural temperament and characteristics. The family, however, is the socialization agent that provides meaning to these animal bonds (Melson, 2001).

Conclusion

It is our position that all people should have the opportunity to interact with companion animals in some context. During childhood, such interactions further a child's social cognition, or "ideas about self and other beings" (Melson, 2001, p. 190). As children form bonds of attachment with one or more nonhuman animals, they learn to become nurturers. Often, that care and concern for a companion animal extends to a more generalized sense of responsibility for other creatures and stewardship for the environment. The humane values that enable a person to care for other species can inspire them to become better human beings. As Henry Bergh, founder of the American Society for the Prevention of Cruelty to Animals, asserted in 1874, "Men will be just towards men when they are charitable towards animals" (quoted in Ascione, 1999). While human beings are capable of developing complex concepts such as sympathy and empathy in the absence of exposure to companion animals, surely personal characteristics that are so valuable to society merit a wide range of opportunities for development. Anthropomorphic arguments aside, the very traits that we admire in animals—sensitivity, compassion, courage, loyalty, fortitude, cooperation, resourcefulness, and generosity, according to von Kreisler's (2001) list—are the traits that human beings can develop more fully in themselves within meaningful contexts of caring for animal companions. For it is often by welcoming other species into the circle of our human families, at home and in the classroom, that we teach ourselves and our children to become more humane.

References

Arluke, A. (2000). Secondary victimization in companion animal abuse: The owner's perspective. In A. L. Podberscek, E. S. Paul, & J. A. Serpell (Eds.), *Companion animals and us: Exploring the relationships between people and pets* (pp. 275-291). New York: Cambridge University Press.

Ascione, F. R. (1999). The abuse of animals and human interpersonal violence. In F. R. Ascione & P. Arkow (Eds.), *Child abuse, domestic violence, and animal abuse:*

Linking the circles of compassion for prevention and intervention (pp. 50-61). West Lafayette, IN: Purdue University Press.

Ascione, F. R., Weber, C. V., & Wood, D. S. (1997). The abuse of animals and domestic violence: A national survey of shelters for women who are battered. *Society and Animals, 5*(3), 205-218.

Barker, S. B., & Randolph, R. T. (1988). The human-canine bond: Closer than family ties? *Journal of Mental Health Counseling, 10*(1), 46-56.

Beck, A. M. (1999). Companion animals and their companions: Sharing a strategy for survival. *Bulletin of Science, Technology & Society, 19*(4), 280-285.

Beck, A. M., & Katcher, A. H. (1996). *Between pets and people: The importance of animal companionship* (Rev. ed.). Lafayette, IN: Purdue University Press.

Bekoff, M. (2002). *Minding the animals: Awareness, emotions, and heart.* New York: Oxford University Press.

Berny, P. J., Cote, L. M., & Buck, W. B. (1995). Can household pets be reliable monitors of lead exposure in humans? *The Science of the Total Environment, 172*(2), 163-173.

Boat, B. W. (1999). Abuse of children and abuse of animals: Using the links to inform child assessment and protection. In F. R. Ascione & P. Arkow (Eds.), *Child abuse, domestic violence, and animal abuse* (pp. 83-100). West Lafayette, IN: Purdue University Press.

Bodson, L. (2000). Motivations for pet-keeping in ancient Greece and Rome: A preliminary survey. In A. L. Podberscek, E. S. Paul, & J. A. Serpell (Eds.), *Companion animals and us: Exploring the relationships between people and pets* (pp. 27-41). New York: Cambridge University Press.

Brooks-Gunn, J., Duncan, G. J., & Maritato, N. (1997). Poor families, poor outcomes: The well-being of children and youth. In G. J. Duncan & J. Brooks-Gunn (Eds.), *Consequences of growing up poor* (pp. 1-17). New York: Russell Sage.

Children's Defense Fund. (2001). *The state of America's children 2001.* Washington, DC: Author.

Covert, A. M., Whiren, A. P., Keith, J., & Nelson, C. (1985). Pets, early adolescents, and families. *Marriage and Family Review, 8*(3-4), 95-108.

DeViney, E., Dickert, J., & Lockwood, R. (1983). The care of pets within child abusing families. *International Journal for the Study of Animal Problems, 4*(4), 321-329.

Endenberg, N., Hart, H., DeVries, H. W. (1990). Differences between owners and nonowners of companion animals. *Anthrozoos, 4*(2), 120-126.

Fifield, S. J., & Forsyth, D. K. (1999). A pet for children: Factors related to pet ownership. *Anthrozoos, 12*(1), 24-32.

Flynn, C. P. (2000). Woman's best friend: Pet abuse and the role of companion animals in the lives of battered women. *Violence Against Women, 6*(2), 162-177.

Franklin, A., Tranter, B., & White, R. (2001). Explaining support for animal rights: A comparison of two recent approaches to humans, nonhuman animals, and postmodernity. *Society and Animals, 9*(2), 127-144.

Frith, G. H. (1982). Pets for handicapped children. *Pointer, 27*(1), 24-27.

Geballe, S., & Gruendel, J. (1998). The crisis within the crisis: The growing epidemic of AIDS orphans. In S. Books (Ed.), *Invisible children in the society and its schools*

(pp. 47-66). Mahwah, NJ: Lawrence Erlbaum.

Headey, B. (1999). Health benefits and health cost savings due to pets: Preliminary estimates from an Australian National Survey. *Social Indicators Research, 47*(2), 233-243.

Heath, S. E. (2000). An epidemiological study of public and animal health consequences of pet ownership in a disaster: The January 1997 flood of Yuba County, California. *Dissertation Abstracts International, Section B: The Sciences and Engineering, 60*(11-B), p. 5384.

Heath, S. E., Kass, P. H., Beck, A. M., & Glickman, L. T. (2001). Human and pet-related risk factors for household evacuation failure during a natural disaster. *American Journal of Epidemiology, 153*(7), 659-665.

Hess, E. (1998). *Lost and found: Dogs, cats, and everyday heroes at a country animal shelter.* San Diego, CA: Harvest Books/Harcourt.

Kidd, A. H., & Kidd, R. M. (1997). Changes in the behavior of pet owners across generations. *Psychological Reports, 80*(1), 195-202.

Lacroix, C. A. (1999). Another weapon for combating family abuse: Prevention of animal abuse. In F. R. Ascione & P. Arkow (Eds.), *Child abuse, domestic violence, and animal abuse* (pp. 62-81). West Lafayette, IN: Purdue University Press.

Loar, L. (1999). "I'll only help you if you have two legs," or why human service professionals should pay close attention to cases involving cruelty to animals. In F. R. Ascione & P. Arkow (Eds.), *Child abuse, domestic violence, and animal abuse* (pp. 120-136). West Lafayette, IN: Purdue University Press.

May, R. (1972). *Power and influence.* New York: W.W. Norton.

McCrindle, C. M. E. (1998). The community development approach to animal welfare: An African perspective. *Applied Behaviour Science, 59*(1), 227-233.

Melson, G. F. (2001). *Why the wild things are: Animals in the lives of children.* Cambridge, MA: Harvard University Press.

Moore, A. (2001). Ground rules for dogs, cats—and kids. *Prevention, 53*(9), 209-211.

National Coalition for the Homeless. (1996, October). *Facts about homeless families and children in America.* Washington, DC: Author.

Nebbe, L. J. (1997). The human-animal bond's role with the abused child. *Dissertation Abstracts International Section B: The Sciences and Engineering, 58*(3-B), 1568.

Ogden, P. (1999a). Emerald cowboys. *Life, 22*(3), 25-27.

Ogden, P. (1999b). *Pony kids.* New York: Aperture Foundation.

Paul, E. S., & Serpell, J. (1992). Why children keep pets: The influence of child and family characteristics. *Anthrozoos, 5*(4), 231-244.

Podberscek, A. L., Paul, E. S., & Serpell, J. A. (Eds.). (2000). *Companion animals and us: Exploring the relationships between people and pets.* New York: Cambridge University Press.

Polakow, V. (1998). Homeless children and their families: The discards of the Postmodern 1990s. In S. Books (Ed.), *Invisible children in the society and its schools* (pp. 3-22). Mahwah, NJ: Lawrence Erlbaum.

Raupp, C. (1999). Treasuring, trashing, or terrorizing:

Adult outcomes of childhood socialization about companion animals. *Society & Animals, 7*(2), 141-149.

Regoli, R. M., & Hewitt, J. D. (2003). *Delinquency in society* (5th ed.). Boston: McGraw-Hill.

Salzman, M. (2000). Pet trends. *Vital Speeches of the Day, 67*(5), 147-153.

Schoen, A. M. (2001). *Kindred spirits: How the remarkable bond between humans and animals can change the way we live.* New York: Broadway Books.

Serpell, J. (1996). *In the company of animals: A study of human/animal relationships.* New York: Cambridge University Press.

Serpell, J. (1999). Guest editor's introduction: Animals in children's lives. *Society and Animals, 7*(2), 87-94.

Sims, V. K., Chin, M. G., Eckman, M. L., Enck, B. M., & Abromaitis, S. M. (2001). Caregiver attributions are not just for children: Evidence for generalized locus of power schemas. *Journal of Applied Developmental Psychology, 22,* 527-541.

Soave, O. A. (1998). *The human/animal bond: A cultural survey.* San Francisco: Austin & Winfield.

Stewart, K. (1993). Victims or pets. *The Australian and New Zealand Journal of Family Therapy, 14*(1), 45-47.

Tuan, Yi-Fu. (1984). *Dominance and affection: The making of pets.* New Haven, CT: Yale University Press.

Vachss, A. (1993). *Another chance to get it right.* Milwaukie, OR: Dark Horse.

Weber, C. V. (1999). A descriptive study of the relation between domestic violence and pet abuse. *Dissertation Abstracts International Section B: The Sciences and Engineering, 59*(8-A), p. 4492.

Wells, D. L., & Hepper, P. G. (1997). Pet ownership and adults' views on the use of animals. *Society & Animals, 5*(1), 45-63.

Chapter 4

A Friend at School: Classroom Pets and Companion Animals in the Curriculum

—Naomi Guede
Netherlands/Antilles

Mark G. Twiest, Meghan Mahoney Twiest, and Mary Renck Jalongo

—Virginie Dereppe
Belgium

> *As a beginning elementary teacher in Macon, Georgia, I wanted to reach my 6th-grade students and create a sense of community in my classroom. It seemed only logical to include animals at school, given my love of animals and my husband's job as a curator of science at the city's museum, which housed a sizable live animal collection. I had no idea at the time that as a result of this animal-friendly approach my room would become the most popular room in the building and would be visited by just about every student in the school. Nor did I expect my students to take such pride in being a member of my class. They were the ones who monitored the door when other students would come to see the snakes or feed the gerbils a piece of lettuce retrieved from a lunch tray. An amazing sense of ownership and curiosity spilled over into the curriculum, as well as empathy for all living things and the joy of shared learning.*
>
> *—Meghan Twiest*

As adults, we often identify ourselves as either being "animal people" or not. As teachers, we have the option of choosing whether or not to share our classroom space and time with companion animals. We can be advocates for bringing animals and children together in the classroom, or we can determine that such experiences should occur elsewhere.

This chapter will examine the pros and cons of having animals in the classroom, offer guidelines for choosing classroom animals, and suggest necessary precautions. Information about how to integrate animals—classroom pets, visiting animals, and animals on school grounds and beyond—into the curriculum is also included.

Access to Animals in the Classroom

Contemporary students have much less free time and often less opportunity and inclination to explore the outdoor world than their peers a generation ago did. With structured activities, parent work schedules, and safety concerns more of a consideration today than in the past, children are less free to roam and observe nonhuman creatures in their natural environments. Additionally, many children grow up in urban environments where there are not only fewer natural places to explore, but also limited space in which to interact with nonhuman animals (e.g., prohibitions in apartment buildings against pets).

In contrast, many educators have childhood memories of investigating such creatures as worms, ants, butterflies, birds, salamanders, and crayfish in their natural environments. Often, observation turned the curious mind to collection, and grasshoppers, worms, and fish were carefully gathered in jars and brought home. Putting together a suitable home for the animals to live in was given utmost consideration by the young collector. How closely these contrived environments came to simulating the natural habitat and meeting animals' requirements may have varied widely, but there is little doubt that life lessons were learned in the process.

The nurturing relationship between children and the animals they keep often provides a unique opportunity for growth and development of both species. Interactions with animals affect children's social growth and communication, and "there is strong evidence that the mere presence of animals alters a child's attitude toward him- or herself and improves the ability to relate to others" (Rud & Beck, 2000, p. 313).

Building on Natural Interest

Orlans (1977) argues that students normally show a natural interest in and fondness for animals and that teachers bear responsibility for channeling that natural curiosity and affection into a serious study that leads to understanding of life processes. "Among the objectives of keeping classroom animals are an appreciation for all forms of life, an opportunity to observe and perceive, and the challenge to develop a spirit of reasoning and inquiry based upon a sound sense of values" (Orlans, 1977, p. 1).

In its publication *NSTA Pathways to the Science Standards* (Lowery, 1997), the National Science Teachers Association (NSTA) stresses that teaching inquiry skills should be an integral part of the elementary science curriculum. Constructivist teaching and learning techniques require students to exert more effort than simply reading about science facts and memorizing them for tests. Animals in the classroom provide numerous opportunities for students to observe, predict, communicate, measure, and maintain records about their classroom animal companions. These kinds of opportunities are consistent with the latest research on effective teaching and learning environments in science.

Possible Drawbacks of Animals in the Classroom

There are, of course, some risks to keeping a classroom animal. Many animals can bite, scratch, carry parasites, or get loose. In addition, some children may have allergies to certain animals or phobias about them. Animals also need care over weekends and vacations, and the teacher is generally responsible for the cost of feeding and housing the animals and for finding appropriate care for ill or injured animals. Fortunately, the risks can be minimized by carefully choosing the animal to meet your expectations, and by caring for it appropriately. With care, you can provide an enriching and positive learning experience for your students.

For example, when choosing a pet that will be handled frequently by children, it is important to first teach the animal to trust and accustom it to being handled. Through frequent handling by a caring adult, the animal will find such contact to be an enjoyable routine. Children, particularly those who are inexperienced with animals, must learn to resist the urge to squeeze small animals. A regular routine for protecting children's clothing and school property also needs to be rehearsed (for instance, placing a clean, folded bath towel underneath a rodent when removing it from its cage). As health precautions, children must wash their hands after handling an animal or cleaning its enclosure (to avoid contracting salmonella, SARS, and other communicable diseases), should never be permitted to go barefoot in areas where animals are kept (to prevent contracting worms), and should not come in direct contact with animal saliva or excrement (Aronson, 1993). Even some pet foods, such as rawhide dog chews, are potentially dangerous to humans and can carry salmonella.

Concept Development and Companion Animals

"Is a bee an animal?" If you answered, "No, a bee is an insect," then your answer was incorrect. Whether we are speaking of insects, birds, mammals, or any other type of living creature not in the plant family, all are members of the animal kingdom. Osborne and Freyberg (1985) found that many adults and children have such misconceptions. In a subsequent study, 180 preservice and inservice teachers contributed data from more than 2,100 K-8 students (Barman, Barman, Cox, Newhouse, & Goldston, 2000). Interestingly, K-2 students correctly identified more organisms as animals than did students in grades 3-8. Another question posed in the study was: "People are mammals, so does that mean humans are animals as well?" The correct answer is "yes," yet 80 percent of the children in the primary grades, 68 percent of 3rd- to 5th-graders, and 50 percent of middle school students answered "no."

When asked to explain their rationale when identifying organisms as animals or not, primary age students would often identify body parts as a characteristic of an animal, reasoning, for example, that if a creature had a leg or head, it must be an animal. Many others said they were unsure *why* it was an animal, but that it just "was." Older students tended to name characteristics common across animals, such as breathing, or the ability to move or reproduce. Ironically, in some cases, younger children (who have had fewer formal learning experiences about animals in schools) actually demonstrated a better understanding of

what an animal is (Barman et al., 2000).

Through experiences with real, live animals, students can build biological concepts and understanding of animal care (Johnson & Solomon, 1997; Toyama, Lee, & Muto, 1997). The child who has to really search to see a toad amid bark and leaves more fully appreciates how animals hide; the child who hears a guinea pig make whistling noises in response to the rustle of its plastic food bag develops a greater sense of duty to care for the animal.

How One Culture Values Insects in Children's Learning

The Japanese culture and society has valued insects, such as crickets, since the Heian period (794-1185 AD), and "autumn singing insects" (crickets) in cages are still considered a welcome present to be brought into the house and listened to (Laurent, 2000). Not only are they valued in their homes, but mushi— crickets, singing grasshoppers, cicadas, dragonflies, ladybugs, rhinoceros beetles and stag beetles—are a lively part of a young child's formal education. Activities include catching the mushi, observing and listening to them, recording the observations, breeding them, creating homes for them, and singing songs about them.

An alignment between the various types of mushi and the developmental stages of the child is present to a certain extent. Young children first play with ladybugs, then progress slowly up to catching dragonflies, which requires more skill. Children eventually work up to playing with rhinoceros beetles, which involves building small carts for their insects to pull. These activities are perceived to be psychological experiences that can be interpreted as the foundation of "being taught about nature" (Laurent, 2000). These experiences also give children an opportunity to become immersed in their education through active involvement, something that educators strive for continually.

Choosing a Pet for the Classroom

If you have decided that you would like to keep one or more animals in your classroom, the obvious question is "Which one(s)?" Many teachers include their students in this decision and children's books about classroom pets can enable children to make more thoughtful decisions (Young & Paznokas, 2003, for an annotated list). Research on the wide variety of organisms to choose from gives your students another opportunity for active engagement in science. Meeting the needs of this new class member in terms of a suitable habitat, care, and feeding can lead to many interesting discussions, as students share their own experiences and the information that they have researched. Planning for a classroom pet is an important step, one in which students can be ideally involved.

Points To Consider When Choosing a Classroom Pet

No animals should be kept in the classroom unless:

- They are hardy and can survive captivity
- Their natural habitat can be somewhat duplicated there
- Their normal behavior can be expressed in the available enclosure
- They can adjust to the normal classroom environment
- They can be properly cared for over the weekends and holidays. (Kramer, 1989)

When most teachers consider an animal for the classroom, the animals that first come to mind are guinea pigs, mice, rabbits, gerbils, or hamsters. These are common classroom pets, because they display all of the characteristics just described. For this reason, many teachers choose these animals for their first experience with a classroom pet. However, it is important to let students experience different types of animals as well.

There are certainly many other animals to choose from and they vary in the amount of care they need to be kept happy and healthy. They range in size and complexity from protozoa, daphnia, mealworms, fish, and praying mantises to exotic lizards, snakes, rodents, and rabbits. The following questions, which have been adapted from *Guidelines for Classroom Pets* (Boekhout, 2002), should help you determine which classroom pet might meet your needs and those of your students.

Questions To Consider:

1) What are the school policies regarding pets? Find out who else has classroom companion animals in your school or school system. Make sure you adhere to administrative policies so that, if some sort of incident does occur, you have followed the correct procedures. Check into insurance and liability issues before establishing classroom policies.

2) Are there any children who are allergic to specific animals? Many children, especially in the younger grade levels, have allergies. This may significantly influence the type of animal that would work well in your classroom. Check the children's records and be sure to send a letter home to the parents before any animal is purchased. Above all, avoid acquiring a pet only to have to relinquish it.

3) Are YOU ready to accept responsibility for the animal? Even though all children get excited about taking care of a new classroom pet, keep in mind that the novelty may wear off, and yet the animal will still need and deserve the best of care. This is a long-term commitment, and you will need to be a role model of responsible pet ownership for your students.

4) What is your objective for having a pet? Do you want children to have something that is easy to care for and tolerates being handled? Do you want students to see the animal living in its unique microhabitat? Do you want a typical kind of pet, or something unusual for the children to observe? Will the pet be integrated into a specific part of the curriculum? Thinking through such questions in advance will result in a better decision.

5) What grade level are you teaching? Younger children need more docile (and resilient) pets. Avoid getting animals that eat live prey or are notorious for eating their own young, since this may be traumatic for young children.

6) Are you willing to spend time caring for a classroom companion animal when school is not in session? Are you willing to take a classroom animal home for vacations and summer breaks? It is always nice when children can participate in

Classroom Animal Suitability Chart

Animal	Diet	Life Span	Pros	Cons	Suitability
Hamsters	Hamster food, fresh fruits, vegetables, hay	2-3 years	Exceptionally clean	Nocturnal animals that shouldn't be disturbed during the day; prone to nip	Not very suitable
Guinea pigs	Commercial pellets fortified with Vitamin C, fresh fruits, vegetables	5-7 years	Sociable, seldom bite, are diurnal (awake during the day) and have unique personalities, won't escape as easily	Require a calm habitat and daily exercise	Very suitable
Gerbils	Commercial pellets, hay, fresh fruits, vegetables	4-6 years	Very clean, active, and sociable	Fast moving and can be difficult for young children to handle	Very suitable
Rabbits (dwarf)	Fresh fruits, vegetables, hay, commercial pellets	7-12 years	Sociable, quiet, diurnal, can be litter box trained	Require a large habitat, enclosure is soiled quickly, needs exercise	Suitable
Domestic rats and mice	Fresh fruits, vegetables, hay, commercial pellets	2-4 years	Sociable and adventuresome day and night	Can nibble on fingers, can be hurt if squeezed, and can escape from someone's grasp	Suitable
Tropical fish	Tropical fish food	2-3 years	Very low maintenance and inexpensive to feed	Require a heater	Very suitable
Coldwater fish (e.g., goldfish)	Goldfish food	Up to 10 years	Easiest of fish to keep, do not require expensive equipment	Enclosure is quickly soiled by fish; water must be changed properly so the fish does not become stressed	Very suitable *Note: Marine or saltwater fish are recommended only for the experienced aquarist
Guppies (a more hardy tropical fish)	Guppy food	2-3 years	Easy to keep, bear live young if kept in a healthy, warm environment	Adults will consume their offspring, so they must be kept separate until they grow larger	Very suitable
Lizards: can be semi-aquatic, arboreal, or desert creatures, which determines the type of habitat	Herbivores: fresh fruits and vegetables, calcium supplements; Carnivores: live prey, although some will eat ground hamburger	Dependent on the species		Some need a very large enclosure; require a heat source	Not very suitable *Note: Iguanas are not recommended because they are susceptible to disease and do not tolerate handling well
Mealworms	Cornmeal or bran; apples, potatoes, or wet paper towel for moisture	7 months for the entire life cycle, 4-6 months in the mealworm stage	All students can have their own to observe; easy to care for, can easily observe the life cycle	Can be hurt or lost if children aren't careful	Very suitable
Birds (ring-doves)	Bird pellets; need grit to digest their food	Approximately 5-10 years	These domesticated versions of the mourning doves are interesting to observe and may reproduce	They should not be handled; once socialized, may need to be taken home at night and over weekends	Generally not recommended—some birds are noisy, nocturnal, and/or sensitive to drafts; children may be allergic to bird dander

Figure 4.1

caring for an animal over these periods of time, but this, too, takes effort to make the necessary arrangements for transportation and to get permission from responsible parents.

7) How much money are you willing to spend on the pet?

The costs associated with classroom companion animals are rarely covered by the school. Usually, teachers have to purchase the animal and its enclosure, as well as food and items to maintain the habitat. Some stores do give discounts to teachers, and it is worth looking into that possibility.

After you have selected the animal that would work best in your classroom, there are many places to find specific information about it. Figure 4.1 summarizes some of the most commonly considered animals and their suitability for classroom settings.

A Cautionary Word About Wild Animals

No wild animals should ever be kept in the classroom for an extended period of time. Most young wild animals that are found require too much care and are not generally fit to survive in the classroom. If the children caught them, they should be observed and returned to the place they were found that day. Baby birds who got pushed out of the nest for some reason may have parasites and do not belong in the classroom. Spiders from the wild are very difficult to keep and do not make good classroom pets. Other insects may carefully

Classroom Animal Suitability Chart (continued)

Animal	Diet	Life Span	Pros	Cons	Suitability
Green anoles (a suitable lizard)	Only live insects such as mealworms and other soft-bodied insects	2-3 years	Clean, wonderful to observe as they change colors	Plants in the enclosure need to be misted every day or two for the anole to get water	Suitable
Chinchillas	Chinchilla pellets and fresh vegetables	Up to 15 years	Easy to care for, love attention, very affectionate, clean themselves with dust baths	Nocturnal and need exercise out of their cages at night; may be considered an exotic animal and require a special permit	Moderately suitable
Earthworms	Good soil and food scraps	Healthy colony can be maintained indefinitely if kept cool	All students can have an individual earthworm to observe; easy to keep	Earthworms must be kept moist when being observed	Suitable
Aquatic snails	Fish food, aquatic vegetation	Population can be maintained indefinitely	Easy to keep; great to observe	Aquatic snails can multiply quickly	Suitable
Land snails	Fresh fruits and vegetables	2-3 years	With moist environment and adequate food, can be left unsupervised over vacations	Need high humidity to be active	Suitable
Daphnia (water fleas)	Algae	Will continuously regenerate	Easy to keep, interesting to look at under a magnifying glass or microscope	Stressful conditions may deplete the population	Very suitable
Hermit crabs	Fresh fruits, including apples, bananas, grapes; dry dog food or meat scraps	Can live many years if cared for properly	Student can observe them and keep track of the shells the hermit crab chooses as it grows larger	Need warm conditions, 70° F and above	Suitable

Generally speaking, animals should be purchased when they are young so they will get used to the classroom environment and to being handled.

Figure 4.1

be brought in for observation for one day, but then must be returned safely to where they were found, as their chances for survival in the classroom are very low. State and federal laws protect many species, and it may be illegal, as well as unwise, to keep these wild animals in the classroom.

Local wild animal species that can be observed in the classroom for a brief period include insects, small reptiles, and amphibians. Once a captured animal becomes a part of your classroom, the larger environment outside of the school is now open for examination and discussion. Important concepts can be discussed, such as animal habitats, adaptation, food chains and food webs, and the interconnected roles of every organism in nature.

As one elementary teacher explained,

> When the kids in the school learned that I had animals in my classroom, children with captive animals started appearing in my room. If they made all the effort to catch a cricket, keep it in a jar overnight, get a ride to school rather than taking the bus so that nothing happened to it, and bring it safely to my desk with the biggest smile I'd ever seen, I was not going to ignore it!

This teacher built upon children's natural curiosity about, and fascination with, animals to teach important lessons about the care of animals and preservation of the environment.

Introducing a Classroom Pet to Children

Dixon (2002) states, "We have a moral obligation as science teachers to foster respect for the environment" (p. 2), and having animals in the classroom is an effective way to learn such lessons. After the new member of the classroom has been selected, it is necessary to provide a suitable environment in which to house it. The variety of environments is as wide as the kind of animals you can select from, but the basic needs of the classroom pet are no different than the human animal's—food, water, and shelter top the list. Teachers and students alike must take the time to research the needs of their classroom animal companion; information can be found online, at

the library, and from more experienced classroom pet keepers.

Once the basic needs of the animal are met, a regular care and feeding schedule needs to be established. Feeding, cleaning, handling, and making detailed observations of the animal all represent opportunities for learning. Make the care and maintenance of a classroom pet part of the classroom routine. Remember to make plans for weekends and vacations, so that the animal's demands do not become a burden to the classroom teacher or the maintenance staff.

Consult the guidelines of the National Science Teachers Association on the responsible use of animals in the classroom (Hampton, 1997). Undue stress on any organism can lead to illness and a premature death. For example, amphibians should not be handled by a succession of students with dry hands, because they need to be kept moist. Similarly, a reptile that is kept in an environment that is too hot or cold may perish. Teach students about each companion animal's requirements.

Integration Into the Curriculum

When a pet first enters the classroom, it can be expected to cause quite a commotion. Even having an animal in residence at the beginning of the school year will cause excitement. There will be moments when, no matter what else is occurring in class, the antics of a classroom animal will be more engaging than the lesson plan. One middle school teacher describes a particular interruption of her reading lesson:

> I was in the middle of a great reading lesson. My embellishment of the story was terrific, my timing perfect, and it felt like it was a great learning moment. That was, until I found my students all staring at the [terrarium] that housed the gerbils. At that moment, one of the small bundles of fur decided it was time to walk to the other side of the enclosure. My students were witnessing the first steps of the young creature, and the most wonderful reading lesson in the world could not compete with this exciting event!

Once the inevitable arguments about when each student will get to hold or feed the new classroom pet are resolved, the pets can be incorporated into your educational objectives in countless ways. Students will need to research and read about the animals. The animal(s) may be the subjects of stories presented in a reading series or the subject of children's books specifically about classroom animal companions, such as *Third Grade Pet* (Cox, 1998) and *Cool Cat, School Cat* (Cox, 2002). Making observations and inferences about the classroom animal can enhance the science curriculum. This is what has been observed, but what does it mean? Why does the animal have the appearance that it does? Is it to protect it by helping it blend into the natural environment? Does it stand out to attract a mate? What about the animal's protective covering? Will it keep the animal warm, help it stay dry, or help it move across a dusty desert floor?

Students also may make observations about how the animal eats, how and where it sleeps, and how it communicates with others. Children can learn a great deal about the life cycle by observing animals in the classroom. It is possible for children to observe the miracle of life in its many forms. They may watch tadpoles hatch, care for young fish as they are born, or observe a nest of newborn, blind, pink mice.

Sadly, children also may experience death as part an animal's life cycle. Personal experience has demonstrated that children often go through the same stages of grief for an animal as they do for a friend, relative, or family member. It is an appropriate time for them to understand that it is normal to have feelings of anger, grief, and denial, and that it is okay to feel this way when a pet or a loved one has died.

Animals and the Science Standards

All science education standards at the federal and state levels address concepts associated with animals in a variety of ways. Current standards are also consistent with research that supports integrating science as a process with science content. The National Science Education Standards (National Research Council, 1996) state that less emphasis should be placed on separating science knowledge and science processes and more emphasis on integrating all science concepts. In grades K-4, the life science content standards address characteristics of various organisms, along with their related environments and life cycles. In grades 5-8, these concepts are examined in depth to include the study of structure, reproduction, populations, and diversity.

Classroom animals can complement the standards. They also can provide opportunities for students to construct meaning for themselves. The standards encourage teachers to provide learning experiences that integrate science skills and content instead of using more traditional didactic strategies (Klausner, 1996). It is no longer sufficient to *tell* students about science; they need to *experience* it. Companion animals provide such opportunities.

Curriculum Resources for Teachers

Although few published curricula address classroom pets specifically, many address animals in general, including:

- The *Full Option Science System* (FOSS, 1993) includes a module specifically on insects. This module encourages students to use the process skills in science while learning content specific to insects.
- *Science and Technology for Children (STC)* (National Science Resource Center, 1994), a hands-on science program for children in grades 1-6, contains three units (*Organisms, The Life Cycle of Butterflies,* and *Animal Studies*) that encourage children to observe, predict, and hypothesize about animals and behavior.
- *Great Expectations in Math and Science* (1996) has developed many instructional guides for teaching about animals. One guide centers on the theme of ladybugs, which are not usually thought of as classroom pets. This instructional unit affords students numerous opportunities for doing science, teaching them about the life cycle of ladybugs. Information about ladybugs' eating habits and their role in the environment shows students a small, but important part of the food web. This information is developmentally appropriate for young children, preschool-1.

At the risk of stretching the concept of companion animals a bit, if a more typical classroom companion animal is not an option, other organisms can be observed, easily and economically, in the classroom with a hay infusion. This entire ecosystem of micro- and macroscopic organisms is contained in a gallon jar. There is no cost associated with the establishment of this colony as only a jar, some fresh water, hay, and an inoculation of pond or ditch water is required. The only expense involves acquiring the tools necessary to observe these organisms. Hand lenses and inexpensive microscopes are all that is needed to watch this miniature, self-contained world.

Additional curricular resources include:

• Barker, L., & Brown, J. (1997). *Animals and us: How we live together. Nature. Teacher's Guide.* New York: Educational Publishing/Thirteen-WNET.
This curriculum guide about the relationship between humans and other animals is designed to accompany the public television series *Nature.* The Teacher's Resource Guide includes a synopsis of each program, objectives, an activity to prepare for viewing the video, a vocabulary list, discussion questions, suggested reading, and a student worksheet. (ERIC Document Reproduction Service No. ED 460843) [Accompanying videos: WNET Video Distribution, P.O. Box 2264, South Burlington, VT 05407-2284.]

• Perry, P. J. (1997). *Exploring the world of animals: Linking fiction to nonfiction.* [Literature Bridges to Science Series, K-5]. Englewood, CO: Teacher Ideas Press.
This teacher resource helps students connect narrative fiction about animals with expository nonfiction about animals. The book is divided into four interdisciplinary themes: 1) pets, 2) farm animals, 3) woodland animals, and 4) wild animals. For each theme, teachers will find plot summaries for the books, suggested discussion topics, and projects for learners that build library research skills while integrating science, social studies, math, and the arts. In addition, curriculum guides that emphasize the elementary science, math, and environmental studies curriculum are available (Vasant & Dondiego, 1995).

• Teaching Units on Companion Animal Care.
Several major organizations, including the American Kennel Club, American Veterinary Medicine Association, the Humane Society of the United States, American Pet Products Manufacturers Association, and Pedigree Petfoods have units of study on animal care. *Animal Sheltering*, published by the Humane Society of the United States, publishes articles about companion animal care (www.hsus2.org/sheltering/magazine/currentissue/). Another good source of information on animal care is 4-H, such as the Florida 4-H's Web site (www.florida4h.com/Curriculum/Bibliography/bibliography.htm). Children can take a self-scoring quiz to determine if they are responsible companion animal keepers (Musselman, 1999).

• Units on Humane Education.
The study of companion animals is often linked with humane education and peace curriculum in social studies (Freund, 1989). Animal Link is a helpful site for educators and children (www.animalink.ab.ca/HumaneEducation/humaneeducation4b.htm) that provides various articles and other resources on humane education. Also worthwhile is the Animals Aloud! Teaching Compassion project supported by the Doris Day Animal Foundation, which encourages teachers to read animal-friendly books aloud to young children every day each October (see www.ddaf.org/aloud.html); it also includes information on other curriculum guides on humane education (Nelson & Ryther, 1980; Raphael, Coleman, & Loar, 1999). The National Association for Humane and Environmental Education (www.nahee.org) publishes a magazine for older children, *KIND* (Kids in Nature's Defense), and produces teacher guides, calendars, lesson plans, and reproducibles, as well as lists of recommended books and other media. Increasingly, books for children are exploring careers in caring for animals (Goodman, 2000; Jackson, 2000).

The Internet has a wealth of online resources to help you choose and then care for a classroom companion animal. By simply typing the words "classroom pet" into your favorite search engine,

Hillary

This is the story of how my kitten Hillary came into my family. It all started on one Friday in July. My grandmother and I went to the Humane Society to look at the animals there. This is something that we do whenever I am visiting her. Little did I know that this would be the beginning of a long and wonderful friendship. This is Hillary's story.

"Meow! Woof!" those were the cries of the animals as we walked into the Humane Society. We took our normal rounds, looking at the dogs first and working our way around to the cats. We didn't see many dogs that we were particularly attracted to, so we went on to the cats. Immediately, I ran over to this cage full of adorable kittens. They were in one of those cages that holds a whole litter of kittens in them. All of a sudden, one of the kittens jumped up and started climbing the cage! When she reached the top, she started pawing and trying to reach me. I was instantly attracted to her and asked Joni if we could get her. She said that no, we'd have to wait for my parents to make that decision. I was heartbroken as I walked out of the building. But, I reminded myself, I still had two days to convince my parents to get her.

All weekend all that my parents could hear about was Corrie this, Corrie that. Her actual name was Carrie, but the a was very round. Finally, they said that they would go and see this cat before we went home if I would just stop bugging them! They said this knowing that the Humane Society wouldn't open until 11:00 and they were planning to leave early.

At last it was time to go see her. That was **ALL** that my parents said that we were going to do. I knew better. I knew that this was the cat that I wanted, the cat that I belonged with.

We went into the Humane Society when it opened. She was still there, much to my delight. One of my worst fears was that she was going to be adopted before my family and I could get to her. She repeated the performance that she had given to Joni and I, and how could my parents say no? I went home with a perfect little kitten. To this day we are best friends. One might even say we are soul mates. Hillary definitely made a good choice when she decided to make me her owner!

—Burkely Twiest (assisted by Hillary Twiest)

you will be greeted with thousands of hits. Teachers.Net offers support in terms of not only care guidance, but also curriculum ideas and activities. Many teachers and schools have their own Web sites, where they share information about their own unique pets and the ways they have used these animals in the classroom.

Other Web sites that offer detailed lesson plans are:

The Busy Educator's Guide to the World Wide Web: www.glavac.com/updates.htm

Kathy Schrock's Guide for Educators - INDEX A-B: www.school.discovery.com/schrockguide/indexa-b.html

Material for Teachers - K-12 Curriculum Activities: www.4sos.org/teach_mat/k-12.asp

Companion Animals in the Curriculum: Promising Practices

While most curriculum developers seem to assume that an interest in companion animals is a topic best suited for early childhood, it is actually a lifespan topic. Although it is customary for teachers who work with children in the primary grades to provide a curriculum theme that focuses on pets, a one-time coverage of the topic is insufficient.

Children's ideas about pet care change with age; therefore, it is important to revisit the topic of pets across the grade levels (Beck, 1993). Whereas the 1st-grader might understand some basic concepts about pet care, most adolescents are capable of thinking about pets in more sophisticated ways, such as in terms of ethical treatment.

Animals merit a place in the curriculum across the grades. Children can develop knowledge (e.g., about particular types of animals, their habits, and living requirements); physical skills (e.g., measuring food and water, arranging suitable habitats for specific animals); higher order thinking skills (e.g., observational skills and ways of representing data, gathering school-wide information about classroom pets); attitudes (e.g., self-efficacy in structuring appropriate environments for animals, responsible pet care, cooperation with classmates); and values (e.g., building a commitment to protect the environment or rescue homeless animals). Specific suggestions for incorporating companion animals in the curriculum at different levels follow.

Recommended Activities
Mary Renck Jalongo

Infants/Toddlers:
Parent Education and Classroom Pets
An "Educating for Parenting" curriculum in Philadelphia focuses learning to care. It encourages a parent to visit school with a newborn (Unit 1), an infant (Unit 2), and a toddler (Unit 3) as a way to build positive home/school relationships and to coach families in how they can nurture children's healthy development. One experience that is a featured part of all three units and visits is choosing and caring for a class pet (Heath, 1995).

Early Childhood:
Democracy in Action
A kindergarten teacher uses the decision to acquire a classroom pet as a way to teach children about the democratic process. The children plan a pet campaign, participate in the voting process, and elect an animal (Gunnels, 1997). Additionally, curriculum projects involving pets can span the curriculum for young children, integrating all of the curricular areas (Kostelnik, 1991; Raines & Canady, 1991; Warner & Bockelmann, 2000). Geiss (1997), for example, has used art masterpieces of pets to create a board book/puzzle set for young children.

Elementary School-Wide Project:
Companion Animals
A project in one elementary school focuses on animal behavior and care. Each participating teacher is responsible for setting up an animal learning center that provides information about the animal, its habitat, and its other requirements. The centers rotate to different classrooms on a monthly basis, giving every student the opportunity to observe, learn about, and care for a total of 14 unusual animals. The program's learning activities cover such curricular areas as zoology, art, language arts, music, mathematics, and science (Benham, 1991).

Later Primary:
Research on Animals
Children who are writing reports about various animals can visit My Virtual Reference Desk's Pets and Animals Encyclopedia at www.refdesk.com/pets.html, or conduct a search at LycosZone (www.LycosZone.com) to discover many interesting facts about pets from authoritative sources.

Later Primary:
Interdisciplinary Curriculum Project
The study of companion animals is naturally interdisciplinary (Freeman & Sokoloff, 1994; Seil, 1995). In one 4th-grade classroom, an interdisciplinary unit about dogs was so successful that the dog that came to visit for two weeks became "a new breed of teacher's pet" and stayed for the entire year (Owens & Williams, 1995).

Later Primary/Early Adolescence:
The Living Library
In Dade County, Florida, students in the intermediate grades can borrow classroom pets from The Living Library, taking an animal to the home or classroom on a short-term loan basis. The program materials include a parental permission form in English and Spanish, a daily pet care checklist, lesson plans for teachers, recommended resources, and supplementary reading (Griffin, 1990).

71

Early Adolescence:

Animal Rights

As children mature, their ability to deal with abstractions and to function as advocates for proper treatment and care of animals increases accordingly. Two Web sites that might be of interest to children are the Animal Rights Law Project (www.animal-law.org) and a group that protects the rights of laboratory animals (www.labanimalwelfare.org). The children's book *Saving Lilly* (Kehret, 2001) deals with the ethical treatment of circus animals, while *Unforgettable Mutts: Pure of Heart, Not of Breed* (Derrico, 1999) takes issue with pedigree as a basis for assessing a dog's worth.

Across the Grades:

Interesting Questions

Some questions about our animal friends are easily answered (e.g., Do brown cows really give chocolate milk?), others require a bit more investigation (e.g., Can our classroom turtle feel me touching him through his shell?), and still others persist into adulthood (e.g., How does my dog know I am coming home several minutes beforehand?—see Sheldrake, 2000). What child or adult has not had the experience of watching classroom or family pets that are asleep and wondering what they dream about or observing an animal's behavior and wondering why an animal responds in a certain way or wondering how animals think about things. Often, the questions that are raised by companion animals' behavior elicit intense emotions and deal with abstractions that intrigue early adolescents. One particularly sensitive question concerns how a culture decides which animals are food and which are to become companions. The practice of euthanasia is another difficult issue: When is it fair to destroy an animal? What is the appropriate role for the pet owner? For the veterinarian? Is it wrong for a wealthy nation to spend thousands of dollars on pet care when people throughout the world are without such care? And so on. Older children may also be fascinated by historical accounts of legendary animals such as *The Pawprints of History: Dogs and the Course of Human Events* (Coren, 2002).

Later Primary/Early Adolescence:

Animal Sanctuaries

One way that children can show their care and concern for animals is to investigate the efforts of animal sanctuaries (e.g., www.bestfriends.org, www.kindplanet.org). A chapter book for children, *The Animal Rescue Club* (Himmelman, 1998), suggests steps that children can take to protect other living creatures.

Organizations That Support the Inclusion of Animals in the Classroom

Many professional organizations (see Figure 4.2), including advocacy groups such as the World Society for Protection of Animals and In the Company of Animals, support teachers who decide to make animals a part of the classroom. The National Science Teachers Association offers a variety of publications that deal with the care of classroom animals. Science supply houses like Delta and Carolina Biological have all of the hardware you need, from aquaria to terraria to help care for your new classroom pet. Locally owned pet stores also are an excellent source of help, as are professional journal articles (Hodges, 1991; Hurst, 1998).

Animals Outside the Classroom

Perhaps you are not ready to become a full-time classroom pet keeper. You can still include animals in your curricular objectives. Children are naturally curious about living creatures, and many exist right outside the classroom walls in the schoolyard. Your schoolyard may already be a haven for such diverse animals as insects, reptiles, and small mammals, depending on your local ecology. Even in a city environment, the briefest patches of grass and trees abound with birds, insects, and other animals.

Your school environment can be enhanced to accommodate a diverse animal population by including bird and squirrel feeders; bird boxes (where birds can roost and build nests); bushes, trees, and flowers; and brush piles and rock piles. A wide variety of activities can take advantage of areas immediately around your school. "Obviously the best way to learn about a spider or a squirrel is to observe it in its natural habitat. Watching a video, coloring a drawing, or reading a story are all valuable learning tools, but the BEST way to learn about the environment and its organisms is to go outside and experience the environment firsthand" (Cronin-Jones, 1992). In schools that have access to more space, trails and special microhabitats can be established. These types of habitats can range from small butterfly gardens to ponds and wetland environments. Often, entire grade levels can work together to develop these habitats. Once these areas are established, your entire school can take advantage of the learning opportunities.

Organizations for Children To Investigate

Mary Renck Jalongo

Delta Society (www.deltasociety.org)
A group that focuses on the role of animals in human health and therapy programs. Provides certification guidelines, educational materials, and gives the Beyond Limits™ Awards for Service and Therapy Animals.

The Fund for Animals (www.fund.org)
A group that takes political action "to speak for those who can't"—animals of all types. Updates on state and federal legislation, campaigns to protect animals, and a variety of publications, posters, and buttons are available at this site. The Fund for Animals has taken a strong stand against wearing fur and trapping animals. The group also operates a refuge for a wide variety of animals in Texas called Black Beauty Ranch.

Goldman Environmental Foundation and Goldman Environmental Prize (www.goldmanprize.org)
Founded in 1990, this international organization promotes protection of the natural environment and honors grassroots environmental heroes from around the world who have worked to protect the environment. A cash prize of $750,000 "offers these environmental heroes the recognition, visibility, and credibility their efforts deserve."

The Humane Society of the United States (www.hsus.org)
A national organization of activists who lobby for humane and ethical treatment of all creatures—not only pets, but also wild animals and animals raised for food. The Humane Society is responsible for various public awareness campaigns.

The Jane Goodall Institute (www.janegoodall.org)
An organization, established by Jane Goodall, dedicated to preservation of the natural environment and to protecting apes. Contributors can support efforts to rehabilitate apes (e.g., acting as a chimpanzee guardian through donations).

The Heifer Project International (www.heifer.org)
An international organization that uses donations to educate low-income people throughout the world about domestic livestock and supply animals that can generate income and greater independence.

The Latham Foundation for the Promotion of Humane Education (www.latham.org)
An organization committed to: 1) fostering a deeper understanding of and sympathy with those creatures—animals—that cannot speak for themselves; 2) inculcating the higher principles of humaneness upon which the unity and happiness of the world depend; 3) emphasizing the spiritual fundamentals that lead to world friendship; and 4) promoting the child's character through an understanding of universal kinship. The group has educational materials, such as videos on various types of animal-assisted activities and therapy.

American Society for the Prevention of Cruelty to Animals (www.aspca.org/site)
The ASPCA "exists to promote humane principles, prevent cruelty and alleviate fear, pain and suffering in animals" and is one of the oldest and largest international nonprofit organizations in existence. It offers information on pet adoption opportunities, humane education, animal care and medicine, pet shelter management, and animals rights advocacy.

Figure 4.2

Animal-Assisted Activity: Effects of Companion Animals on Children's Reading

Mary Renck Jalongo

Why Bring a Dog to Reading Class or the Library?

Visitation programs that bring animals, particularly dogs, to school as a way to encourage children's reading are a relatively recent phenomenon in the United States (Glazer, 1995). The most well-known of these programs is the Reading Education Assistance Dogs (R.E.A.D.) program, which was begun in Salt Lake City in 1999 with the support of the Intermountain Therapy Group (www.therapy animals.org). Preliminary findings from the research were very encouraging. All of the students who participated in R.E.A.D. for 13 months improved at least two grade levels in reading proficiency and some improved as much as four grade levels, according to ITA Executive Director Kathy Klotz (Bueche, 2003). Media coverage has resulted in greater public awareness of such programs, and similar programs have been instituted in communities throughout the United States (http://pawsforhealth.org). While dogs are the most commonly used companion animal in animal-assisted activities, other animals, such as cats, rabbits, and birds, are sometimes used.

Certified therapy dogs used to facilitate children's reading take advantage of children's natural tendency to open up in the presence of animals, and an animal's calming effect on children experiencing stress. First of all, children *talk to animals*. In a study of 10-year-old Scottish children, Dr. Alasdair Macdonald, a psychiatrist, discovered that 84 percent of the children talked to their pets; more surprising, 65 percent believed the pets understood the meaning of the words they were using. Among adolescents who own horses, more than 70 percent confide in the animals, talking out their problems in the isolation of the barn while grooming and caring for the animal (Serpell, 2000, p. 125). Second, the presence of mellow companion animals tends to *moderate stress*. Both tactile and visual contact with pet animals can be physiologically calming (Katcher, Friedmann, Beck, & Lynch, 1983). In a review of the literature, Friedmann, Thomas, and Eddy (2000) concluded that the moderating effect of an animal's presence on stress responses may be influenced by such things as the type and familiarity of the setting, the type of stressor, and the child's perception of and relationship with the animal. Despite these sources of variation, the presence of a calm, attentive dog moderated the stress responses more than the presence of an adult—and even more than the presence of a supportive friend—when children were reading aloud, presumably because the animal is nonjudgmental. A number of experimental and quasi-experimental studies confirm that "three categories of human-animal association provide physiological benefits to individuals: people explicitly looking at or observing animals or pictures of animals; people being in the presence of animals but not interacting with them; and people touching or interacting with them" (Friedmann, Thomas, & Eddy, 2000, p. 137).

How Are Therapy Dogs Used To Promote Reading?

Visitation programs that bring companion animals into the classroom or library as a way to encourage children to read have several characteristics in common:

1. Collaboration. Usually, several organizations are involved: the school and/or library; the organization that provides animal-assisted therapy personnel; and the agencies that locate, train, certify, and provide health care for the dog. In the Reading With Rover program in the state of Washington (www.kcls.org), companies such as Barnes and Noble and Home Depot collaborate by offering their retail stores as sites where trained animals can be field tested for their ability to adjust to new environments and

Figure 4.3

74

interact with many different people in a public setting.

2. Certification. Both the personnel in the programs and the companion animals are specially selected, trained, and registered. The most well-known training programs for volunteers and their canine companions are sponsored by the Delta Society (www.deltasociety.org) and Therapy Dogs International, Inc. (www.tdi-dog.org). Animals selected as reading companions are gentle, calm, and adaptable.

3. Programming. Animal-assisted activities involve much more than just bringing a family pet to school. In Utah's Reading Education Assistance Dogs, or R.E.A.D., program (www.therapy animals.org), three things are taken into consideration: book selection (e.g., matched to age, reading level); interest (reading material is focused on an animal theme); and motivation (each book is "pawtographed" with a paw print of the dog and, if a child advances to the next level, he or she gets to keep the book).

In sum, animal-assisted activities show great promise for motivating children to complete academic activities, not only in reading, but also across the curriculum (Nebbe, 2003).

References

Bueche, S. (2003). Going to the dogs: Therapy dogs promote reading. *Reading Today, 20*(4), 46.

Friedmann, E., Thomas, S. A., & Eddy, T. J. (2000). Companion animals and human health: Physical and cardiovascular influences. In A. L. Podberscek, E. S. Paul, & J. A. Serpell (Eds.), *Companion animals and use: Exploring the relationship between people and pets* (pp. 125-142). New York: Cambridge University Press.

Glazer, S. M. (1995). Assessing the influence of visitors on learning. *Teaching K-8, 26*(3), 112-113.

Katcher, A. H., Friedmann, E., Beck, A. M., & Lynch, J. J. (1983). Looking, talking, and blood pressure: The physiological consequences of interaction with the living environment. In A. H. Katcher & A. M. Beck (Eds.), *New perspectives on our lives with companion animals* (pp. 351-359). Philadelphia: University of Pennsylvania Press.

Nebbe, L. (2003). Animal-assisted activities/Therapy as an animal and human welfare project. Retrieved from the World Wide Web Psychologists for the Ethical Treatment of Animals www.PSYETA.org

Reading Education Assistance Dogs (R.E.A.D), Intermountain Therapy Animals. {*Includes frequently asked questions, printable brochure, and other resource materials on using dogs to promote reading.}* www.therapyanimals.org

Serpell. J. A. (2000). Creatures of the unconscious: Companion animals as mediators. In A. L. Podberscek, E. S. Paul, & J. A. Serpell (Eds.), *Companion animals and us: Exploring the relationship between people and pets* (pp. 108-124). New York: Cambridge University Press.

Figure 4.3, continued

Insects can be found in all environments, and their interesting eating and social habits often can be observed and studied. Ants, for example, have a complex social organization and live in colonies in underground tunnels or in galleries in dead wood. Grasshoppers and crickets can easily be brought into the classroom for brief periods of time to be observed, perhaps in conjunction with reading trade books depicting these animals.

If it is not possible to develop a nature trail on the school grounds, short field trips can be taken to local parks to observe animals in their habitats at different times of the year. Many parks have educators on staff who can enhance your students' experience and may even provide instruction free of charge. Your students can get exercise and fresh air while observing animals in their natural habitats.

In addition to observing the wildlife around your school building, you may want to invite pets as visitors into your classroom. The best way to ensure safety with both the students and the animals is to invite people who own animals that have been professionally trained to be around children. Even very friendly family pets can be unpredictable in an unknown setting, around many excited children. Family pets also may not have updated shots, which is another good reason to keep family pets at home. Specifically trained animals and handlers offer many wonderful opportunities for your students, such as animal-assisted activities (see Figure 4.3).

Other professional organizations, such as the local herpetological society or 4-H organization, have handlers who will bring other types of animals into the classroom. Check with these associations or local pet stores to see if someone would be available to come into the classroom. These people have specific animals that are docile around people and are used to being handled, again making for a less stressful situation for all involved. Many museums, aviaries, and zoos sponsor outreach programs that will bring animals to your classroom or auditorium for assemblies. These organizations have trained docents (a teacher in residence at a museum) who use animals that are acclimated to groups of children.

You may want to take your students on a field trip to a local zoo, farm, aviary, museum, or aquarium. This provides students the opportunity to see a wide variety of animals in an environment that simulates the natural habitat of animals, such as the simulated rainforest that houses gorillas at the famous San Diego Zoo. Most of these nontraditional science education settings have docents who can provide instruction for your students. The best way to integrate these kinds of visits is with lessons in your classroom, both before and after the field trip. Students who arrive with background knowledge and appropriate expectations are much more likely to benefit than those who see the field trip as a day off. Teachers need to build their background knowledge as well. For example, it is important to be knowledgeable about the ethical issues affecting animals in zoos (Hancocks, 2001) rather than uncritically accepting whatever is available. By providing opportunities for students to anticipate their trip, they can plan to look for information and opportunities to engage in the subject matter. Follow-up instruction in the classroom after the field trip gives students the chance to share their observations and construct additional meaning.

Other Ways To Include Animals in Your Curriculum

Many nontraditional science education settings have Web cams that allow you to observe animals online. Web cams have the advantage of allowing students to view the animals over an extended period of time and at different times during the day, including feeding time. These cameras offer constantly updated images from all over the world. Many zoos keep cameras on their animals and broadcast the images over the Internet. Web cam

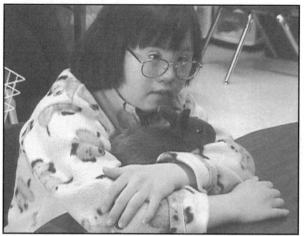

Photo courtesy of Marsha Robbins

Girl with Down syndrome holds a bunny.

observation can be as commonplace as Puppycam or as exotic as African wildlife at game preserves.

Virtual field trips can be an excellent alternative to the real thing. Again, the key is integration into the curriculum. An array of interesting trips can be found by typing the key words "virtual field trip" and "education" into your favorite search engine.

Adoption of a class animal is yet another possibility. Many agencies deal with endangered animals in an effort to raise awareness and funds for the protection of the species through tracking, observation, and monitoring. In return, your class can "adopt" a particular animal for a year. During this time, you will be sent information about your adopted pet and receive progress reports about where the animal is and what it is doing. This is a wonderful way for children to feel they are making a difference, see an animal as an individual in need of help, and learn more about the species. In addition, students learn wonderful social studies skills as they track the whereabouts of their adopted animal.

Although not as "up close and personal" as the real thing, many high-quality videos and CDs and DVDs provide wonderful photography showing the beauty and complexity of the animals that live on our planet. Many cable and satellite systems carry the *Animal Planet* cable channel, which is dedicated to information and stories on a wide range of different animals worldwide.

Finally, the availability of print resources on animals, both in books and in periodicals, is overwhelming. Some of the best print resources you can get for the classroom are the *Peterson Field Guides, The Audubon Society Field Guides,* and the *Golden Guide* series. The first two are written for the general public and provide a wealth of information in easy-to-understand terms. Photographs and drawings for identification are included so when a curious student brings a turtle she found into class, you and your students can use these guides not only to identify it but also to learn more about the organism. The *Golden Guides* are written for elementary age students and give readers an opportunity to learn about animals on their own. All of these guides are relatively inexpensive and should be part of every school's library.

Conclusion

Many contemporary children are deprived of opportunities to act upon their natural curiosity about animals and their natural desire to affiliate with other forms of life. Companion animals in the classroom can enrich the lives of children, develop a sense of classroom community, and enhance the curriculum in countless ways. Many teachers fondly recall from their own childhoods a wide range of opportunities for bonding with and caring for animals. We need to extend the same opportunity to all children, particularly those who may not otherwise have the chance to care for and about other living creatures.

References & Resources

Aronson, S. S. (1993). Ask Dr. Sue: Going barefoot and having animals. *Child Care Information Exchange, 91,* 57-58.

Barman, C. R, Barman, N. S., Cox, M. L., Newhouse, K. B., & Goldston, M. J. (2000). Students' ideas about animals: Results from a national study. *Science and Children, 38*(1), 42-46.

Beck, A. (1993). Pets foster kids' nurturing skills. *Futurist, 27*(1), 8-12.

Benham, D. C. (1991). A short stay, a long-lasting lesson. *Science and Children, 29*(3), 19-21.

Boekhout, N. (2002). *Guidelines for classroom pets.* Retrieved October 5, 2002, from http://teachers.net/gazette/AUGoo/coverb.html

Coren, S. (2002). *The pawprints of history: Dogs and the course of human events.* New York: The Free Press.

Cronin-Jones, L. (1992). *The schoolyard wildlife activity guide.* Tallahassee, FL: Nongame Wildlife Program, Florida Game and Freshwater Fish Commission.

Derrico, K. (1999). *Unforgettable mutts: Pure of heart, not of breed.* Troutdale, OR: New Sage Press.

Dixon, N. (2002). *The care of live animals in the classroom.*

Retrieved September 3, 2002 from www.usask.ca/education/idea/tplan/scilp/careanim.htm

Freeman, C. C., & Sokoloff, H. J. (1994, April). *Toward a theory of thematic curricula: Constructing new learning environments for teachers and learners.* Paper presented at the Annual Meeting of the American Educational Research Association, New Orleans, LA. (ERIC Document Reproduction Service No. ED 3769290).

Freund, C. A. (1989). *A peace education curriculum for preprimary children.* (ERIC Document Reproduction Service No. ED 312 089)

Full Option Science System. (1993). Berkeley, CA: Lawrence Hall of Science.

Great Expectations in Math and Science. (1996). Berkeley, CA: Lawrence Hall of Science.

Griffin, J. (1990). *The living library.* Miami, FL: Dade County Education Fund. (ERIC Document Reproduction Service No. ED 357 972).

Gunnels, J. A. (1997). A class pet campaign: Experiencing the democratic process. *Dimensions of Early Childhood, 25,* 31-34.

Hampton, C. (1997). *Classroom creature culture, algae to anoles.* Arlington, VA: National Science Teachers Association.

Hancocks, D. (2001). *A different nature: The paradoxical world of zoos and their uncertain future.* Berkeley, CA: University of California Press.

Heath, H. (1995). *Education for parenting/learning to care. (Units 1, 2, and 3).* Haverford, PA: Conrow Publishing. (ERIC Document Reproduction Service Nos. 437 152, 437 153, and 437 154).

Hodges, J. L. (1991). Spiders and boas and rats, oh my! *Science and Children, 28*(4), 22-25.

Hurst, C. O. (1998). Cats, dogs, and other fauna. *Teaching Pre-K-8, 28*(5), 74.

Johnson, S. C., & Solomon, G. E. A. (1997). Why dogs have puppies and cats have kittens: The role of birth in young children's understanding. *Child Development, 68*(3), 404-420.

Klausner, R. (1996). *Time* Special Issue.

Kostelnik, M. (1991). *Teaching young children using themes.* Springfield, IL: GoodYear.

Kramer, D. C. (1989). *Animals in the classroom: Selection, care and observations.* Reading, MA: Addison-Wesley.

Laurent, E. L. (2000). Children, "insects" and play in Japan. In A. L. Podberscek, E. S. Paul, & J. A. Serpell (Eds.), *Companion animals and us: Exploring the relationships between people and pets* (pp. 61-89). New York: Cambridge University Press.

Lewis, R. (1998). *Life.* New York: McGraw-Hill.

Lowery, L. (Ed.). (1997). *NSTA pathways to the science standards.* Arlington, VA: National Science Teachers Association.

Musselman, K. (1999). Are you a responsible pet owner? *Hopscotch, 10*(5), 14-15.

National Research Council. (1996). *National science education standards.* Washington, DC: National Academy Press.

National Science Resource Center. (1994). *Science and technology for children.* Burlington, NY: Carolina Biological Supply Company.

Nelson, D., & Ryther, S. (Compilers). (1980). *Animal*

activities: A handbook of humane education ideas. Resources and materials for elementary school teachers. Middlebury, VT: Addison County Humane Society. (ERIC Document Reproduction Service No. ED 243 731).

Orlans, F. B. (1977). Animal care from protozoa to small mammals. Menlo Park, CA: Addison-Wesley.

Osborne, R., & Freyberg, P. (1985). Learning in science. Portsmouth, NH: Heinemann.

Outdoor Biological Instructional Strategies. (1981). Lawrence Hall of Science. Hudson, NH: Delta Education.

Owens, R., & Williams, N. (1995). A new breed of teacher's pet. Teaching Pre-K-8, 28(2), 50-51.

Raines, S. C., & Canady, R. J. (1991). More story stretchers: More activities to expand children's favorite books. Mt. Rainier, MD: Gryphon House.

Raphael, P., Coleman, L., & Loar, L. (1999). Teaching compassion: A guide for humane teachers, educators, and parents. Alameda, CA: The Latham Foundation.

Rud, A. G., & Beck, A. M. (2000). Kids and critters in class together. Phi Delta Kappan, 82(4), 313-315.

Seil, A. (1995). Across-the-curriculum ideas. Learning, 24(2), 72.

Sheldrake, R. (2000). Dogs that know when their owners are coming home. New York: Three Rivers Press.

Toyama, N., Lee, Y. M., & Muto, T. (1997). Japanese preschoolers' understanding of biological concepts related to procedures for animal care. Early Childhood Research Quarterly, 12(3), 347-360.

Vasant, R., & Dondiego, B. L. (1995). Cats, dogs, and classroom pets: Science in art, song, and play. Ridge Summit, PA: TAB Books.

Warner, L., & Bockelmann, S. (2000). Studying dogs and puppies: Two examples of emergent curriculum. Texas Child Care, 24(3), 10-16.

Young, T. A., & Paznokas, L. N. (2003). Classroom pets: Books about animals in the classroom. Book Links, 13(2), 53-58.

Children's Books

Cox, J. (1998). Third grade pet. New York: Holiday.

Cox, J. (2001). Cool cat, school cat. New York: Holiday.

Geiss, T. (1997). Pets: Five 12-piece puzzles and five masterpiece paintings. New York: Knopf. (board book/puzzle set).

Goodman, S. E. (2000). Animal rescue: The best job there is. New York: Simon & Schuster.

Himmelman, J. (1998). The animal rescue club. New York: HarperTrophy.

Jackson, D. M. (2000). The wildlife detectives: How forensic scientists fight crimes against nature. New York: Houghton.

Kehret, P. (2001). Saving Lilly. New York: Simon & Schuster.

Chapter 5
Animals That Heal: Animal-Assisted Therapy With Children

—Austen Linder
USA

Mary Renck Jalongo,
Marsha R. Robbins, and Marjorie L. Stanek
with Dana M. Monroe
and Nancy Patterson-Uhron

One morning, on my way into the office, I encountered an unusual sight in the College of Education. Three animals—a therapy dog, a 20-pound Chinchilla rabbit, and a cockatiel—were being loaded onto the elevator to become part of a presentation for the special education majors about animal-assisted therapy. I chatted with the presenter, Marsha Robbins, told her about this book, and asked her for her business card. Not long afterwards, I mentioned this project in a graduate class and Dana Monroe, a doctoral candidate and program director of a school for autistic children, offered to contribute to the book. Then, while at the doctor's office, I met Nancy Patterson-Uhron, the director of Simple Blessings Farm, where Shetland ponies are raised to become the companions of children with special needs. As the book began to take shape, some of the material that Marjorie Stanek had written seemed more suited to this chapter. And that is how this author team for this chapter was formed—chance meetings, shared interests, and common goals.

In the chapter title we refer to two key terms: animal-assisted therapy and healing. What, exactly, do they mean? Animal-assisted therapy involves the use of specially trained companion animals as adjuncts in a goal-directed intervention with clients. Professionals in the health and human services fields involve companion animals in their practice as a way to motivate clients to participate in and continue with a treatment plan. How can an animal accomplish therapy goals? Allow us to introduce you to Moses.

Moses
Marsha R. Robbins

Moses is a hero at Pioneer Education Center. He loves all the kids and seems to instinctively know who is sad and who is happy. He is gentle with the fearful, and playful with the confident. Moses listens to stories even when the reading is tentative, and walks in the sunshine with the students who are learning to walk. He has been on television numerous times to attract support for many deserving causes, but his head isn't in the clouds. His heart still belongs to the kids at Pioneer. Moses is a dog.

How did Moses become our hero? The experience of Tammy, a girl with cerebral palsy, helps to explain. Tammy has very low muscle tone and walks with a lot of ataxia. Up until recently, she needed a walker to hold her trunk steady. Tammy is so unsteady on her feet that the teachers hold their breath when she attempts to walk across the room. Despite these physical challenges, Tammy one day announced that she wanted to walk Moses. The teachers went into the hallway, fully expecting to have to intervene and prevent this determined little girl from falling. What they saw instead was a child who stood still for a few moments, gathered her composure, and summoned up every ounce of motor control. Tammy then began walking very deliberately and slowly. Instantly, with no command or direction, Moses slowed down and matched his gait to Tammy's pace. Ordinarily, Moses is a flying dynamo who catches frisbees for hours and never puts on his brakes. At that moment, however, he acted like a calm, older dog and walked in a manner that none of the teachers had seen from him before. The child and dog made a fine pair strolling down the hall together. Tammy had mustered extraordinary physical control to walk Moses, and he instinctively understood what to do. Her teacher was speechless when she looked out into the hall, and the rest of the staff stopped in their tracks. It was a wonderful moment.

Moses' life could have been very different. He found himself at an animal shelter at a very young age, in a scary room full of big, barking dogs. He was dejected. His former owner didn't have the time for him and was put off by his high energy level. Moses was very bright and, when he got bored, would improvise activities of

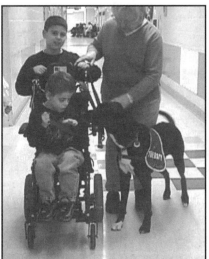

Moses the therapy dog and friends.

photo courtesy of Marsha R. Robbins

his own design—chewing shoes, digging holes, and barking endlessly. Then a teacher with a friendly smile came into the kennel. She stopped in front of Moses' crate and talked to him in a soft voice as she touched him through the side of the bars. He leaned into her touch and when she invited him out to interact, he leaned into her hug and put his head on her shoulder. It was love at first sight. Moses had a home.

Within weeks after leaving the shelter, Moses had sailed through basic obedience and breezed through advanced obedience training. He was working and loving it. Then he went on to get his Therapy Dogs International Title. Therapy Dogs International, Inc. is an organization based in New Jersey that grants therapy dog licenses to dogs who pass rigorous obedience testing, extensive temperament testing, and stringent health tests. The dogs who pass the evaluation receive photo identification cards that entitle them to go into hospitals, nursing homes, and schools to visit and spread canine joy. Moses passed his test before he was a year old and earned his red, white, and blue superdog cape. Those colors are special; they indicate that Moses was once a homeless dog destined for—if shelter statistics are any indication—euthanasia.

Moses became a regular guest at Pioneer Education Center. He knows every student and staff member and is as much at home beside a wheelchair and a walker as he is curled up on the sofa in the living room of his home. He can go from room to room visiting and bringing smiles, and he is happiest when he is doing just that! His testimony is a condition we refer to as "chronic happy tail." Moses walks and wags, sits and wags, or snuggles and wags. At the end of each visit, you can be sure that his tail is the most tired part of his body.

The students at Pioneer have multiple disabilities. They require much more extensive care than most children, such as frequent doctor visits, numerous hospitalizations, and long recuperation periods. Taking care of a family pet is often more than their family resources can support. Moses can be their pet at school. When children master a new skill, they beam with pride. For a child in a wheelchair, walking an 80-pound black lab/great Dane mix is just such a thrill. Moses strolls comfortably beside the wheelchair, his hyperactive tail creating a breeze. With a single word, children can make Moses sit politely and shake hands for a doggy cookie. That is a stupendous accomplishment when you only weigh 40 pounds yourself.

Moses is an important part of the students' learning experience. They learn that they can control something much bigger than themselves. It is much more fun to try to control a big, slurpy, black dog than to fight your disability. It is much more self-affirming to learn that even if you can't walk, you CAN walk a dog. Moses teaches them all of these things. He may have started out as a shelter dog, but he has become a hero to the youngsters at Pioneer. He shows them, on a daily basis, what they CAN DO, in the face of the daily reminders about what they can't. He makes them proud to be who they are.

One sunny day last November, a little boy named David asked if he could walk Moses outside. He took the leash and put it around his wrist as he wheeled his wheelchair through the back door of the school. The boy and the dog took a few laps around the track behind the school, and then, when David was tired, they headed back to the doorway of the classroom. Upon arrival inside the classroom, David announced emphatically, "I never walked a dog before. I'M GOOD AT IT!" And Moses, somebody's throw- *away pet, has discovered what he is good at, too.*

As Moses' story highlights, animal-assisted therapy is more than merely throwing animals and children together. It requires specialized training, not only for the companion animal but also for the practitioners. One certification program for teachers that is offered in conjunction with People

Animals and Nature (PAN) culminates with earning an Animal-Assisted Therapy and Education certificate (AAT/E). Information on this program and other animal therapy programs is available at the Web sites of the Latham Foundation (www.latham.org) and the Delta Society (www.deltasociety.org).

The animals that are most commonly found in animal-assisted therapy programs are dogs and cats, although rabbits, horses, llamas, and birds also are used. Figure 5.1 summarizes some of the approaches that are used in animal-assisted therapy.

Another word that we use in this chapter's title is "heal," because the ultimate goal of animal-assisted therapy is to heal. As Benjamin Shield and Richard Carson (1989) observe in *Healers on Healing*, "Love is the one common denominator that underlies and connects all successful healing. For healing means not only a body without disease or injury, but a sense of forgiveness, belonging, and caring as well" (quoted in Schoen, 2001, p. 143).

How does Boomer, 12-year-old Caitlin's dog, promote healing? First of all, Boomer protects Caitlin, who has severe epilepsy, by warning her, in advance, that a seizure is about to occur. Boomer's ability to anticipate a seizure meets a health and human services goal, as it builds Caitlin's independence and confidence. With Boomer as her early warning system, Caitlin can get herself to a safe place, away from curious stares, and avoid injuring herself by falling. In addition, she can trust Boomer to curl up with her and be there, waiting patiently, until she recovers.

This service dog has contributed to other people's healing as well. A vocational services program affiliated with the local middle school has found opportunities for adolescents with special needs to work with the local animal shelter. The middle school students have learned to care for and select dogs that appear to display a level of sensitivity that would make them appropriate candidates for specialized training. This is how Boomer was found for Caitlin. Each time one of their homeless animals is successfully trained and "graduates," the students attend a celebratory luncheon. Boomer also spent time at a residential facility for young adolescents who have been tried and convicted as juveniles. Three professionals—a

Approaches to Animal-Assisted Therapy

Animals can be an important support for children meeting a wide range of challenges (Melson, 2001).

Animal-Assisted Activities for Typically Developing Children Under Stress

Numerous studies have demonstrated that most of us tend to calm down in the company of a gentle animal (Schoen, 2001). Stroking a companion animal's fur can slow a rapid pulse, reduce high blood pressure, relax tense muscles, and return breathing to normal rates (Freidmann, Thomas, & Eddy, 2000). Companion animals are active and fun, but they are also nonjudgmental playmates that are usually willing to accede to our wishes (George, 1999). The parrot that bobs his head excitedly while a high school student practices a difficult musical piece, the cat that curls up on a computer while a 7th-grader struggles with his first research paper, the guinea pig that whistles a welcome home to a lonely latchkey child, and the pot-bellied pig that offers grunts of encouragement as a 2nd-grader reads aloud all help to mitigate daily types of stressors that affect children. Animals also can exert a positive effect on emotions vicariously as children read stories about them, such as *Cinderella Dogs: Real-life Fairy Tale Adoptions From the San Francisco SPCA* (Glassner, 2001) and experience an emotional catharsis.

Therapy for Children Who Have Been Abused or Neglected

By entrusting them with the care of animals, children who have been victims or witnesses of violence and are experiencing serious problems in school and in life can make progress toward healing (Roseberry & Rovin, 1999). Some of the animals are disabled wildlife, others are farm animals, and still others are strays or exotic animals (Ross, 1999; www.gchimney.org). Often, this bond with an animal serves as an important first step in learning to trust human beings. The development of awareness and empathy in children leads to caring, and that caring can change their attitudes about violence (George, 1999). It is not unusual for abused children to resist human touch, and so animals often function as an intermediary in the process of learning that touch can be a way of expressing kindness rather than anger (Rathmann, 1999). Adolescent group therapy that focuses on anger management skills has been successful when animals are an adjunct to the treatment (Hanselman, 2001). As UK researcher Doyle (2001) asserts, companion animals often serve as "nonhuman lifelines" of great importance to children.

Therapy for Children Who Are Ill or Hospitalized

It has taken many years for pediatric health care professionals to accept the presence of animals in medical facilities. Concerns about safety, infection control, and allergies have been key barriers. Gradually, however, the medical community has become persuaded that the presence of these animals—if carefully controlled and supervised—can make contributions to the overall well-being of many children (Belcher, 2002; Brodie, Biley, & Shewring, 2002). One important advance in bringing therapy dogs into hospitals is the emergence of rigorous programs that certify animals. Therapet, for example, requires the dogs to complete an obedience class, a temperament class, and a three-hour, on-site hospital training session. Even after the animals are certified, they retrain annually and are retested biannually in order to "earn their cape" and maintain their certification. In terms of the possible health benefits of human-animal interactions, the presence of friendly animals (usually dogs) can significantly lower behavioral distress during a physical examination, and reduce the anxiety of chronically ill children who had to submit to painful medical procedures (Johnson, Odendaal, & Meadow, 2002; McConnel, 2002).

Therapy in Corrections Facilities

Increasingly, those who work with children showing a pattern of escalating involvement in criminal activities recognize that caring for and training animals can lead to positive outcomes for both people and companion animals. Some programs teach shelter dogs basic obedience skills to make them more adoptable. Others work with dogs to prepare them to become service animals of various types, such as those that assist persons with visual or auditory impairments, orthopedic impairments, or epilepsy or diabetes. In many corrections facilities, the opportunity to work with the animals represents a powerful privilege that inmates will work hard to retain. In this way, the dogs make a contribution not only as family pets or service dogs, but also as ways of rehabilitating prisoners. See Animal Planet's show *Cell Dogs* to understand how these programs operate.

Figure 5.1

corrections officer, a psychologist, and an animal handler—have collaborated to offer a service dog training program in which the facility residents can earn the right to participate. The residents who worked with Boomer and other dogs have improved their lives by knowing that they are doing meaningful work and seeing the positive outcomes.

When people hear about therapy animals, they usually think of visitation programs. The Animal-Assisted Therapy Foundation, or Therapet, explains the difference between a visitation program and AAT as follows:

A visitation program occurs when animals accompany their owners to a facility and visit with the patients. The main goal of this type of program is socialization. On the other hand, an Animal-Assisted Therapy program occurs when animals are used by the therapist in goal-directed treatment sessions, as a modality, to facilitate optimal patient outcomes. Regardless of the type of program, all animals should be temperament tested, given a complete veterinary screening, and receive obedience training before beginning to work with patients. (Source: www.therapet.com)

Aaron Katcher has conducted extensive research on the child-animal bond, focusing on children with severe attention deficits, hyperactivity disorders, or violent and aggressive behavior (Beck & Katcher, 1996). His approach to therapy was unusual yet highly effective; Katcher created a menagerie of small animals and provided children with 2-5 hours per week of learning about and caring for the animals. Based on over 10 years of data, the "companionable zoo" has been responsible for helping children to learn impulse control and exhibit more prosocial behaviors. With the support of the Devereux Foundation, Katcher has promoted the use of similar methods in special education classes in Philadelphia. Animals can be remarkably effective healers of broken spirits as well as sick or injured bodies. Figure 5.2 provides an overview of ways that companion animals can become adjuncts in therapy and support children's healing.

The premise of this chapter is that "co-species healing exists" (Schoen, 2001) and that animal-assisted therapy is a legitimate and effective adjunct to more traditional therapies. How did AAT begin?

History of Animal-Assisted Therapy

The contention that animals might contribute in some significant way to the human animal's well-being is far from new. Across cultures and belief systems, animals have been deified, honored, or afforded special status. Companion animals were part of the practice of enlightened professional practice early in the 19th century, long before research supported AAT. Florence Nightingale (1820-1910), the humanitarian whose competence and compassion inspired the nursing profession, advised that "a small pet animal is often an excellent companion for the sick, for long chronic cases especially" (cited in Vidrine, Owen-Smith, & Faulkner, 2002). Decades later, the intuitive appeal of this practice in nursing is being supported by theory and research in work with chronically ill children (Spence & Kaiser, 2002); a San Francisco-based group called Pets Are Wonderful Support (PAWS) provides carefully selected animal companions for HIV patients of all ages. Decades ago in Vienna, Sigmund Freud (1856-1939) met his patients in the company of his family dogs, two chows. Although Freud did not argue publicly that animals could function as healers, his pets were part of his practice long before anyone uttered the phrase "animal-assisted therapy." Today, the staff of a modern mental and physical health care facility in Bethel, Germany, is using a variety of animal-assisted activities and therapies to promote the well-being of its more than 9,000 residents.

Although many enlightened thinkers, great humanitarians, and prominent professionals throughout modern history have testified to the healing and humanizing effect of animals on children and adults, it wasn't until the 20th century that the first scholarly paper was written on the subject (Serpell, 1986). In 1903, W. Fowler Bucke analyzed over 1,200 children's writings to determine the value and support the children drew from their companion dogs. Bucke was a pioneer in the field of therapy animals, arguing that dogs were useful for lonely or unwell children because they relieved the child's "solitude" (Serpell, 1986, p. 93).

In 1969, Boris Levinson, a noted child psychotherapist, proposed the idea of pet-facilitated psychotherapy. Through his pivotal work, *Pet-Oriented Child Psychotherapy* (1969), Levinson was responsible for a major step forward in public awareness of the healing value of animals. Levinson noticed that some severely withdrawn and previously unreachable children opened up more when his dog, Jingles, entered the room during a therapy session. The dog served as an initial means of reaching these troubled children. Children would often project their feelings onto the dog, and say things to and share feelings with the nonjudgmental animal that they would not otherwise share (Levinson, 1969). Levinson (1971) argued that pets were valuable to children, and he gathered observational data and designed the first empirically testable methods to support his beliefs. At the time, Levinson was ridiculed by many of his contemporaries, who held to the opinion that animals had no power to connect emotionally with human beings. There were numerous jokes about psychoanalysis "going to the dogs," and much of Levinson's work was challenged or dismissed by critics. Nevertheless, convinced of

---

How Animals Help Children Heal

Companion animals are part of the construction of identity. It is no mistake that people refer to themselves as "a cat person" or as "horse people." Interactions with companion animals throughout life affect who we are and who we become.

Companion animals provide a constant presence. They are always there, always at our beck and call. They rejoice when we arrive, and they seek out our company.

Companion animals offer unwavering acceptance. Even at times when humans would prefer not to be around us because we are sick or grouchy or need a bath, companion animals accept us. They are nonjudgmental.

Companion animals usually are willing to go along with our agendas. They look on or rest quietly as we work, or they become very animated when we initiate play.

Companion animals are sensitive. They learn to attune themselves to us. They make special provisions as they interact with people; for example, being especially gentle with a baby or a frail, elderly person.

Companion animals encourage us to smile. We find them comical and we allow ourselves to be foolish in front of them. We want to talk about their antics with others.

Companion animals remind us of what is important. Our lives tend to emphasize worries about the past and anxieties about the future, but animals exist in the here and now, and they have the capacity to bring us back to it. In doing so, they exert a calming influence and reduce our stress.

References: Graham, 2000; Lasher, 1996, 1998; Schoen, 2001

Figure 5.2

the contributions of companion animals as he pursued his professional practice with children, Levinson (1969) continued to argue for the use of animals in psychotherapy. Other studies followed that eventually persuaded the experts, as well as the general public, that animals could facilitate emotional healing (Arkow, 1985).

Lasher (1996, 1998) refers to the close emotional bonds between companion animals and people as "attunement." She contends that it is nonhuman animals' openness that enables them to sense when a person is upset or that something is wrong. When a caring, trusting interspecies bond is formed, a companion animal becomes capable of responding to humans in ways that are calming and comforting. This connection is the essence of AAT.

In the past 40 years, researchers have begun to understand that animals can play important roles in somatic health and that the potential contributions of pet-facilitated therapy are considerable (Brodie & Biley, 1999). Many tangible health benefits have been found to result from human-companion animal interactions (Becker, 2002). Research indicates that pet ownership may play a role in cardiovascular health. The presence of a companion animal also has been correlated with a better recovery process in those who have already suffered a heart attack, enabling them to live longer and healthier lives than those in comparison groups who do not have companion animals (Freidmann, Thomas, & Eddy, 2000). Companion animals have been used to improve the moods of chronically ill or bedridden patients, and are now becoming a common sight in hospitals and other facilities, as depicted in Esordi's (2000) photo essay book, *You Have a Visitor: Observations on Pet Visitation and Therapy*.

The behavior of patients in various treatment facilities showed many positive changes after animal therapy was implemented. According to Serpell (1986), behavioral indicators suggest that patients who have contact with therapy animals are more alert and responsive, as evidenced by their increased willingness to talk, smile, and laugh. Animal-assisted therapy and animal visitation programs also encourage patients to take a greater interest in their surroundings, interact more with other patients and with staff members, and—perhaps most important— evidence a greater will to live (Serpell, 1986). These results are especially dramatic in those patients who had been severely withdrawn prior to the introduction of a therapy animal.

Of course, animal-assisted therapy can take place outside of a residential institutional setting. There has been a proliferation of animal therapy programs for children who are emotionally disturbed, mentally disabled, physically disabled, or who have multiple developmental challenges. One type of animal-assisted therapy that is becoming more widely available is teaching horseback riding skills to children with special needs. Riding can offer a variety of both physical and mental benefits to children, but it is especially valuable for physically handicapped children, many of whom have had to use a wheelchair for most of their lives.

First of all, key physical benefits can result from equine-assisted therapy programs. Horseback riding's rhythmic motion helps to increase the strength and flexibility of the large muscle groups in children who use wheelchairs. According to the North American Riding for the Handicapped Association (NARHA), equine-assisted activities have been shown to improve muscle tone, balance, posture, coordination, and motor development.

Second, working with horses can contribute to the emotional well-being of children with physical handicaps, emotional disturbances, and learning disabilities (www.NARHA.org, 2003). The connection with the horse frequently gives children a confidence and a sense of freedom that they do not normally experience. For most of these children, it is an incredible feeling of power to communicate and cooperate with such a large animal. Growing evidence—anecdotal, clinical, and empirical—suggests that children with mental and physical challenges progress much more rapidly after they have participated in equine-facilitated therapy.

Riding programs are not the only type of therapy programs involving horses, however. Nancy Patterson-Uhron is a Licensed Practical Nurse and the Community Director for Personal Ponies, Ltd., and explains that program in the following segment:

Personal Ponies at Simple Blessings Farm
Nancy Patterson-Uhron

photo courtesy of Nancy Patterson-Uhron

Personal Ponies is a nonprofit organization that was founded in 1986 by Marianne Alexander, our National Director. Marianne's dream was to do something special for special kids. She discovered the incredible sensitivity of the UK Shetland Pony to children with disabilities and witnessed firsthand their power to change children's lives.

Our mission is to bring smiles, laughter, and "pony magic" to the young and the young-at-heart.

Sarah and Sam the pony.

Thanks to the tireless efforts of Marianne, the organization has grown from humble beginnings and two tiny ponies into a national nonprofit organization involving hundreds of volunteers throughout the United States. Ponies are offered to promoters to serve their communities, and are offered to differently abled children to enrich their lives. We now have programs in every state, and have placed ponies with many hundreds of children. We have hundreds more on our waiting list.

Shetland ponies' size makes them less intimidating to young and physically fragile children, and also makes them more appropriate as "backyard companions." Furthermore, the Shetland's long life span often spares the child from having to cope with loss. The quiet, gentle companionship of a huggable little Shetland enriches the lives of children who are differently abled. The ponies are a bright spot of friendship and comfort in their lives, which are otherwise sometimes burdened by frustrations and fears related to their developmental or medical conditions.

A child named Sarah illustrates how the Personal Ponies program works. In September, Sarah and her extended family came to visit our farm. Sarah was born with hydranencephaly and had been expected to live only days, but was now about to celebrate her 8th birthday—she was a miracle, indeed! As only the brainstem portion of her brain was intact, she was totally blind, wheelchair bound, nonverbal, and had to receive tube feedings. Yet when Sarah met Sammy the Shetland pony, she began to smile, vocalize, and even attempted to stand up! We became friends and worked closely with Marianne, the founder of Personal Ponies, to find Sarah a pony all her own. Sarah had been struggling with various health problems and had recently had pneumonia, so we wanted to get her a pony as soon as possible. Sadly, Sarah only had her pony for one week before she became ill again with pneumonia and passed away. Currently, Sarah's gramma, mom, and sisters all participate in promoting the program and taking the two little Shetlands that touched Sarah's life to various community functions. The Personal Ponies, Ltd. Program affects the lives of those who participate in it in many ways.

As Nancy's experiences suggest, most professionals who become involved in these programs devote time, effort, and money to them because they have personally witnessed the positive effects on children.

How Does Animal-Assisted Therapy Work?

Gertz (2002) reported on two Dalmatians, Trapper and Hawkeye, that were trained by Therapy Dogs International, Inc. (TDI) and brought to Manhattan following the September 11th tragedy. The most remarkable experience with these therapy dogs occurred at the Red Cross Family Assistance Center. A 7-year-old boy had been so traumatized by the death of his parent from the disaster that he had stopped talking; although volunteers had tried repeatedly to comfort the boy and get him to interact, he remained inconsolable and uncommunicative. When the two dogs arrived, one put his head in the boy's lap while the other began to lick his face. As the adults looked on, the boy who had been so inexpressibly sad began talking to the dogs softly. Later, when adults spoke to the child, he gently touched the black spots on the dogs' coats and spoke aloud to the therapy dogs, rather than speaking directly to the adults.

As this child's response illustrates, the role of animals in human beings' lives has undergone a transformation in modern society (Fine, 2000). Animals first joined up with humans to be exploited as workers, then we began caring for them as pets, and now the animals care for us, both physically and psychologically. Figure 5.3 lists some of the organizations (and their Web sites) that have been leaders in animal-assisted therapy.

There are at least two roles for companion animals that enable them to enter into the realm of animal-assisted therapy.

First, animals can function as a *social lubricant*. A companion animals can function as a "go-between" through its attentive, patient, kind, uncritical, and affectionate behavior. These animals invite attention and spark conversation. The power of companion animals to ease tensions and promote more positive social interactions is

Organizations in Animal-Assisted Therapy

American Dog Trainers Network
    www.inch.com/~dogs
American Miniature Horse Association
    www.minihorses.com/amha
Animal Assisted Therapy Foundation/Therapet
    www.therapet.com
Assistance Dogs and People Together (ADAPT)
    www.inch.com/~dogs/service.html
Assistance Dogs of America
    www.assistancedogsofamerica.org
Assistance Dogs for Living
    www.marilynpona.com/adl.html
Assistance Dogs International (ADI)
    www.adionline.org
Association of Professional Humane Educators
    http://aphe.vview.org
Canine Companions for Independence
    www.caninecompanions.org
Delta Society
    www.deltasociety.org
Devereux Kanner Nurture Fund
    www.devereux.org/site/PageServer
Discovery Dogs
    www.marin.org/partners/partner_org.cfm?orgID=2959
Dog-Play
    www.dog-play.com
Dolphins Plus
    www.pennekamp.com/dolphins-plus
Guide Dogs for the Blind
    www.guidedogs.com
Guide Dogs of America
    www.guidedogsofamerica.org
Harcum College & Devereux Foundation Animal
Assisted Therapy & Education Certificate Program
    www.activitytherapy.com/pet.htm
Hearing Dogs, Inc.
    http://hometown.aol.com/IHDI/IHDI.html

Hearing Dog Resource Center
    www.bigfreebies.com/main/content/12/22/175.html
Horseback Outdoor Recreation and Specialized Equipment and Services (HORSE)
    www.latham.org/shop/prodserv_Type.asp?Type=Video
Independent Assistance Dog Partners (IAADP)
    www.sonic.net/~lalovell/sca/disabilities/servicedogs.html
International Federation of Guide Dog Schools (IFGDS)
    www.inch.com/~dogs/service.html
The Latham Foundation for the Promotion of Humane Education
    www.latham.org
Mona's Ark Occupational Therapy Program
    www.latham.org/shop/prodserv_Type.asp?Type=Video
North American Riding for the Handicapped Association
    www.narha.org
National Association for Search and Rescue
    www.nasar.org
National Education of Assistance Dogs Service (NEADS)
    www.neads.org
Paws With a Cause
    www.pawswithacause.org
Pets Are Wonderful Support (PAWS), San Francisco
    www.pawssf.org
Personal Ponies
    www.personalponies.org
Prison Pet Partnerships Program
    http://members.tripod.com/~prisonp/
Seeing Eye Guide Dogs
    www.thepuppyplace.org
Super Dog Animal Assisted Therapy
    www.superdog.com/therapy.htm
Therapy Dogs International, Inc.
    www.tdi-dog.org

Figure 5.3

gaining such acceptance that companies in Tokyo pay $4,000 a month for a service called Pet Plan 110, which will bring a dog, cat, or pig to corporate offices each day (Von Kreisler, 2001). Observational studies suggest that a child with special needs who arrives in a classroom with a companion animal is far more likely to interact with peers, and that the positive interactions are more apt to continue (Innes, 2000).

Second, animals can become *ambassadors* who make people more aware of the issues that others are facing. Dutchess, a German shepherd, is one such animal. As a Guide Dog for the Blind, she makes the rounds in her community along with her owner, Nathan, and a representative from the national organization. They visit schools and groups such as Cub Scouts, 4-H, and the Lions Club to demonstrate how dogs can be trained to assist human beings with serious visual impairments. In fact, Dutchess' life reflects a long pattern of bringing people together. First, Dutchess was raised by a reputable breeder and evaluated as a puppy by an expert in animal-assisted therapy. After she was weaned, a family with a 9-year-old girl volunteered to be puppy raisers. The family raised Dutchess, socialized her, and taught her to be a calm, obedient animal. Next, Dutchess was enrolled in an advanced training program. After she was thoroughly trained, Dutchess met her new owner, Nathan, who is legally blind due to macular degeneration. Dutchess trained with Nathan and became his best friend as well as a way for Nathan to gain greater independence. Despite having the limited life span of a dog, Dutchess has touched many lives and brought many people together.

As James Serpell (1986) concludes, after many years of empirical research on companion animals, "There is something spiritually uplifting about interacting with other species. By so doing, it heightens awareness of our interrelatedness . . . humans and animals establish a profound, at times heart-rending bond with one another" (p. 106). Sometimes therapeutic results from the interaction between children and companion animals are unanticipated, however, and the animals are unusual.

You Dirty Rat!
Marsha R. Robbins

Mack was a rat. No, I mean it! He was a white lab rat who had come into my life via my Psychology of Learning Class at the University of Pittsburgh. I had taught him to work through mazes in Skinner boxes to find water and food. He and I had worked paw-in-hand for 15 weeks, exploring the theories of learning. We were a successful team. Then it was the end of the term, and I asked what the university did with these educated rodents. HE WAS TO BE FED TO A SNAKE! Now that Mack was too smart to be trained again, he was of no use to the university. But he mattered to me. Together, we had wandered through the maze of materials to be learned. He deserved better than becoming a snake's entrée, so he came home with me. Then he came to work with me.

I was working in a classroom filled with kindergarten and 1st-grade students who had physical disabilities. Our class was in a mainstream elementary school. A little caged mascot seemed like a good idea, and as I believe in exploding myths, the rat came to school. The students were young enough that they hadn't heard you weren't supposed to like rats. They named the rat "Mack," because that is the first word that they had learned to read. He had a nametag on his cage and he was always willing to help them finish off any snack that they could fit between the bars of the cage. The kids loved him. They would hold him and feed him and nobody noticed that he had a scaly pink tail or yellow teeth. Each day after lunch, the children had the chance to visit with Mack and fill him with food they had smuggled out of the cafeteria. The students loved talking to Mack, and reading to Mack, and giving him treats. They were proud to read his nametag and he was delighted to help out with still another human learning program. (Rodent pride is evidenced in a hearty appetite for contraband food.)

There was one little boy in that class who didn't read Mack's name as he approached the cage. He didn't speak at all. His name was Vinnie, and he had never uttered a single word in his four years at school. His mother assured us that he talked at home all the time, but he had never made a sound in school from the moment that he joined our early intervention class.

88

One day in mid-April, as the teacher and I were chatting about the plans for the afternoon lessons, we heard a strange little voice in the back of the room. "Mack, do you want another cheese twist?" We were startled because no new students had entered the room. We both turned quickly to look in the direction of the voice, and what do you think? There, by the cage of the white lab rat, stood Vinnie, offering a bit of his lunch. He went on to offer a pretzel to the rat, and gently pushed the salty snack through the bars as the teacher and I stood in the back of the room with tears streaming down our cheeks.

For four years, numerous professionals had tried to reach Vinnie. He had been in speech, in play therapy, and in special education since he was 2 years old. No mere human could entice Vinnie to speak, however. It took a rat to make him feel so relaxed that he forgot to remain silent.

Vinnie went on to talk to his friends that year, and by the end of the following school year he was reading to his rodent buddy and answering questions in class. Who could have ever imagined that it would be a  *rejected laboratory rat who would undo Vinnie's code of silence.*

Children With Special Needs and Interactions With Companion Animals

The use of pets in animal-assisted therapy with special populations of children has a long history (Mallon, 1992; Nebbe, 1997) and has gained general acceptance (Fine, 2000). Psychotherapists have brought pets into their practice (Reimer, 1999), personnel in residential treatment programs have extolled the virtues of pet ownership for children (Levinson, 1971), and elementary counselors have written case studies that offer success stories about pets and special populations (Nebbe, 1997). Animal Systems is a company that provides workshops in advanced techniques of animal-assisted therapy. They explain their mission as follows:

We try to get people to understand that their relationships with animals mirror their relationships with other people. For instance, when we're working with adoles-

cent boys who have issues with anger, we'll pair them with a younger horse or a dog who is also emotionally out of control. As the boys work with the animal, teaching the animal to keep itself under control, they begin to recognize similarities to their own behavior. If it goes well, the boys grasp that being able to control their own emotions is a more adaptive strategy to life than being constantly stirred up. (Schoen, 2001, p. 72)

Likewise, special educators have studied how animals can be used to teach practical life skills to children with visual impairments (Lieberman, 1974), have used dogs to promote prosocial behavior in autistic children (Redefer & Goodman, 1989), and have used animals to motivate children with multiple handicapping conditions (Cox, 1968).

Sunshine and Song
Marsha R. Robbins

Some children have disabilities that are so severe only the most creative teaching methods facilitate involvement in the learning process. Armen was one of those children. Armen was born with serious birth defects. He was blind, had a significant hearing loss, and had serious physical disabilities. Armen received his nourishment through a G-tube (gastro-intestinal tube). Armen had cerebral palsy and could only move his head and hands voluntarily. When I met him, he had scoliosis to a degree that precluded sitting in a chair for more than the time that it took to ride the bus to and from school. His days in school were spent in assorted reclining positions to accommodate digestion and breathing.

In spite of all these challenges, Armen was a delight. When you would touch him or offer sensory stimulation, he would flash a smile to rival any toothpaste commercial. There were only three staff members in the classroom and eight students. That seems like a reasonable ratio until you consider the fact that most of the students really needed one-to-one interaction to benefit from the activities. If the students needed to go to the bathroom, it took two of the adults to facilitate the process, leaving just one adult in the classroom. During such times, I always attempted to have the students involved in an independent leisure activity, but it was particularly challenging finding such activities for Armen. He could only process tactile input, and synthetic means were only briefly satisfying to him. If he was touching a tactile ball, made up of varied textures and surfaces, it would move out of reach. Music was his favorite pastime, but when the music was loud enough for him to hear, no other aural communication could be effective above the din. He would not use earphones. Armen really made me THINK!

One day, a pet store in the community called to ask a favor of me. They had a bird that had a significant birth defect. It was a cockatiel with a ruptured air sac (the name given to the breathing organs of a bird), and they didn't think he would survive for long. Since I had already established a reputation for animal rescue in our community, they wanted to know if I would consider taking this bird for the time that he had left. The alternative was euthanasia, since the pet store environment was too stressful for him and nobody would buy a defective bird.

They knew the right number to call when they called me; after getting approval from my principal, I went to get the fledgling bird. Cockatiels have bright orange cheek patches that look like circles of rouge. This one was a pied cockatiel, which means he had a bright yellow head with patches of gray over his body. The rest of him was white. He had an outgoing personality and chirped merrily, despite his affliction, so it only took a moment to dub him "Sunshine."

Sunshine and I bonded quickly, and the next week he went to the school. He had a cage right next to the elevated mat where Armen laid. Over the course of the next few days we noticed an interesting behavior. When Sunshine would sing his midday song, Armen would move his head from side to side like he did when he heard music that he enjoyed. Sunshine's song wasn't very loud, so we initially found no connection between the two behaviors. After all, Armen was supposed to be nearly deaf.

As we watched Armen's response for the next two weeks, however, he consistently rocked his head whenever the bird sang. It seemed unlikely that he was hearing Sunshine, but it was worth investigating. We would watch Armen. When Sunshine would chirp, he would rock with his toothiest grin. We decided to test the theory that the bird's song was eliciting Armen's response. When Sunshine would chirp, Armen would grin, and then we would take the bird out of the room. Armen's grin would disappear. We repeated the trials with 100 percent correspondence. Even though the child could not hear a human voice, he evidently could hear the pitch of the bird's song, and he obviously liked what he heard.

Finally, a leisure activity that could stimulate Armen when humans couldn't be there next to him! He could be happy and enjoy the bird independently.

I am a firm believer that if one is good, then more is better. Within two weeks I had brought two lovebirds into the classroom, and Armen's joy was multiplied. Cockatiels engage in periodic song, but lovebirds chatter endlessly. Whenever Armen entered the classroom, his smile was spontaneous. The birds greeted him instantly, and from that day on he was never alone in the classroom, devoid of interaction. When the humans were busy elsewhere, the songs went on, and Armen had acquired an independent leisure activity that brought him joy, Sunshine, and song.

Autistic children also can benefit from interaction with companion animals. Law and Scott (1995) noted that some children with PDD/autism "exhibit excessive anxiety or fear when in contact with animals," and so they developed a school-based program in which children were taught to "feed, handle, soothe, clean, and groom a variety of animals" (p. 17). Program evaluations indicated that pet care bolstered the self-confidence and self-esteem of students with PDD/autism, and offered opportunities for socialization with other pet caregivers and the larger school population. Dana Monroe is the Director of Educational Services for several programs that are designed to support children with autism and related developmental disorders. In the vignette below, she describes the unique style of interaction between a child with autism and his companion animal.

Canine to Five: Big Brother With Paws
Dana M. Monroe

Billy hobbles out of bed and down the hall to the bathroom. Behind him follows his golden retriever, Molly, who stretches out her paws against the carpet, then lets out a morning yowl. The sound of the dog is meaningless to Billy, who is now pacing erratically in front of the bathroom sink, chanting the word "bathroom." Over and over, Billy swings from one end of the bathroom to the other with a frantic and anxious expression on his face, his arms flailing next to him in a repetitive motion, like hummingbirds flying near his head. Molly, a beautiful nearly white-haired dog, watches Billy for a moment, prances into the master bedroom, and begins nudging Billy's mother to wake up. She awakes and follows Molly down the hallway to the bathroom. Billy's mother finds him feverishly pacing and crying; she now understands that Billy has forgotten what he is supposed to do in the bathroom and he needs guidance to complete his task. Luckily, Molly recognizes when Billy needs help. The story of Billy Robertson and his dog Molly proves that animals can bring very special experiences to our lives.

Molly became part of the Robertson family on Billy's first birthday. Billy's father brought her home for him in hopes that the dog would bring Billy out of the shell that he seemed to be hiding in. Billy's parents, Linda and Buck Robertson, had begun noticing that Billy didn't seem to be developing like other children in the neighborhood, although their pediatrician insisted that Billy would catch up in due time. It seemed that Billy didn't want to interact with anyone and he cried inconsolably throughout the day. In a desperate attempt to soothe Billy, Buck decided to buy a puppy for his son, and that is how the relationship between Billy and Molly began.

Molly was a playful pup, bouncing and yelping and frolicking all over the house. She would desperately try to jump into Billy's play area, but he never really acknowledged that she was there. Of course, that didn't stop her, and she persisted in becoming a part of whatever he was involved in, even though Billy continued to ignore her. On Billy's third birthday, Buck and Linda decided to seek outside help for Billy and, through a doctor's evaluation, they discovered that Billy had a developmental disorder called autism. It took several years, but the family adjusted to the different needs of their son, and Billy became a unique and interesting young child with a very supportive family. Molly still tried to be with him, although Billy didn't seem to care if she was in the room or not. At one point, Buck felt that Molly seemed to be depressed because Billy refused to interact with her; despite the rejection, she still tried to nuzzle with him on the floor or lick his face while he was playing with his toys. Molly always dropped her ball in front of Billy in hopes that he would throw it to her, but Billy never did.

It wasn't until Billy was about 6 years old that Buck and Linda started noticing the very special relationship that Molly and Billy shared. It wasn't the typical boy-dog interaction, yet they did have a unique connection. Unfortunately, Billy's disorder caused him to be isolated from his peer group, as he engaged in many strange behaviors and had no formal way of communicating with others except for a small vocabulary or screeching when he was angry. These behaviors seemed to scare others, but not Molly. She never seemed to care that Billy would bang his head and scream as loud as he could; she would sit close by and wait patiently until he finished. It was as if Molly understood that Billy needed to do these things, and she accepted him as he was. Buck and Linda started noticing that Molly would consistently alert them if Billy had run too far down the street by scratching her nails on the top of their feet. If Molly dug deep into her shoes, Linda knew that Billy was in danger in the neighborhood. Molly was usually right, and she was rewarded for her watchful eye with a bacon strip.

Little by little, in every aspect of Billy's life, the family began to realize how much Molly protected Billy. They saw Molly follow Billy around the cul-de-sac when he was riding his bike, or watched her wait beside him for the school bus. Molly was like his shadow, and she kept him in view no matter where they were. The strangest part of the relationship, the Robertsons admit, is that Billy has never acknowledged Molly. He has never reached out to pet her long coat, never smiles when she comes running toward him, and has never engaged in any play with Molly. The Robertsons believe that Billy has never even made eye contact with Molly; nevertheless, they are sure that he knows she is there. They have watched Billy move over on the sidewalk so that Molly can walk beside him; although he never calls her or watches her, this simple gesture lets *everyone know that he knows she is with him. Billy never slams a door in the house, and he always takes an unusual amount of time entering and leaving through a door. After careful evaluation, the Robertsons have deduced that Billy is holding the door open for Molly. He never looks down, he never checks to see if she has made it through; he just takes extra time with the door. Most people wouldn't acknowledge these behaviors as anything but coincidence, but the Robertsons consider them testimony to the power of pets. Billy rarely engages with anyone, humans or animals, but their golden retriever somehow has been able to establish her own relationship with him. The Robertsons have nicknamed Molly "Canine to Five" because it seems like she is always on the job watching her friend Billy. Her unconditional love towards Billy demonstrates on a daily basis that the ability to nurture is not just a human trait.*

Billy's story illustrates the reciprocity that human beings have with animals: "People expect reciprocity from animals and, consequently, enter into special, intimate primary relationships with them" (Menache, 2000, p. 44) in which companion animals can function as mediators of nonverbal communication.

Animals' Capacity To Connect With Humans

People from contemporary Western cultures are sometimes surprised to discover that many indigenous peoples throughout history did not regard themselves as superior to animals (Suzuki & Knudtsen, 1998). Rather, nonhuman and human animals were regarded as interdependent elements in a web of life. In many contemporary tribal cultures, animals continue to be treated with respect as fellow inhabitants of the earth, even those animals that are hunted for food (Erikson, 2000). During Rene Descartes' day, such attitudes were dismissed as primitive and the "civilized" world believed animals to be senseless brutes devoid of thought and feelings. At various points in Western history, the academic community has sought to identify some uniquely human trait that makes people superior to other life forms, such as the ability to use tools, solve problems, and use language. Further study of animals would contradict these arrogant assertions. The current line of demarcation has to do with the emotional lives of animals, as some scientists argue that animals are incapable of emotion, acting only on instinct or in order to get some benefit.

In their best-selling book, *When Elephants Weep: The Emotional Lives of Animals,* McCarthy and Masson (1996) synthesize both empirical and anecdotal evidence from a variety of professional fields to argue that animals do indeed have emotional states. Stories abound of animals who surprise us with their sensitivity (cats who respond to an owner's distress); protectiveness (a pet pig that chases away intruders); courage (dogs that go into battle, sniff out explosives, or help to catch criminals); and self-sacrifice (a mare that lashed out with her hooves against a bear that was threatening her owner) (Von Kreisler, 2001). With the advent of new technologies that make it possible to record brain activity, studies reveal patterns of brain activity in animals that are remarkably similar to that of human beings in comparable emotional states, such as when both are frightened (Diamond & Hopson, 1999). Researcher Temple Grandin (1996) believes that animals' emotions might best be represented as a collection of visual images that they draw upon to interpret experiences and that the animal's early life is a critical time when such images are developed and committed to memory.

Such theories about animals' capacity for emotional responses have intuitive appeal for anyone who has worked with an abused animal. Monty Roberts (1998), a widely respected horse trainer noted for his gentle methods, explains that he can be in the presence of an abused animal and infer the particular type of maltreatment from the animal's behavior. People who work with shelter animals know this, too. The dog who is "head shy" and ducks or cringes when a hand reaches out is responding to hurtful mental images of past abuse.

Conclusion

When the conversation turns to animal-assisted therapy, we are claiming something even more profound than an animal's ability to experience fear, pain, joy, or sorrow. We are contending that some companion animals are capable of *responding appropriately* to a human being's emotional state and *adjusting their animal behavior* in ways that accommodate the person's needs. Can companion animals really do this? Observations and observational research suggest that they can, if they are selected based on temperament (rather than on some superficial criteria for appearance), and given appropriate training and ample opportunity to evolve into therapy animals. As anyone who works with service dogs can attest, the particular characteristics of the task interact with the individual strengths of the animal. The dogs that provide various types of emotional support are quite different from those selected to rescue people from icy waters or those chosen to sniff out drugs in a high school locker. Development of both nonhuman and human animals not only depends on the interaction of nature and nurture, but also on the particular context and specific types of interdependency between the two species. Rather than dismiss animal-assisted therapy as the anthropomorphic imaginings of pet enthusiasts, we need to observe these remarkable creatures at work and learn new ways of measuring the effects of animal-assisted therapy on children.

References

Arkow, P. (Ed.). (1985). *Dynamic relationships in practice: Animals in the helping professions.* Alameda, CA: Latham Foundation.

Beck, A. M., & Katcher, A. H. (1996). *Between pets and people: The importance of animal companionship* (2nd ed.). West Lafayette, IN: Purdue University Press.

Becker, M. (2002). *The healing power of pets: Harnessing the amazing ability of pets to make and keep people healthy.* New York: Hyperion.

Belcher, D. (2002). Pet-assisted therapy at Mount Sinai in New York. *American Journal of Nursing, 120*(2), 71.

Brodie, S. J., & Biley, F. C. (1999). An exploration of the potential benefits of pet-facilitated therapy. *Journal of Clinical Nursing, 8*(4), 329-337.

Brodie, S. J., Biley, F. C., & Shewring, M. (2002). An exploration of the potential risks associated with using pet therapy in healthcare settings. *Journal of Clinical Nursing, 11*(4), 444-456.

Cox, L. V. (1968). The Maryland School for the Blind summer day school program for pre-school multi-handicapped children. *International Journal for the Education of the Blind, 18*(4), 97-99.

Diamond, M., & Hopson, J. (1999). *Magic trees of the mind: How to nurture your child's intelligence, creativity, and healthy emotions from birth through adolescence.* New York: Penguin.

Doyle, C. (2001). Surviving and coping with emotional abuse in childhood. *Clinical Child Psychology and Psychiatry, 6*(3), 387-402.

Erikson, P. (2000). The social significance of petkeeping among Amazonian Indians. In A. L. Podberscek, E. S. Paul, & J. A. Serpell (Eds.), *Companion animals and us: Exploring the relationships between people and pets* (pp. 7-27). New York: Cambridge University Press.

Esordi, R. L. (2000). *You have a visitor: Observations on pet visitation and therapy.* San Diego, CA: Blue Lamm Publishing.

Fine, A. H. (Ed.). (2000). *Handbook on animal-assisted therapy: Theoretical foundations and guidelines for practice.* San Diego, CA: Academic Press.

Freidmann, E., Thomas, S. A., & Eddy, T. J. (2000). Companion animals and human health. In A. L. Podberscek, E. S. Paul, & J. A. Serpell (Eds.), *Companion animals and us: Exploring the relationships between people and pets* (pp. 125-142). New York: Cambridge University Press.

George, M. H. (1999). The role of animals in the emotional and moral development of children. In F. R. Ascione & P. Arkow (Eds.), *Child abuse, domestic violence, and animal abuse* (pp. 380-392). West Lafayette, IN: Purdue University Press.

Gertz, K. R. (2002). The hero dogs of 9/11: Some came to rescue, others to heal. *Family Circle, 115*(7), 83-84, 86-89.

Glassner, P. (Ed.). (2001). *Cinderella dogs: Real-life fairy tale adoptions from the San Francisco SPCA.* San Francisco: Kinship Communications.

Grandin, T. (1996). *Thinking in pictures: And other reports of my life in autism.* New York: Vintage.

Graham, B. (2000). *Creature comfort.* New York: Prometheus.

Hanselman, J. L. (2001). Coping skills with adolescents in anger management using animals in therapy. *Journal of Child and Adolescent Group Therapy, 11,* 159-195.

Innes, F. K. (2000). The influence of an animal on normally developing children's ideas about helping children with disabilities. *Dissertation Abstracts International Section A: Humanities and Social Sciences, 60*(11-A), p. 3897.

Johnson, R. A., Odendaal, J. S., & Meadow, R. L. (2002). Animal-assisted interventions research: Issues and answers. *Western Journal of Nursing Research, 24*(4), 422-440.

Lasher, M. (1996). *And the animals will teach you.* New York: Berkeley Books.

Lasher, M. (1998). A relational approach to the human-animal bond. *Anthrozoos, 11*(3), 130-133.

Law, S., & Scott, S. (1995). Pet care: A vehicle for learning. *Focus on Autistic Behavior, 10*(2), 17-18.

Levinson, B. M. (1969). *Pet oriented child psychotherapy.* Springfield, IL: Charles C. Thomas.

Levinson, B. M. (1971). Household pets in training schools serving delinquent children. *Psychological*

Reports, 28(2), 475-481.

Lieberman, G. (Ed.). (1974). *Daily living skills: A manual for educating visually impaired students.* Washington, DC: Bureau of Education of the Handicapped (ERIC Document Reproduction Service No. ED 098 776).

Mallon, G. P. (1992). Utilization of animals as therapeutic adjuncts with children and youth: A review of the literature. *Child and Youth Care Forum, 21*(1), 53-67.

McCarthy, S., & Masson, J. (1996). *When elephants weep: The emotional lives of animals.* New York: Delacorte.

McConnel, E. A. (2002). About animal-assisted therapy. *Nursing, 32*(3), 76.

Melson, G. F. (2001). *Why the wild things are.* Cambridge, MA: Harvard University Press.

Menache, S. (2000). Hunting and attachment to dogs in the pre-modern period. In A. L. Podberscek, E. S. Paul, & J. A. Serpell (Eds.), *Companion animals and us: Exploring the relationships between people and pets* (pp. 42-60). Cambridge, UK: Cambridge University Press.

Nebbe, L. J. (1997). The human-animal bond's role with the abused child. *Dissertation Abstracts International Section B: The Sciences and Engineering, 58*(3-B), 1568.

Rathmann, C. (1999). Forget Me Not Farm: Teaching gentleness with gardens and animals to children from violent homes and communities. In F. R. Ascione & P. Arkow (Eds.), *Child abuse, domestic violence, and animal abuse* (pp. 393-409). West Lafayette, IN: Purdue University Press.

Redefer, L. A., & Goodman, J. F. (1989). Pet-facilitated therapy with autistic children. *Journal of Autism and Developmental Disorders, 19*(3), 461-467.

Regoli, R. M., & Hewitt, J. D. (2003). *Delinquency in society* (5th ed.) Boston: McGraw-Hill.

Reimer, D. F. (1999). Pet-facilitated therapy: An initial exploration of the thinking and theory behind innovative intervention for children in psychotherapy. *Dissertation Abstracts International: Section B: The Sciences and Engineering, 60*(5-B), 2363.

Roberts, M. (1998). *The man who listens to horses.* New York: Ballantine.

Roseberry, K. B., & Rovin, L. M. (1999). Animal-assisted therapy for sexually abused adolescent females: The program at Crossroads. In F. Ascione (Ed.), *Child abuse, domestic violence, and animal abuse: Linking the circles of compassion for prevention and intervention* (pp. 433-442). West Lafayette, IN: Purdue University Press.

Ross, S. B. (1999). Green chimneys: We give troubled children the gift of giving. In F. R. Ascione & P. Arkow (Eds.), *Child abuse, domestic violence, and animal abuse* (pp. 367-379). West Lafayette, IN: Purdue University Press.

Schoen, A. M. (2001). *Kindred spirits: How the remarkable bond between humans and animals can change the way that we live.* New York: Broadway Books.

Serpell, J. (1986). *In the company of animals.* New York: Cambridge University Press.

Shield, B., & Carson, R. (1989). *Healers on healing.* New York: Putnam.

Spence, L. J., & Kaiser, L. (2002). Companion animals and adaptation in chronically ill children. *Western Journal of Nursing Research, 24*(6), 63-80.

Suzuki, D., & Knudtsen, P. (1998). *Wisdom of the elders.* New York: Bantam.

Vidrine, M., Owen-Smith, P., & Faulkner, P. (2002). Equine-facilitated group psychotherapy: Applications for therapeutic vaulting. *Issues in Mental Health Nursing, 23*(6), 587-603.

Von Kreisler, K. (2001). *Beauty in the beasts: True stories of animals who choose to do good.* New York: Tarcher/Putnam.

Chapter 6

Global Companion Animals: Bonding With and Caring for Animals Across Cultures and Countries

Jyotsna Pattnaik

—Julia Schulte-Strathaus
Germany

I am in tears, while carrying you to your last resting place as much as I rejoiced when bringing you home in my own hands fifteen years ago. (Epitaph recovered from an ancient pet cemetery, as cited by Bodson, 2001, p. 32)

Zarko, you were very special to me, and I love you still. Wherever you are now, I hope your eyes are bright and your teeth sharp and your coat glossy, and the lady cats adore you as much as I did. I will never forget you. (Epitaph posted on a virtual pet cemetery by Bronwyn Halls (n.d.) of Melbourne, Australia)

These examples bear testimony to the universality of pet-keeping practices as well as to the strong emotional relationship between human beings and their pets across eras and cultures. Demographic reports from various countries demonstrate a worldwide increase in the number of pet-owners. The Urban Management Animal Coalition (1995) reported that 60 percent of households in Australia own a pet. A survey conducted by a European pet food association in the year 2001 determined that approximately 55 million European households own a pet (The Pet Food Manufacturers' Association, 2001). In 2001, amid religious and official rulings against owning dogs, the first-ever dog show was held in Iran (Daragahi, 2002). At present, theorists and researchers from a variety of fields reject the notion that "pet-keeping is a product of western wealth, decadence, and bourgeois sentimentality," instead highlighting the beneficial aspects (cognitive, emotional, socio-moral) of children's relationships with animals (Serpell, 1986, p. 53). For example, Melson (2001) writes, "Animals may function as a meaning

95

system through which children make sense of both themselves and their surrounding environments" (p. 12).

Using a global perspective, this chapter will focus on: the status and role of animals across cultures, celebrations for companion animals, the kinds of animals kept by children, classroom animal companions around the world, worldwide efforts to involve children in protecting the well-being of animals, children's literature and tales about pets, what the world's children say about their companion animals, and the implications of the child/companion animal bond for the world's teachers.

The Status and Role of Animals Across Cultures

It is important to understand that the practice of pet-keeping is a function of age-old cultural perceptions toward the status and role of animals. For example, animals occupy a significant place in the mythology of various cultures. Goats took a center stage in Greek mythology, the owl signified wisdom and prosperity in Western myths, snakes symbolized eternity and renewal and functioned as pets for the Greeks and Romans, and animals in Celtic and Welsh mythology represented fertility and vitality (Nooden, 1992). In some Native American mythologies, the buffalo represents steadfast endurance to rise above one's weaknesses and the owl symbolizes wisdom, truth, and knowledge. For Buddhists, the lizard represents conservation and agility, the turtle represents a long and meaningful life, and the deer is perceived as a messenger of universal love.

The mouse, rat, lion, elephant, water buffalo, and the peacock and other birds are all depicted in Hindu mythology as companion animals for gods and goddesses. Cambefort (1994) found evidence of beetle worship in cultures around the world, including ancient Egypt, Indian tribes from South America, and Germany. One finds the utmost form of compassion toward animals in the Buddhist practice of nonviolence toward animals. Buddha is believed to have taken the physical form of animals (such as a dog, monkey, deer, and fish) in his various rebirths.

Animals have been credited with at least three broad roles by various cultures. First is the role of *animals as teachers*. In this role, animals have been used to convey cultural wisdom, as reflected in proverbs from various cultures, such as: "You can cage a bird but you cannot make it sing" (French-Jewish) or "A chattering bird builds no nests" (Chinese). Additionally, moral lessons often are conveyed through folklore that features animals, such as Aesop's Fables and the Jataka Tales from India. The view that pet animals serve educational and emotional purposes is gaining wider acceptance, as teachers in many countries have begun to include pet animals as integral members of their classroom communities.

The second major role is the *animal as healer*. In the Shamanic traditions (practiced by Siberian tribes and aboriginal people in other parts of the world), ceremonies are performed to evoke the power of animals to heal the dispirited, the depressed, and the physically ill (Harner, 1990). Originally proposed by child psychotherapist Boris Levinson, the technique of "pet therapy" now is frequently used with children in hospitals. Green Chimneys, a social service agency in the United States, promotes positive interaction between animals and emotionally disturbed children as a way to help these children cope with their difficulties.

The third enduring role is *animals as friends and companions*. The theme of animals' profound devotion to their owners is repeated in stories from around the world. For example, Erickson (2001) describes a myth from a particular Amerindian tribe in which a former pet bird saves the life of his master (a hunter who is stuck in the trees) from other birds. In an Amerindian belief, the pet-human relationship continues even after death, and such animals as birds and monkeys guide their masters to their final abode. In modern times, dogs are used as companions for children with special needs (Hart, Hart, & Bergin, 1987) and for people with visual and physical impairments. This human-animal bond of companionship and service has inspired individuals and groups who fight against cruelty toward animals and lobby against the use of animals for medical research or testing for cosmetic products (Coleman, 2000).

Celebrations for Pets and Animals

Many cultures around the world hold human religious celebrations for animals. Basso (1973) reported that Kalapalo Indians in Brazil followed the same burial ritual for animals that they used when burying infants who die during childbirth or before being named. In India, ceremonies are conducted symbolizing the cow as a form of God. At the Pueblo State Historic Park in downtown Los Angeles, thousands of pet owners gather with their pets the Saturday before Easter to have their animals blessed with a sprinkling of holy water in a ceremony conducted by a Cardinal of the Catholic Church. This event is considered to be a way of expressing appreciation for the many services that animals have rendered to the human community (Dresser, 2001).

Companion animals are often commemorated after death as well. Pet cemeteries existed in ancient Greece and Rome as they do now in many contemporary societies. With the advent of the Internet, virtual pet cemeteries (such as www.myCemetery.com) provide yet another way of commemorating pets. These Web sites allot virtual "plots" to pet owners, where they can write tributes to their beloved pets that have died.

Companion Animals Across the Cultures

Anthropologists report that pet-keeping was a very common practice among aboriginal peoples around the world. For example, anthropologists report that pets and young animals are suckled by women in many aboriginal communities world-wide and are treated with utmost affection by their human mothers. Part of the initiation ceremony for Dinka youth in Southern Sudan is that, upon entering puberty, each boy is given a special bull as a brother. The boy is expected to converse with the bull and to compose poetry about it as part of his rite of passage into adulthood (Schwabe, 1994). Wallabies, opossums, and dingoes served as pets for Australian aborigines, while deer, wolves, raccoons, turkeys, turtles, and varieties of birds were frequently kept as pets by Native Americans. Polynesians typically kept pigeons, parrots, and lizards as pets. During their study of tribal communities, anthropologists have observed returning hunters bringing small, live, wild animals as gifts for their children from their hunting trips (Laughin, 1968). Pet monkeys are also very common in tribal communities.

Rituals and stories from various cultures reflect a strong affectionate relationship between domesticated animals (e.g., cattle, sheep, and goats) and their keepers. When the author asked children in a rural village in India to write stories about their pets, some of the children wrote stories about their pet cows. Elephants also are kept as pets, especially in the southern states of India. Camels are kept as pets in the desert areas of India and Middle East.

Types of Companion Animals

Historians believe that dogs were the first domesticated animal in the world and that goats were the second. Nigerians trace the domestication of dogs to the beginning of the creation; in Nigerian folklore, dogs are believed to drive away evil spirits (Ojoade, 1990). Presently, dogs are the most popular pet throughout the world.

In many Muslim communities, however, dogs are considered unclean and contact with a dog is followed by a ritual washing. This view, however, appears to be changing.

Cats were first domesticated in Egypt some 3,000-4,000 years ago (Serpell, 1986), and cats are now the second most popular pets (after dogs) throughout the world. Twenty-six percent of Australian households own a cat. Cats are gaining in popularity as pets over dogs in recent years in Britain and in the United States. The Chinese believe that cats bring good luck, and they keep cats in shops and homes.

Birds are a favorite of many pet owners around the world. The eagle is a most important bird for many Native Americans, and an oft occurring symbol. The parrot is also a favorite pet bird in cultures around the world. Bahti (1990) maintains that parrots occupy a special place in Hopi religious thoughts and practices, as manifested in the use of parrot feathers on religious articles and the identification of parrots with the direction of south. The parrot used to be a favorite pet in many households in India. After passage of the Wildlife Protection Act of 1978, however, homeowners now must have a license to keep a wild bird as a pet; thus, the number of households with parrots has declined. A native of Australia, the budgerigar, more commonly known as a parakeet, is now the most popular pet bird throughout the world.

Some of the fancy varieties of goldfish, such as veiltails, were first bred in the 16th century in China. Goldfish were first bred in the United States in 1878, and there are now many goldfish farms in the United States.

The idea of insects as companion animals (e.g., the *mushi* in Japan) may not appeal to many. Laurent (2000) argues, however, based on Serpell and Paul's (1994) definition of a pet, as well as on research with Japanese children, that the insects so popular with Japanese children are indeed pets, and not toys, as some have suggested. Various kinds of mushi, such as the rhinoceros beetle and the stag beetle, as well as the suzumushi cricket, are a great attraction for children at Japanese pet fairs, and at department and pet stores.

First originated in Japan, virtual and electronic pets such as Tamagotchi, Poo-Chi, and the cyber spider have become very popular in the world market in recent years (see Chapter 9). Debate exists over whether these virtual pets are toys or pets. Equipped with artificial intelligence software and sophisticated sensory technology, many of the electronic pets such as the Poo-Chi puppy, the Meow-Chi cat, and Polly the robotic parrot (manufactured by Tiger Electronics) are designed to be interactive and do many things that their real-life counterparts do. At present, researchers at Purdue University are conducting a study to compare children's responses to virtual pets and live pets.

Companion Animals in Classrooms Around the World

Classroom companion animals are very common in some countries, especially the United States, the United Kingdom, Canada, and Australia. Some classrooms have resident animals, while others have animal visitors. The organization Teacher's Webshelf provides a forum where classroom teachers from Australia, Canada, New Zealand,

Photo courtesy of Shireen DeSouza

Three children from Ecuador care for a dog.

Puerto Rico, Spain, South Asia, the United Kingdom, South Africa, and the United States can discuss and share thoughts about their classroom pets on the Web. Teachers describe their previous and current classroom pets and the animal-related topics and activities that they have implemented in their curriculum. Some of these teachers have expressed their own love for and devotion to animals as well as their efforts to foster these feelings in their students. For example, a teacher from Australia writes:

My long-term goal is to have the opportunity to hand rear an orphaned Australian animal, with the help and enthusiasm of my partners, my classroom kids. I feel an experience such as this would bring children to a full, realistic understanding of our duty, as adults, and as human beings, to care for this world and its inhabitants.

Animal protection groups provide important information regarding classroom companion animals. For example, the Web site of the British Columbia Society for the Prevention of Cruelty to Animals (2002) provides detailed descriptions of common classroom companion animals (such as life span, size, origin, and diet), as well as the pros and cons of keeping these animals inside the classroom (see Chapter 4). For example, whereas guinea pigs and hamsters are recommended as the most suitable classroom pets, rabbits are recommended only for higher grade levels and red-eared slider turtles are not recommended for the classroom at all. The Web site also provides guidelines for classroom companion animals, discusses practical concerns, and offers strategies and suggestions to teachers who are interested in keeping an animal in the classroom (see Chapters 4, 8, and 9).

Unfortunately, companion animals are not an integral part of the community in many classrooms around the world. A variety of objections are raised to keeping animals in the classroom, including unfavorable cultural perceptions toward animals, limited space, school policies, or narrow perceptions of education (with an academic emphasis). As urbanization rapidly spreads all over the world, the resultant crowded housing conditions, lengthy commutes, limited opportunities for outdoor activities, and the lack of socialization opportunities with people in the community will further alienate children from the natural world, particularly contact with animals. Therefore, an even greater need exists for teachers in urban classrooms across the world to keep classroom companion animals as a way to counteract the monotony, loneliness, social alienation, and disconnection from the natural world that students may experience. Furthermore, because animals play a very important role in the mythology and society of many cultures around the world, a classroom companion animal also may serve to maintain continuity between children's cultural heritage and their everyday lives.

Worldwide Efforts To Involve Children in Protecting the Well-Being of Animals

Unfortunately, while the trend of keeping companion animals is gaining worldwide popularity, incidences of cruelty and negligence toward pets and domesticated animals are also on the rise. Animal protection societies in many countries are striving to involve children in their efforts to protect and rescue animals. For example, the World Society for the Protection of Animals (WPSA, 2002) mascot, Pepe the bull, is used as a symbol of their opposition to bull fighting, and the campaign has gained children's support in Mexican schools. The WSPA has opened Kindness Clubs around the world. Approximately 35,000 children (of all ages) in 32 countries across Africa are enrolled in these WSPA-sponsored Kindness Clubs, which are led by schoolteachers. The clubs provide children training and education about the needs and importance of animals, respect for animals, animal welfare problems, and how to look after a variety of common pets and domesticated animals. Children in Kindness Clubs also participate in free veterinary clinics hosted by the school. In Malaysia, the Ipoh Society for the Prevention of Cruelty to Animals (2002) reports that large numbers of children visited their booths, set up at schools, to learn about responsible pet care and the local government rulings on companion animals. In Romania, the "Children Love Animals Foundation" is a nonprofit organization that promotes the philosophy of the affective and educational relation between children and animals. The Petcare Information and Advisory Service, from Australia, has initiated many school programs, including presentations on pet care in schools.

Special days are set aside at the international level to remember the importance of animals in our lives and our responsibility toward them. Some important days, such as World Animals Day on October 4 (celebrated on the feast day of St. Francis of Assisi, the patron saint of animals) and the World Zoonoses Day on July 6 (established to teach people the importance of vaccinating their pets, domesticated animals, and themselves), are observed throughout the world.

What the World's Children Say About Their Pets

Whether it is a story in the local newspaper or scholarly research, classroom practice or pediatric medicine research, exploring and highlighting children's attachment to their companion animals has become an important part of modern society. Rud and Beck (2000) describe a contest sponsored by a community newspaper in which schoolchildren from the United States were asked to contribute favorite stories about their pets. Interestingly, one boy described the family dog as the "first child" of the parents.

Kidd and Kidd (1995) reported that "pet-owning children placed their self-figures significantly closer to their pet-figures than to their family member-figures" (p. 239), indicating the strength of the bonds between children and their pets. Summarizing his research with children in Kenya, Moses Mutuku (2002) writes, "In a way, these drawings seem to reflect children's need for companionship, security, and appreciation for beauty" (personal communication). A similar theme emerged from the writings of children in Bangalore, India (Geocities, n.d.). Children seemed to feel happy about the things that they do with and for their companion animals. In their writings, children shared their own fondness for their pets as well as the pets' fondness for them. Children also discussed the important contributions of their pets to their family—such as guard-

ing the home from thieves and strangers and chasing away other, uninvited animals.

Children's emotional attachment is reflected more strongly in the memories that they share about the companion animals that they have lost to death. An excerpt from a child's posting in a virtual cemetery (www.mycemetery.com/pet/) is provided here to highlight this point. Melanie Gillis (n.d.), a 14-year-old girl from Calgary, Canada, writes, "Misty and I were very attached. I would not be alive today if it wasn't for her. I lay choking in my crib when she awoke my parents. . . ." For many, animals are not only playmates, but also protectors and rescuers.

Implications for the World's Teachers

Animals occupy a central place in the physical and emotional lives of children across the world, as evident in a wide array of products, places, and hobbies that are of interest to children, such as nursery rhymes, books, oral tales, lullabies,

Photo courtesy of Shireen DeSouza

Gabriel demonstrates how he dances with his dog.

videos, software programs, stickers, toys and games, live and virtual pets, zoos, and other animal attractions. Therefore, it is imperative that teachers validate these important aspects of children's lives in the curriculum, as well as involve children in animal welfare activities at the local, national, and international levels.

Implication 1: Appreciate the Importance of the Child-Pet Relationship. Although the importance of the child-companion animal relationship has been documented by scholars from diverse fields of study, most teachers and administrators across the globe have not sufficiently explored its educational implications. Yet, it is important for teachers to become aware of experts' views on the child-pet relationship in terms of the developmental benefits, especially in the social domain such as their social competence, empathy, and pet attitudes (Poresky & Hendrix, 1989); the educational benefits, such as animals' power to motivate learning, cooperation, and expression among children (Kaufman, 1997); the emotional benefits, such as the calming effect of dogs on children (Friedman, Katcher, Thomas, Lynch, & Messent, 1983); and the moral benefits, such as children's capacity to develop greater empathy by tending to an animal's needs (Myers, 1998). Knowledge of these dimensions of the child-pet relationship will help teachers to design appropriate curriculum.

Implication 2: Integrate Animals Into the Classroom Community. Naturalist Jane Goodall (2002) was once opposed to the practice of keeping classroom pets because of the potential for exploitation of the animal. Now, however, she says:

I have come to think differently after seeing, with my own eyes, the incredible difference that meeting an animal can make in the life of a child. Of course, such a program must be really well run and the animals protected from any kind of harm. And some animals simply are not suitable. But domestic animals as well as quiet, wild animals who cannot be released into the wild and who are used to people—can serve as wonderful ambassadors from the animal kingdom. It seems worth it, indeed, when you see a child's eyes filled with wonder.
(Goodall & Bekoff, 2002, p. 71)

A carefully selected classroom pet can be an important addition to the classroom community. Yet, classrooms in many developing countries are extremely crowded. Therefore, keeping a classroom pet will pose a significant challenge to the teacher in such schools. In such situations, collaboration might offer a solution. Perhaps one or two small animals can be kept in a common area in the school so that the children may spend time with the animals on a rotating basis. If an area cannot be designated for pets, children and teachers might carefully screen animals that could visit the school. In communities where unfavorable attitudes exist toward companion animals, teachers may serve as animal advocates and share with parents and community members the growing body of compelling research evidence in support of the child/companion animal bond.

Implication 3: Animals As a Focal Point of the Curriculum Through Designing Thematic Units. Thematic units that are age- and grade-appropriate will help foster a broad understanding among children regarding the importance of companion animals in people's lives. For example, thematic units—such as "ways that pets are similar, yet different"—may help children to learn about animals' habitats, diet, common diseases and required immunizations, unique characteristics, and contributions to the well-being of their owners in particular as well as to the entire community.

Gabriel feeds the chickens.

Photo courtesy of Shireen DeSouza

101

Children may read literature (fiction/non-fiction), pet magazines, and Web-based resources; write to children in other countries through pen-pal or E-pal arrangements; and interview people from other countries to obtain information on the topic. These units may be organized around "World Animal Day" or other special days to honor animals (as some communities do in India). Additionally, teachers may designate a special "companion animal day" when the children can celebrate animals in their home lives and in their classrooms.

Implication 4: Incorporate Global and Multicultural Folktales and Stories. Experts suggest that children's literature can be used very effectively to influence children's cognitive, emotional, and moral development. More specifically, children's books about companion animals can facilitate an understanding of the reality and permanence of death, as well as the idea that death is part of the life cycle (Davis, 2000); foster a feeling of connection and empathy with other living beings without resorting to overly didactic approaches (Miller, 2001); and help children progress from intellectual understanding of moral elements (such as responsibility, fairness, and friendship) to compassionate action (Lake, 2001). Although contemporary children's literature from various cultures focusing on the human/companion animal relationship abounds, folktales (sometimes limited to the oral version only) still dominate this field in many cultures across the world. Therefore, besides using children's books from various countries and cultures, teachers need to collect oral tales about pets and animals from parents and community members of different ethnic groups, or through connecting with children, teachers, parents, and other adults via the Internet. This section provides a selection of multicultural books and stories related to pets that fit the themes of fostering an empathic attitude toward animals and understanding the mutuality in human-animal companionship.

Fostering an empathic attitude toward animals. Some books feature an animal as the main character and present the story from the animal's viewpoint. Canadian author Jacqueline Ward has published a series of nonfiction, picture books about farm animals and the events in their lives. For example, *Jack's Lunch* (Ward, 2000) is based on the story of a dog, Jack, who makes many mistakes in his search for a perfect meal. Australian author John Heffernan has written books with a similar theme. For example, *Spud* (Heffernan, 2000) is the story of a blue heeler pup that must adjust to living with new owners and learning the skills of survival. These books can foster empathy among children toward pet animals and encourage children to perceive and treat pet animals with the respect and affection that is due to all living beings.

Understanding the mutuality in human-animal companionship. Some books emphasize the important dimensions of humans' connections with nonhuman animals. The phrase "A friend in need is a friend indeed" comes alive in each of these books. *The Dancing Pig* (Sierra, 1999), based on a folktale from Bali, depicts the story of twin sisters who are tricked by a witch and taken to her house. After the girls befriend the animals—a pig, a mouse, and some frogs—the animals rescue them and drive the witch away.

Set on the island of Hokkaido, Japan, San Souci's (2002) picture book, *The Silver Charm,* recounts the story of a little child, Satsu, who disobeys two rules: 1) never lose the tiny silver ship good luck charm, and 2) never go near the ogre's woods. However, with the help of his pet fox cub and a puppy, the boy is saved.

John Heffernan's *My Dog* (2001) received Australia's 2002 Children's Book of the Year for younger readers. The story, set during the crisis in Kosovo, depicts the optimism and courage of a boy whose only companion is a dog that he rescued from a dying man. In the story, the dog serves as a constant and loyal companion amid the horrors of war. A variation of this theme is found in the folktale "Baula," which takes place in a rural village in eastern India. There, a poor woman keeps a pet cow named Baula, whom she loves like a child. In financial need, however, she is forced to sell Baula to a man in her village. The next day, the woman finds the cow standing on her doorstep with tears rolling down her face. The woman returns the money to the buyer to keep her devoted animal companion. This tale is used to

102

convey the important message that people are obligated to be the guardians of their companion animals, even under adverse conditions.

Implication 5: Engage Children in Worldwide Efforts To Protect Animals. As mentioned before, animal protection groups worldwide strive to involve children in animal welfare activities and educate children about the role of nonhuman animals in human beings' lives. Teachers need to contact local, national, and international animal welfare societies and establish a school-wide animal awareness day. Teachers may recruit parent and student volunteers to form a local Friends of the Animals club. Such a club could host a variety of animal awareness and welfare activities, as well as sponsor events inside and outside the school. For example, the club may organize debates and essay competitions among children that focus on such topics as the issues facing animals in a particular community, or the need for global advocacy for animals. With the help of local veterinarians, the club may host free clinics for pets and other animals in the community and involve children in various ways in the clinic activities. A group of teachers from various countries may create a Web site that highlights events and activities hosted by the Friends of the Animals club in their school and invite other teachers to engage their students in similar activities.

International efforts to protect animals are also a way for children to learn about their obligations to the animals that fascinate and entertain them, such as reconsidering traditional ways of exploiting animals. For example, a number of cities have responded to the exotic animal trade by banning circuses. In 2000, India imposed a countrywide ban; in 2001, Rio de Janeiro imposed a citywide ban. Children need only to type in the words "animal protection" on an Internet search engine to access tens of thousands of sites devoted to animal rights. The world's largest database of

An Indian girl poses proudly with her cow.

Photo courtesy of Jyotsna Pattnaik.

information about animal protection groups is The World Animal Net Directory (www.worldanimalnet.org), with more than 13,000 listings and 6,000 links. An online publication with an international focus on animal rights is *Animals' Agenda* magazine (www.animalsagenda.org). Older students who seek to apply their research skills to the issues surrounding animal rights will be interested in a reference guide edited by Kistler (2000) called *Animal Rights: Subject Guide and Bibliography With Internet Sites.*

Conclusion

Since the beginning of recorded history, various kinds of nonhuman animals have been integrated into family and community life. Today, interest in the human/companion animal bond is growing worldwide, and professionals in many fields are seeking to unravel the many dimensions of these interspecies connections. To keep pace with these developments, teachers need to integrate animals into the classroom community and harness the benefits that accrue from child-companion animal interactions. Professionals dedicated to the care and education of children will need to address the inevitable cultural clashes that surface when an animal that is a beloved companion animal in some cultures is considered a food source in others, or when some members of a social group consider their treatment of animals to be perfectly acceptable, while others consider it to be abusive (Burgess-Jackson, 1998; Cavalieri, 2001). Attitudes toward companion animals can build bridges of understanding across cultures, but they also can be a point of friction that leads to misunderstanding, disrespect, and prejudice. As Jane Goodall (1990) points out in her book *Through a Window: My Thirty Years With the Chimpanzees of Gombe*, the Western world is inclined to express outrage when they see animal abuses elsewhere—such as a peasant beating a weary donkey struggling to pull an oversize load—yet willing to overlook abuses committed in the name of science, such as injecting a baby primate with human diseases in the laboratory as part of a medical experiment. It is far easier to pass judgment on others who act out of selfishness and cruelty than it is to look at ourselves and challenge what we take for granted where animal rights are concerned. As educators, we bear responsibility for carefully treading an intersecting line, one axis of which is respect for other cultures and customs, and the other, our duty to protect animals is both human and nonhuman.

References

Bahti, M. T. (1990). Animals in Hopi duality. In R. Willis (Ed.), *Signifying animals: Human meaning in the natural world* (pp. 134-139). London: Unwin Hyman.

Basso, C. B. (1973). *The Kalapalo Indians of Central Brazil.* New York: Holt, Rinehart, & Winston.

Bodson, L. (2001). Motivation for pet keeping in ancient Greece and Rome: A preliminary survey. In A. Podberscek, E. Paul, & J. Serpell (Eds.), *Companion animals and us: Exploring the relationship between people and pets* (pp. 27-41). Cambridge, UK: Cambridge University Press.

British Columbia Society for the Prevention of Cruelty to Animals. (2002). *Choosing the right classroom pet!* Retrieved July 2002, from www.spca.bc.ca/rightpet.htm

Burgess-Jackson, K. (1998). Doing right by our animal companions. *Journal of Ethics, 2*, 159-185.

Cambefort, Y. (1994). *Beetles as religious symbols.* Retrieved August 18, 2002, from www.insects.org/ced2/beetles_rel_sym.html

Cavalieri, P. (2001). *The animal question.* New York: Oxford University Press.

Coleman, V. (2000). *Animal rights, human wrongs. A blueprint for a better society.* Devon, Exeter, United Kingdom: Blue Books.

Daragahi, B. (2002). *Once banned as unclean—now unleashed.* Retrieved September 10, 2002, from www.csmonitor.com/2003/0621/p09s02-wome.html

Davis, J. (2000). When a pet dies: Books can help children learn to grieve. *Texas Child Care, 24*(3), 28-33.

Dresser, N. (2001). The horse bar mitzvah: A celebratory exploration of the human-animal bond. In A. Podberscek, E. Paul, & J. Serpell (Eds.), *Companion animals and us: Exploring the relationships between people and pets* (pp. 90-107). Cambridge, UK: Cambridge University Press.

Erickson, P. (2001). The social significance of pet-keeping among Amazonian Indians. In A. Podberscek, E. Paul, & J. Serpell (Eds.), *Companion animals and us: Exploring the relationship between people and pets* (pp. 7-26). Cambridge, UK: Cambridge University Press.

Friedman, E., Katcher, A. H., Thomas, S. S., Lynch, J. J., & Messent, P. R. (1983). Social interaction and blood pressure: Influence of animal companions. *Journal of Nervous and Mental Disease, 171*, 461-465.

Geocities (n.d.). *A kid's page: Children and their pets: Sophia High School.* Retrieved May 17, 2002, from http://geocities.com/Athens/Acropolis/9732/petsop1.htm

Gillis, M. (n.d.). Misty 1979-1988. Plot 1: Virtual pet cemetery. Retrieved September 10, 2002, from www.mycemetery.com/pet/plot_01.html

Goodall, J. (1990). *Through a window: My thirty years with the chimpanzees of Gombe.* Boston: Houghton Mifflin.

Goodall, J., & Bekoff, M. (2002). *The ten trusts: What we must do to care for the animals we love.* San Francisco: HarperCollins.

Halls, B. (n.d.). Zarko. Plot 8: Virtual pet cemetery. Retrieved September 10, 2002, from www.mycemetery.com/pet/plot_08.html

Harner, M. J. (1990). *The way of the shaman.* San Francisco: Harper.

Hart, L. A., Hart, B. L., & Bergin, B. (1987). Socializing effects of service dogs for people with disabilities. *Anthrozoos, 1*(1), 41-44.

Heffernan, J. (2000). *Spud.* Hunter Hill, Australia: Margaret Hamilton Books.

Heffernan, J. (2001). *My dog.* Hunter Hill, Australia: Margaret Hamilton Books.

Ipoh Society for the Prevention of Cruelty to Animals, ISPCA. (2002). *What is new?* Retrieved August 12, 2002, from www.aramisdesign.com/ispca/public.shtml

Kaufmann, M. (1997). Creature comforts: Animal assisted activities in education and therapy. *Reaching Today's Youth: The Community Circle of Caring Journal, 1*(2), 27-31.

Kidd, A. H., & Kidd, R. M. (1995). Children's drawings and attachments to pets. *Psychological Reports, 77*, 235-241.

Kistler, J. (Ed.). (2000). *Animal rights: Subject guide and bibliography with Internet sites.* Westport, CT: Greenwood.

Lake, V. E. (2001). Linking literacy and moral education in the primary classroom. *Reading Teacher, 55*(2), 125-129.

Laughin, W. S. (1968). Hunting: An integrating biobehavior system and its evolutionary importance. In R. B. Lee & I. DeVore (Eds.), *Man the hunter* (p. 309). Chicago: Aldine.

Laurent, E. L. (2000). Children, insects, and play in Japan. In A. Podberscek, E. Paul, & J. Serpell (Eds.), *Companion animals and us: Exploring the relationship between people and pets* (pp. 61-89). Cambridge, UK: Cambridge University Press.

Miller, H. M. (2001). A dose of empathy. *The Reading Teacher, 54*(4), 380-381.

Melson, G. F. (2001). *Why the wild things are: Animals in the lives of children.* Cambridge, MA: Harvard University Press,

Myers, G. (1998). *Children and animals.* Bolder, CO: Westview Press.

Nooden, L. (1992). *Animal symbolism in Celtic mythology.* Retrieved July 24, 2002, from www-personal.umich.edu/~lars/rel375.html

Ojoade, J. L. (1990). Nigerian cultural attitudes to the dog. In R. Willis (Ed.), *Signifying animals: Human meaning in the natural world* (pp. 215- 221). London: Unwin Hyman.

Petcare Information and Advisory Service, The. (n.d.). *School.* Retrieved July 22, 2002, from www.petnet.com.au/schools.html

Poresky, R. H., & Hendrix, C. (1989). *Companion animal bonding, children's home environment, and young children's social development.* (ERIC Document Reproduction Service No. ED 312 087)

Rud, A. G., & Beck, A. M. (2000). Kids and critters in class together. *Phi Delta Kappan, 82*(4), 313-315.

San Souci, R. (2002). *The silver charm:: A folktale from Japan.* London: Random House.

Schwabe, C. W. (1994). Animals in the ancient world. In A. Manning & J. Serpell (Eds.), *Animals and society: Changing perspectives* (pp. 36-58). New York: Routledge.

Serpell, J. (1986). *In the company of animals.* New York: Basil Blackwell.

Serpell, J., & Paul, E. (1994). Pets and the development of positive attitudes to animals. In A. Manning & J. Serpell (Eds.), *Animals and human society* (pp. 127-144). New York: Routledge.

Sierra, J. (1999). *The dancing pig.* San Diego, CA: Harcourt.

Teacher Webshelf. (n.d.). *Teacher Registry: Australia.* Retrieved August 29, 2002, from www.teacherwebshelf.com/classroompets/HomeTeach-Australia.htm

Pet Food Manufacturers' Association, The. (2001). *Pet ownership demographics.* Retrieved August 24, 2002, from www.pfma.com/petownership.htm

Urban Management Animal Coalition. (1995). *National people and pets survey.* Retrieved August 15, 2002, from www.petnet.com.au/People_and_Pets/52UAMR.HTML

Ward, J. (2000). *Jack's lunch.* British Columbia, Canada: Fogbound Books.

World Society for the Protection of Animals. (2002). *Action against cruelty: Bullfighting in Mexico.* Retrieved July 10, 2002, from www.wspa-international.org/action/bullfighting/mexico.html

Chapter 7

Portraying Pets: The Significance of Children's Writings and Drawings About Companion Animals

Patricia A. Crawford
and Moses Mutuku

I wish I had a flying horse for my mom because she love horses like me and my sister and my Dad

—*Emma Brady*
USA

"Why did you do all this for me?" [Wilbur] asked. "I don't deserve it. I've never done anything for you."

"You have been my friend," replied Charlotte. "That in itself is a tremendous thing. I wove my webs for you because I liked you. After all, what's a life, anyway?"

—*from* Charlotte's Web
(White, 1952, p. 164)

So goes the dialogue in E. B. White's classic children's book, a text that quickly became a mid-century favorite and eventually became one of the best-selling juvenile titles of all time. The book's appeal can be found on a variety of levels. Who wouldn't love an adorable, personified pig who always seems to find his way into trouble? Who wouldn't be dazzled by the tale of a clever spider turned scribe, who puts forth her best efforts to love and protect the little pig? And, finally, who wouldn't find resonance in the very profound messages communicated through the relationship between Charlotte and Wilbur: friendship is real; small actions matter; everyone can make a difference; real love endures

107

until death and, in some extraordinary cases, even beyond.

In looking at this text and the powerful themes within its pages, it is important to note that before there was Charlotte, there was Fern. For all of the delightful and fanciful twists within *Charlotte's Web*, the story begins with the tale of a little girl named Fern and her fight to save Wilbur's life. Although readers do not encounter the mature, spectacular Charlotte until page 33, young, well-grounded Fern can be found on the very first page, where she declares her outrage at the idea of killing a helpless animal. Fern quickly takes on the role of lover, protector, and advocate, forging a relationship that is every bit as significant as that which will exist between Charlotte and Wilbur:

Fern loved Wilbur more than anything. She loved to stroke him, to feed him, to put him to bed. . . . Wilbur loved his milk, and he was never happier than when Fern was warming up a bottle for him. He would stand and gaze up at her with adoring eyes. (White, 1952, p. 8)

Fern's heartfelt concern and tender care usher her into a helping relationship. This position allows her to be both a receiver of affection and giver of care, a position that psychologists and educators agree is important for the nurturance of security, self-esteem, responsibility, and healthy development (Edwards, 1986; Ferreira & Bosworth, 2000; Noddings, 1992). Children's need to participate in these types of relationships, along with the seemingly natural and universal appeal of animal companions, have helped to make books like Charlotte's Web perennial favorites. From *Old Yeller* (Gipson, 1956) to *Shiloh* (Naylor, 1991), and from *The Tenth Good Thing About Barney* (Viorst, 1971) to *Because of Winn-Dixie* (DiCamillo, 2000), books that probe and celebrate the deep relationships that develop between children and their animal companions have won awards and proved to be an irresistible draw for young readers.

Putting Pencil to Paper

Given children's interest in celebrating this special human-animal bond in the reading part of their literacy lives, there is little wonder that they would also choose to explore this topic as part of their writing lives. Just as children love to read about animals, they also find satisfaction in portraying pets through their writing and drawing. Experts in children's writing affirm the fact that when given support and opportunity, children typically write about things that are compelling, that they know well, and that are both relevant and important to them (Atwell, 1998; Calkins, 1994; Fletcher & Portalupi, 2001; Graves, 1994). In short, children write about things that matter. Both the professional literature and personal experience attest to the fact that animal companions matter deeply to children (Bodsworth & Coleman, 2001; Lagoni, Butter, & Hetts, 1994; Melson, 1998, 2001).

In order to explore children's written and creative representations of their animal companions, we invited a number of teachers and parents to encourage their young writers in this regard. In total, we gathered 92 writing samples from children who ranged in age from 5 to 13 years and hailed from two different countries: Kenya and the United States. The children were invited to write about their pets and to tell about the relationships that they shared with them.

Looking at Children's Writing

As we reviewed the children's responses to our invitation, we could not help but be overwhelmed by their strong voices and their enthusiasm for the topic. Participants from both countries responded in a variety of modes. It became clear that both visual and textual representations mattered to our young authors. While all of the children included written texts as we requested, the majority of them also included illustrations, and a good number also chose to include a photograph.

In terms of writing, children expressed their thoughts by way of a number of different genres. Across cultures, students wrote from both their heads and their hearts. While most of the children expressed their thoughts in prose, others created succinct lists of the reasons why their pets were important to them, such as this one by a Kenyan student (see Figure 7.1):

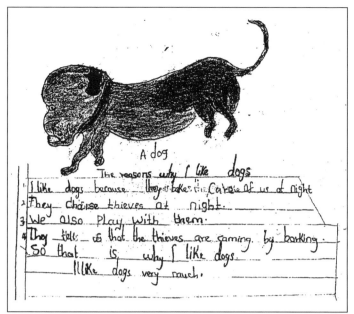

Figure 7.1 (Kenya)

Still others shared their thoughts, hopes, and love for their pets in the form of poetry (see Figure 7.2).

In terms of content, the children's writing

> Morrgie
> Cute, sweet
> Sleeping, cuddling, playing
> Makes me happy
> Gerbil
>
> Morrgie

Figure 7.2 (USA)

represented a veritable zoo of subject matter. Not surprisingly, a number of children from both cultures chose to explore their relationships with dogs and cats. Kenyan children extended their discussions of pets to include parrots, cuckoos, donkeys, pigs, and rabbits, while young writers from the United States also focused on hamsters, gerbils, lizards, horses, rabbits, fish, hermit crabs, birds, and mice.

Reading Between the Lines

In reading the children's writing samples, a number of significant themes emerge that cross cultural lines. The children who participated in this project wrote extensively about the following: the nature of the child-pet relationship, the admiration they felt for their pet, their appreciation for daily interactions with an animal companion, lessons learned from having a pet, and insights gained from pets as they related to the cycle of life.

Relationships: Children hailing from both countries, and representing all age groups, expressed a sincere appreciation for the relationship they shared with their pets. The vast majority of participants clearly viewed their pets as true animal companions, often describing them as "my best friend" or "another member of the family." The children appeared to rely heavily on these relationships, seeing them as a source of strength, encouragement, and love (see Figure 7.3):

Pet Writing

Tell about your pet. How do you feel about your pet? What have you learned from your pet? What does your pet mean to you? You may draw a picture to illustrate your writing on the back of this paper if you like.

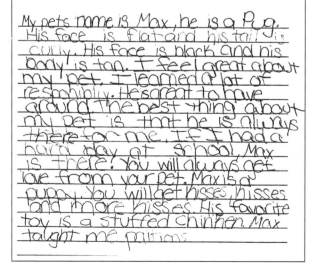

Figure 7.3 (USA)

Admiration of a Pet's Unique Qualities: Our young authors not only elaborated on the general benefits of pet ownership, they also provided rich descriptions of the qualities that made their own pets unique. While many writing samples contained expected references to pets who were "cuddly," "warm," "fluffy," and "cute," others included much more vivid descriptions of a pet's physical characteristics (see Figure 7.4):

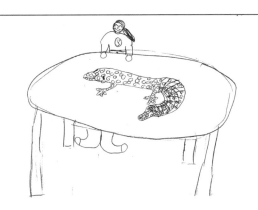

"One day on Christmas morning when I woke up, I ran to the Living Room and what I saw was very odd. I saw a cage with a lizard that had a fat tail like smooshed toothpaste and a body of a dragon. It also had skin that felt like sand and spots like lepord or a cheata! I yelled, 'mom . . . dad!' My daddy came running into the room. I said, 'I wanted a iguana not that thing.' Dad said, 'but sweetey it's a lepard gecko.' 'Oh!?' I said.

A month later my lepard gecko and I grew a very special bond together. It was like having a friend to talk to that would listen. When you have a pet like that it feels really good.

Now I have a male. The day that I brout it home my mom freaked out. You shood get a pet like that. (If your mom isn't afraid of it)."

Figure 7.4 (USA)

Other children focused on their pet's emotional make-up, with one 7th-grader noting, "My dog's name is Monster. He is a bulldog with attitude." Another commented, "Even though you wouldn't think it, crabs do have personalities."

Figure 7.5 (Kenya)

Although the majority of children expressed admiration for their pets' physical characteristics, abilities, and affective qualities, most of the Kenyan children also demonstrated an appreciation for their pets in terms of more pragmatic issues. For example, a number of the Kenyan writers noted that pets were good for breeding; for scaring away such unwanted pests as rats, snakes, and thieves; and even for being a source of food (see Figure 7.5).

Appreciation for Daily Interactions: Children from both the United States and Kenya consistently noted the day-in, day-out delight they felt in sharing everyday life with a pet. Their message was clear: small things matter. Children expressed pleasure in being able to simply watch, pet, cuddle, and play with their pets. They enjoyed the reassurance of being greeted at the door or receiving pet kisses after a long day at school. Some children described the joy they found in playful pet-child rituals. For example, a 7th-grader described the joy she experiences from regular song and dance exchanges with her parrot (see Figure 7.6).

Lessons Learned From Having a Pet: A number of children commented on the fact that they had learned much through their experience of having a pet. Some lessons were poignant: "From my cat . . . I learned how to comfort other people who are sad, like she does." Some were humorous: "One thing I learned from my [bird]: If he goes in your shirt, don't panic or he will bite you." Other lessons were pragmatic, with a number of pieces describing the unhappy ramifications of underfeeding or overfeeding fish: "She exploded." "She died after I didn't feed her for three days straight." Other pieces

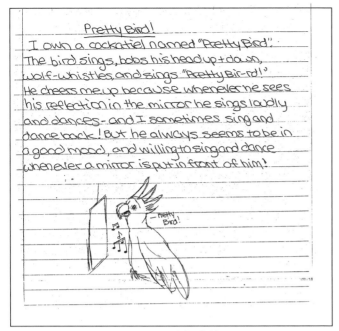

Pretty Bird!

I own a cockatiel named "Pretty Bird". The bird sings, bobs his head up + down, wolf-whistles, and sings "Pretty Bir-rd!" He cheers me up because whenever he sees his reflection in the mirror he sings loudly and dances- and I sometimes sing and dance back! But he always seems to be in a good mood, and willing to sing and dance whenever a mirror is put in front of him!

-Pretty Bird!

Figure 7.6 (USA)

the important elements that undergird the relationships that they share with their animal companions. The children who contributed their writing samples to this study were a diverse lot: boys and girls representing a wide range of ages, hailing from different countries and cultures, and coming from both private and public school systems. Despite this diversity and the unique insights contributed by each individual, a common theme emerges. Like Fern in *Charlotte's Web*, these children care deeply about their animal companions and are learning much through the experience of nurturing and interacting with their pets. Both givers and recipients of care, the children show that having a pet involves much more than a series of isolated child-animal events. Rather, the experience of pet ownership is a rich ongoing relationship that is located at the intersection of the very real issues of love, loss, learning, and life (see Figure 7.8)

pointed to the ways that pet ownership helped children to assume greater levels of responsibility: "I learned that if you have a pet, you're the one who feeds it and spends time with it—not your parents."

Insights Gained About the Cycle of Life: In writing about their pets, many children acknowledged the reality of suffering and the inevitability of the life cycle. Some described medical conditions in great detail, with one 2nd-grade student expressing concern for her poodle's "luxating patella." A number of young authors spoke of the anguish experienced when losing pets in the past. Meanwhile, many others ex-pressed concern about the possibility of losing a pet at some point in the future. Refrains such as Katey's "My pet means a lot to me. I never want him to die" were common, with one child noting that she would "go to pieces" in the event that she lost her dog. The depth of feeling about this potential loss is expressed well by Casey (see Figure 7.7).

Animal Companions: That's Life

By looking at the children's writing samples, it is possible to get a glimpse into

My Pet Dog

I have a dog named Lilly. Lilly is a Jack Russel Terrier. She has white hair with Brown spots she is so cute!

I have learned that my dog hate going swiming and never give your mom the dog because she will hog it!! And never leave the door open because she will run right out the door. My dog is scared of nothing not even cars.

My pet dog means alot alot alot to me if she dies I would be so sad I would not be able to move. I'd cry all day thats how much my dog mines to me.

Figure 7.7 (USA)

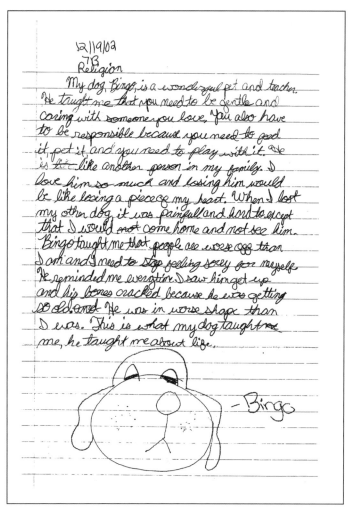

Figure 7.8 (USA)

References

Atwell, N. (1998). *In the middle: New understandings about writing, reading, and learning* (2nd ed.). Portsmouth, NH: Heinemann.

Bodsworth, W., & Coleman, G. J. (2001). Child-companion animal attachment bonds in single and two-parent families. *Anthrozoos, 14*(4), 216-223.

Calkins, L. M. (1994). *The art of teaching writing* (2nd ed.). Portsmouth, NH: Heinemann.

Edwards, C. P. (1986). *Promoting social and moral development in young children.* New York: Teachers College Press.

Ferreira, M. M., & Bosworth, K. (2000). Context as a critical factor in young adolescents' concepts of caring. *Journal of Research in Childhood Education, 15*(1), 117-128.

Fletcher, R., & Portalupi, J. (2001). *Writing workshop: The essential guide.* Portsmouth, NH: Heinemann.

Graves, D. H. (1994). *A fresh look at writing.* Portsmouth, NH: Heinemann.

Lagoni, L. S., Butter, C., & Hetts, S. (1994). *The human-animal bond and grief.* Philadelphia: W.B. Saunders.

Melson, G. F. (1998). The role of companion animals in human development. In C. C. Wilson & D. C. Turner (Eds.), *Companion animals in human health* (pp. 219-236). Thousand Oaks, CA: Sage.

Melson, G. F. (2001). *Why the wild things are: Animals in the lives of children.* Cambridge, MA: Harvard University Press.

Noddings, N. (1992). *The challenge to care in schools: An alternative approach to education.* New York: Teachers College Press.

Children's Books Cited

DiCamillo, K. (2000). *Because of Winn-Dixie.* New York: Scholastic.

Gipson, F. (1956). *Old Yeller.* New York: Harper & Row.

Naylor, P. R. (1991). *Shiloh.* New York: Yearling.

Viorst, J. (1971). *The tenth good thing about Barney.* New York: Atheneum.

White, E. B. (1952). *Charlotte's web.* New York: Scholastic.

Chapter 8

Companion Animals in Books: Themes in Children's Literature

—Jamie R. Bellman
USA

Melissa Ann Renck and
Mary Renck Jalongo
with Jeffrey C. Brewster

Once upon a time, a poor miller left all of his worldly possessions to his three sons. To the eldest, he left the mill; to the second, he left his donkey; to the youngest, he left the cat. Thoroughly depressed, the youngest son looked down at the feline and said, "At least a donkey is useful. However shall I make a living with a cat?"

To his great surprise, the cat answered him encouragingly, telling the young man that things were not so bleak as he feared. "If you get me a pair of boots to protect my feet from the brambles, and a sack with a cord, I may be of service to you, Master!" Feeling that he had nothing to lose, the miller's son did what the cat asked, thereby setting in motion a series of adventures in which, guided by the wily animal's wisdom, he obtained riches, prestige, and love.

Charles Perrault's tale *Puss in Boots* has retained its perennial appeal since he first recounted it in the 17th century. It's been retold, re-illustrated, and anthologized in countless editions. Part of the reason for the story's appeal, of course, is the ongoing fascination humans have for communing with companion animals. Children's literature richly documents that link between people and animals in all of its manifestations, both fanciful and real.

In this chapter, we begin by discussing the pedagogical implications of books about companion animals. Next, we explain the selection criteria for the children's books that are annotated here and clustered around five distinct themes: 1) world folklore about powerful human/companion animal bonds, 2) animals as helpers, 3) animals in need of rescue, 4) children learning to care for companion animals, and 5) children learning to cope with the loss or death of a companion animal. Finally, we offer a selective list of reference books that reviews children's literature titles and offers additional resources to educators for developing interdisciplinary teaching themes that include companion animals.

Pedagogical Implications of Children's Literature About Companion Animals

The rationale for including children's literature about companion animals in the curriculum is consistent with the goals of using children's literature as an educational resource in general: to promote curiosity, interest, and enthusiasm for learning (Johnson & Giorgis, 2001). As Diana Mitchell (2003) points out, books about companion animals are particularly appealing to children because:

Almost every child has had positive experiences with animals and loves to read stories that have animals in them. We love animals because they are soft to pet, respond to us with soulful looks, and live totally in the present, allowing play and fun to take precedence in their lives. We believe that our own animals care deeply about us and are very attuned to us. We love their loyalty, their patience, their wish to spend as much time as possible with us. They make us feel special and needed. We recognize that our animals need us too, and we give them our time and are generous. . . . For all of these reasons, we have a passion for animal stories. (p. 261)

More specifically, there are at least four ways in which books about companion animals contribute to children's learning, commencing in early childhood and continuing into adolescence and beyond.

First, *children's books about animals carry on the traditions of literature, build enjoyment, and foster literary appreciation.* Animals often figure prominently in information books for children, in animal realism (a genre that blends fact and fiction), and as companion animal characters in picture books and high fantasy. Children's literature experts Nodelman and Reimer (2003) contend that it is the shared bond of animality that initially attracts the child to animals in literature. Companion animals are well-represented in the oral storytelling traditions of cultures throughout the world, as well as in published folktales and fairy tales. As children's book author/illustration Jerry Pinkney (2000) points out in the introduction to *Aesop's Fables*, animals have long been used as a way to point out human foibles and teach moral lessons.

Additionally, *pourquoi* stories—stories that explain how an animal came to have certain physical traits, such as the story that attributes the cat's purr to swallowing thunder (Alexander, 2000), are found in many different cultures. Well-known and beloved nursery rhymes, myths, folktales, fairy tales, and classics in children's literature are populated with companion animal characters who become part of the enduring memories of childhood.

Even though the title or author of a picture book experienced during childhood may have been forgotten (or never really known), bits of text and mental images of the pictures often linger long well into adulthood. Consistent with the finding from brain research that simple, powerful visual images tend to make the most lasting impression (Rushton & Larkin, 2001), many adults in the United States can still visualize companion animals from the pages of books, such as those represented in Garth Williams' drawings (Wilder, 1932), or from such book covers as *The Incredible Journey* (Burnford, 1961) or *Where the Red Fern Grows* (Rawls, 1961).

Second, *children's literature about companion animals also serves to construct knowledge and understanding of various companion animal species.* Stories heard and read contribute to children's storehouse of information about companion animals' characteristics, requirements, and behaviors, both typical and unique. The child who acquires (or hopes to acquire) a hamster, for instance, can consult a wide array of information books on matters of proper care. Through literature, it is also possible to imagine what might happen if a child taking a turn to care for the classroom pet hamster at home lost the animal by reading *Wanted . . . Mud Blossom* (Byars, 1993), for example. Likewise, the child who wonders what it would be like to raise an animal can attain an insider's view of the process (Katz, 2002; McNicholl, 2002) or further explore favorite authors and illustrators of children's books by learning about their dogs (Rosen, 1993).

The knowledge that is built by quality books about companion animals can extend far beyond the child's direct experience to incorporate knowledge and understanding that might otherwise be inaccessible. A child from a tropical climate can read Gary Paulsen's (1983) *Dogsong*, for example, and get a sense of the interdependency between a human being and sled dogs, as well as acquire insight into Native American traditions. Often, the insider's knowledge and understanding acquired through reading leads to a line of inquiry that prompts the child to delve deeper into the topic—perhaps by reading nonfiction on a related topic, such as *Dogs of the Iditarod* (Schultz, 2003); exploring other books by the same author, such as *My Life in Dog Years* (Paulsen, 1999); or enjoying a fictional story about sled dog racing, such as *Stone Fox* (Gardiner, 1980).

Broadening the scope of the canine companions theme further might lead the young child to read *Bow Wow Meow Meow: It's Rhyming Cats and Dogs* (Florian, 2003), or the early adolescent to explore Joyce Sidman's (2003) book of poetry *The World According to Dog: Poems and Teen Voices*, or to read edited collections of true stories about dogs (Katz, 2003; Rosen, 2001). For pure flights of fancy that adopt the dog's point of view, young readers might enjoy *Stanley's Party* (Bailey, 2003), the tale of a lonely dog who throws a canine bash, or *Stay! Keeper's Story* (Lowry, 1997), the story of a rags-to-riches dog who ultimately finds a loving home. From there, the older child might branch out to another species and read story collections about horses, such as Coville's *Herds of Thunder, Manes of Gold* (1989) or Rosen's *Horse People: Writers and Artists on the Horses They Love* (2002).

In each case, children's literature about companion animals sheds a different light on the three universal questions of literature identified by Rebecca Lukens (2003) in *A Critical Handbook of Children's Literature*: What are people like? What do they need? Why do they do what they do? Answers to these questions, applied simultaneously to people and to the animals entrusted to their care, are at the heart of children's books about companion animals. Ideally, such books serve to promote interspecies understanding and respect.

Third, *children's literature about companion animals can inspire activism for animal rights.* Books about animals often pose a profound question that is set on a shifting value terrain: How is the status of being afforded to companion animals affected by the historical era, geographic location, cultural context, economic circumstances, religious convictions, ethical concerns, and health issues for people and animals? Take, for example, the current situation with Sudden Acute Respiratory Syndrome (SARS). After it was theorized that animals, particularly chickens, living in close proximity to humans might be carriers of the devastating disease, panic set in and many companion animals were destroyed.

The issue of what personal sacrifices human beings could or should make on behalf of companion animals in a particular situation, as well as how others evaluate the response, is the focus of perennial debate that is chronicled on the pages of children's books. Even though Anna Sewell's (2002) story *Black Beauty* has been criticized for anthropomorphizing horses, it continues to be an all-time favorite. When it was published in 1877, it precipitated a public outcry about the abuse of horses.

Some important questions about animal rights that warrant frequent re-examination include: What constitutes cruelty and unethical treatment to different types of animals, and what should be done about it? When does training cross over into abuse? Under what conditions, if any, is it reasonable to make wild animals into companion animals? Why, when, and how might the dominant culture's attitudes toward animals be challenged?

What response is appropriate when groups of people who live together in society have conflicting views about which animals merit companion animal status? What happens to animals after they die? Should their death be commemorated in any way? What makes a companion animal valuable? Should the criteria be based on objective worth (e.g., famous bloodlines, earnings in competitions, investment made in training) or subjective worth (e.g., importance to a person)?

My Pig Amarillo (Ichikawa, 2003), a story set in Guatemala, underscores a wide range of cultural differences in attitudes toward animals. Pablito is delighted when his grandfather presents him with a baby pig, and he forms a strong emotional tie with the animal. Sadly, the pig disappears without any warning or explanation and is never found. Pablito comes to terms with the loss during All Saints' Day, a religious holiday, when he sends a kite into the sky as a message to his departed pet and hopes for a sign. When grandfather points out a huge, smiling, pig-shaped cloud, the boy is convinced that his former pet is now happy and in heaven. Some individuals and groups may consider the pig that is so dear to Pablito unworthy of companion animal status, others may regard pigs strictly as a food item, and still others consider pigs to be entirely unsuitable, even as food. For others, the implication that a pig has a soul might be offensive. Yet it is possible for readers/listeners to consider the companion animals that matter to them and, through this process of identification, to connect with Pablito via universal themes of love, loss, and coping with grief. Such identification is a necessary first step in protecting the rights of companion animals, whatever species they might be (Bekoff, 2002).

Fourth, *children's books about companion animals offer models of listening, reading, writing, and drawing.* The read-aloud favorites of many teachers are books about companion animals. As such, these books can be used as models for expressive reading, effective writing, appreciative listening, ways of talking about books, and artistic styles. Nonfiction and fiction about companion animals can inspire budding artists and writers to share stories about their own animal friends through the language arts. The range of children's literature about companion animals is enormous. Wordless books, such as Mercer Mayer's (1990)

I decide to call him Amarillo because of his color. *Amarillo* means "yellow" in my language. "Don't be afraid, my little yellow pig," I tell him. "You'll be my best friend." He climbs on my back, and scratches me!

Frog Goes to Dinner, the story of a pet frog who wreaks havoc in a posh restaurant, beckon children to create text and dialogue, and to use art to portray their companion animals' amusing antics. Predictable books, such as Cindy Ward's (1994) *Cookie's Week,* which gives a seven-day account of a mischievous kitten's escapades, invite children to create a book with a similar, day-by-day format. There are picture books that are works of high fantasy for the very young child, such as *While You Were Out* (Lee, 2003), the charming story of a rabbit who enjoys exploring a house while the owners are away. Older readers may prefer such nonfiction books as Betsy Hearne's (2003) *The Canine Connection: Stories About Dogs and People*, which may inspire them to collaborate and generate a collection of stories, perhaps written by a class, an entire school or district, or in collaboration with E-pals from around the world. When children read a work of fiction that unashamedly anthropomorphizes companion animals, such as the

Beverly Cleary (2003) classic *The Mouse and the Motorcycle*, or a work of historical fiction that blends authentic sources with an author's imaginative reconstructions, such as Laurie Myers's (2002) *Lewis and Clark and Me: A Dog's Tale* (which tells the explorers' story from a Newfoundland dog's point of view), it often inspires children to adopt a new point of view in their writing. They also may be inspired to read a related work of historical realism, such as a survival tale from Newfoundland, *The Wreck of the Ethie* (Hyland, 1999), or a synthesis of historical documents about the Lewis and Clark expedition from the *In Their Own Words* series (Sullivan, 2000). Books about companion animals provide particularly varied and interesting models of language arts in use.

Children's books about companion animals also are an important resource for forging interdisciplinary connections that span the traditional subject boundaries (Kaser, 2001). "One of our goals when introducing books is to show teachers how literature can reflect on everyday events. When these connections are made, chances increase for books to capture children's interest and affirm what they know" (Johnson & Giorgis, 2001, p. 210). In *Mapping Penny's World* (Leedy, 2000), which illustrates this concept, the child narrator is studying maps at school and applying the concepts she has learned to invent a map showing the travels of Penny, her Boston bullterrier, around the house, yard, and nearby environs. By beginning with the known (the dog's travels) and linking it with what is becoming known (map skills), the young girl in the story demonstrates how school-based learning influences everyday life outside of school.

When children are given a choice of a topic for an assignment or participate in curriculum design, companion animals often are part of the inquiry. Such projects typically have expansive interdisciplinary implications. A unit on the ethical treatment of animals, for example, leads to study of history, law, philosophy, science, religion, farming, medicine, media studies, and so forth. Often, the place to begin is by building on what a child has experienced directly, such as sitting in the veterinarian's office with an injured cat, as de-

picted in *The Broken Cat* (Perkins, 2003), or debating whether a homeless dog should be brought into a household of cats, as in *Widget* (McFarland, 2001).

Thus, books about companion animals can expand, enrich, and enlarge bonds of understanding, empathy, and responsibility between human beings and animal companions.

Criteria for Selection

In the pages that follow, we offer a selective, annotated list of books about companion animals. Criteria for selection were as follows:

1) **Positive responses from children.** Children's positive responses to the books included here were based on the first author's more than 15 years of work as a children's services librarian in a public library system serving diverse groups of children of all ages, from toddlerhood through adolescence, during story hours, summer reading clubs, in school settings, and so forth. In every case, the books included here are titles that were well-received by children, requested by them, and checked out by them to be further savored at home.

2) **Professional judgment of the books' quality.** Books selected for inclusion earned our professional endorsement as well as the recommendations of reviewers in published sources, including *Booklist*, *Book Links* (American Library Association), *The Reading Teacher* (International Reading Association), *The Horn Book*, and *Riverbank Review*. Additionally, many of the books on the list have been honored by various groups and organizations that have awards programs for children's literature.

3) **Racial, ethnic, and cultural diversity unified by common bonds.** A deliberate effort was made to represent a wide range of companion animals in diverse cultural contexts. The goal was to illustrate that although differences clearly exist, every culture has honored companion animals in some way at some time.

In addition, each book has been evaluated in terms of the liveliness of its writing, how visually stimulating the illustrations are, and whether it has universal emotional resonance in terms of its portrayal of the human/companion animal bond. Although all of the titles are published in English, they have been selected for their representation of world cultures in an accurate, respectful, positive manner.

Folklore on the Human/Companion Animal Bond

An ongoing motif in world folklore is the role of animals as teachers (e.g., *Heetunka's Harvest*, Jones, 1994), givers of gifts (e.g., *Rainbow Crow*, Van Laan, 1989), or sources of power (e.g., *The Story of Blue Elk*, Hausman, 1998). Sometimes, we see frightening predators that must be outwitted or overcome in some way (e.g., *Punia and the King of the Sharks*, Wardlaw, 1997).

Native American Folklore

Bierhorst, J. (2000). *The people with five fingers: A native Californian creation tale.* New York: Marshall Cavendish. Coyote and other animals participate in the creation of humankind.

Cohen, C. (1988). *The mud pony: A traditional Skidi Pawnee tale.* New York: Scholastic. A poor boy becomes a powerful leader when Mother Earth turns his mud pony into a real one.

Dominic, G. (1996). *Song of the hermit thrush: An Iroquois legend.* Vero Beach, FL: Rourke Corporation. The animals and birds hold a contest to see which will sing a song to greet each day.

Goble, P. (1987). *The gift of the sacred dog.* New York: Aladdin Books. The Great Spirit sends the horse to the plains tribes in response to a boy's prayer for help for his hungry people.

Goble, P. (1985). *The great race of the birds and the animals.* New York: Bradbury Press. The Creator calls for a race to settle the question as to whether man or buffalo should have supremacy over the Earth, and thereby become the guardians of creation.

Hausman, G. (1998). *The story of Blue Elk.* New York: Clarion Books. A magical elk helps a mute Pueblo boy find his power.

Jones, J. (1994). *Heetunka's harvest: A tale of the Plains Indians.* Niwot, CO: Roberts Rinehart Publishers in conjunction with the Council for Indian Education. A Dakota woman learns not to be greedy when she steals from the winter store of Heetunka the bean mouse.

Keams, G. (1995). *Grandmother Spider brings the sun: A Cherokee story.* Flagstaff, AZ: Northland Publishing. After a succession of other animals fail in the quest, tiny spider succeeds in fetching a piece of the sun to her side of the world.

Van Laan, N. (1989). *Rainbow crow.* New York: Knopf. Crow sacrifices his beautiful rainbow-colored feathers and lovely singing voice to save the earth from ever-falling snow.

Van Laan, N. (1993). *Buffalo dance: A Blackfoot legend.* New York: Knopf. The origin of the sacred ritual honoring the spirit of the buffalo, in which a young girl saves her tribe from starvation.

Walters, A. (1993). *The two-legged creature: An Otoe story.* Flagstaff, AZ: Northland Publishing. After the first harmonious creation of the world, Man becomes abusive to animals, so that only Dog and Horse remain close.

African Folklore

Aardema, V. (1999). *Koi and the kola nuts: A tale from Liberia.* New York: Atheneum. The son of a chief must make his way through the world with only a sack full of kola nuts and the help of some animals he has treated with kindness.

Diakite, B. (1997). *The hunterman and the crocodiles: A West African folktale.* New York: Scholastic Press. Donso the hunterman learns the importance of living in harmony with all living things when he is captured by a hungry crocodile.

Diakite, B. (1999). *The hatseller and the monkeys.* New York: Scholastic Press. By understanding their natures, a man outwits a tree full of mischievous monkeys.

Hamilton, V. (1997). *A ring of tricksters: Animal tales from America, the West Indies, and Africa.* New York: Blue Sky Press. A collection of 12 animal trickster tales that show the migration of African culture to the Americas via the West Indies.

Troughton, J. (1980). *Tortoise's dream.* New York: Bedrick/Blackie. Tortoise dreams of a wonderful tree that is the origin of all the good things to eat on earth.

Troughton, J. (1989). *How stories came into the world: A folktale from West Africa.* New York: Bedrick/Blackie. When angry Lightning breaks down Mouse's door, Mouse's trove of stories escapes into the world.

Folklore of Asia

Bartoli, J. (1977). *The story of the grateful crane: A Japanese folktale.* Chicago: Albert Whitman. An old childless couple rescues a crane from a trap, and it repays their kindness in a magical way.

Casanova, M. (2000). *The hunter: A Chinese folktale.* New York: Atheneum. Hai Li Bu the hunter learns the language of the animals and sacrifices himself to save his village.

Chang, M. (1994). *The cricket warrior: A Chinese tale.* New York: Maxwell Macmillan. A boy turns into a fighting cricket and becomes the Emperor's champion in order to save his family.

Czerniecki, S. (1997). *The cricket's cage.* New York: Hyperion. A kindly, clever cricket designs the towers of the Forbidden City.

Granfield, L. (1998). *The legend of the panda.* New York: Tundra Books. A young shepherd girl saves a tiny panda cub and earns the undying gratitude of the

118

pandas.

Hamanaka, S. (1993). *Screen of frogs: An old tale.* New York: Orchard Books. A spoiled, rich Japanese man learns to respect nature, just in the nick of time.

Lee, J. (1985). *Toad is the uncle of heaven: A Vietnamese folk tale.* New York: Holt, Rinehart, and Winston. Toad and a group of animals ask for rain from the King of Heaven.

Folklore From Europe

Andreasen, D. (2000). *Rose Red and the bear prince.* New York: HarperCollins. A young girl saves a bear from a dwarf's wicked spell.

Perrault, C. (1990). *Puss in boots.* New York: Farrar, Straus, Giroux. Illustrated by Fred Marcellino. A translation of the French fairy tale in which a boot-wearing cat sets out to gain a fortune for his master.

Folklore From India

Candappa, B. (1996). *The Bharunda bird.* Crystal Lake, IL: Rigby Interactive Library. The tale of a two-headed bird that teaches the value of cooperation.

Demi. (1987). *The hallowed horse.* New York: Dodd, Mead. A young Indian king must find a hallowed horse in order to defeat an evil, multi-headed snake.

Gleeson, B. (1992). *The tiger and the Brahmin.* New York: Simon & Schuster. A Brahmin tricked by a hungry tiger is saved by a humble jackal, thereby learning a lesson he has not encountered in any book.

Folklore From Latin America

San Souci, R. (1995). *The little seven-colored horse.* San Francisco: Chronicle Books. Juanito, a poor farmer, wins the hand of the mayor's daughter with the help of a magical horse.

Folklore From the Middle East

Bahous, S. (1993, 1997). *Sitti and the cats: A tale of friendship.* Boulder, CO: Roberts Rinehart. In this Palestinian tale, a kind old woman is rewarded with wealth beyond her dreams when she assists a stray kitten.

Durkee, N. (1996). *The animals of Paradise.* London, UK: Hood Books. As the animals sit together in Paradise, they entertain each other with stories of their earthly lives among humans.

Lemu, B. (1994). *Animals in Islam.* Plainfield, IN: American Trust Publications. This story offers readers the basis for the Islamic respect of animals.

Salim, U. (1997). *The kind man and the thirsty dog.* Birmingham, UK: Al Hdaayah Publishing & Distribution. A man takes pity upon a thirsty dog, thereby earning remittance of his sins, in this story often attributed to the Prophet Mohammed.

Pacific Islands Folklore

Wardlaw, L. (1997). *Punia and the king of the sharks.* New York: Dial. A Hawaiian fisherman's clever son finds ways to outwit the king of the sharks and get his delicious lobsters from him.

Recurring Themes in Contemporary Children's Books About Companion Animals

Judging from the large quantity of books—both informational and fictional—published about animals each year, there is an ongoing demand among young readers for stories about pets. Some of the major recurring themes include: 1) companion animals who are of service to humans, 2) coping with the death or loss of a much-loved companion animal, 3) dealing with a new pet and providing appropriate pet care, 4) young children's very first interactions with animals, and 5) animals in need of rescue.

THEME 1: ANIMALS AS HELPERS

Animals As Helpers: Nonfiction Picture Books

Alexander, S. (1992). *Mom's best friend.* New York: Macmillan. A blind mother adjusts to her new guide dog.

Arnold, C. (1991). *A guide dog puppy grows up.* San Diego, CA: Harcourt Brace Jovanovich. The life of a guide dog, from puppyhood to its placement with a blind person.

Calmenson, S. (1994). *Rosie: A visiting dog's story.* New York: Clarion. A cheerful Tibetan terrier visits hospitals and nursing homes to brighten the days of the patients there.

Clements, A. (2001). *Brave Norman: A true story.* New York: Simon & Schuster. A blind Labrador retriever rescues a drowning girl from the ocean.

Clements, A. (2001). *Ringo saves the day! A true story.* New York: Simon & Schuster. A cat alerts its owners to the broken gas main in their yard.

Clements, A. (2002). *Dolores and the big fire: A true story.* New York: Simon & Schuster. A brave cat saves her owner from a house fire.

Clements, A. (2002). *Tara and Tyree, fearless friends: A true story.* Simon & Schuster. Two dogs save their master, and each other, when they fall through the ice.

Greenwood, P. (1993). *What about my goldfish?* New York: Clarion. A small boy's pets help him to adjust to a move to a new home.

Herriot, J. (1985). *Only one woof.* London: Michael Joseph. An unusual sheepdog surprises his farmer owner at the sheepherding trials.

Lang, G. (2001). *Looking out for Sarah.* New York: Tailwinds. Perry the Labrador "tells" about his day taking care of Sarah, who is blind.

Martin, A. (1996). *Leo the magnificat.* New York: Scholastic. A homeless cat adopts a church congregation, residing there as unofficial counselor until his death.

Moore, E. (1996). *Buddy: The first Seeing Eye dog.* New

York: Scholastic. The true story of the German shepherd that became the first Seeing Eye dog in America.

Morpurgo, M. (2003). *Kensuke's kingdom.* New York: Scholastic Press. A boy finds himself frightened, alone, and struggling to survive on an island until a dog becomes his companion and helper in this book that earned Britain's Children's Book Award.

Rand, G. (2002). *Little Flower.* New York: Henry Holt. A potbellied pig seeks help when her elderly owner falls and breaks a hip.

Animals As Helpers: Fiction Picture Books

Armstrong, J. (1993). *Chin Yu Min and the ginger cat.* New York: Crown. A haughty Chinese widow learns humility and self-reliance from her pet cat.

Bemelmans, L. (1953). *Madeline's rescue.* New York: Viking. When a hound rescues the intrepid school-girl from the Seine, he becomes a beloved school pet—until the trustees find out.

Cherry, L. (1990). *Archie, follow me.* New York: Dutton. A beautifully illustrated account of the special bond that a young girl shares with her cat.

Goodall, J. (1999). *Dr. White.* New York: North-South. A little white dog visits sick children in the hospital every day to help them recover.

Gregory, N. (1997). *How Smudge came.* New York: Walker & Co. Cindy, a girl with Down syndrome who lives in a group home, tries to find a way to keep Smudge the puppy in this award-winning Canadian title.

Hefferman, J. (2001). *My dog.* Gosford, NSW, Australia: Margaret Hamilton. This award-winning book tells the story of a young boy living in the war-torn former Yugoslavia who finds the courage to survive through the companionship of a small dog.

Jewell, N. (1972). *The snuggle bunny.* New York: Harper. An old man and a bunny find out that they have complementary needs.

Kennedy, P. (1997). *Through Otis' eyes: Lessons from a guide dog puppy.* New York: Hungry Minds, Inc. This book illustrates the joy and sorrow of raising a guide dog puppy, only to surrender it to someone who needs it more.

LeGuin, U. (1988). *A visit from Dr. Katz.* New York: Atheneum. Although she has to spend a day sick in bed, Marianne is cheered by the "treatment" she receives from her two cats.

Middleton, C. (2003). *Do you still love me?* Cambridge, MA: Candlewick Press. A loyal dog is temporarily dethroned by a new baby chameleon, but the story comes to a peaceful and satisfying conclusion.

Okimoto, J. (1990). *Blumpoe the grumpoe meets Arnold the cat.* Boston: Joy Street Books. A man mourning the loss of his dog is cheered by the friendliness of a shy, young cat.

Osofsky, A. (1992). *My buddy.* New York: Henry Holt. A service dog helps a boy with muscular dystrophy.

Polacco, P. (1992). *Mrs. Katz and Tush.* New York: Bantam. A lonely old Jewish woman is presented with a tailless kitten by her young African American neighbor.

Sweeney, J. (2000). *Suzette and the puppy.* New York: Barron's. Through the intervention of Nipper, a puppy, a little girl becomes friends with an elegant lady she meets in the park—who just happens to be world-famous artist Mary Cassatt.

Trottier, M. (2000). *Little dog Moon.* New York: Stoddart Kids. A Tibetan terrier living in a monastery guides two children through the mountains to freedom in Nepal.

Animals As Helpers: Juvenile Fiction

Byars, B. (2000). *My dog, my hero.* New York: Holt. Eight stories of heroic canines, within the framework of a "contest" that is judged by a panel of three.

Cooper, I. (2000). *Absolutely Lucy.* New York: Golden Books. A shy boy is helped to be more outgoing by his beagle puppy, Lucy.

Crisp, M. (2000). *My dog, Cat.* New York: Holiday House. A tiny Yorkshire terrier teaches small 10-year-old Abbie that size is not as important as he thought.

DeVinck, C. (1993). *Augusta & Trab.* New York: Four Winds Press. Augusta's pet cat helps her come to terms with the death of her mother via an emotional journey one year after her loss.

Dicamillo, K. (2000). *Because of Winn-Dixie.* Cambridge, MA: Candlewick. A big, ugly dog teaches Opal how to make friends and let go of some of the sadness left over from her mother's abandonment.

Fleischman, P. (2003). *The animal hedge.* Cambridge, MA: Candlewick Press. When a farmer falls on hard times and has to surrender his livestock, he begins to clip his hedges into animal shapes. As his sons mature, they pursue their dreams and pool their resources to restore real, live animals to the farm.

Hubbard, C. (1999). *One golden year: A story of a golden retriever.* New York: Apple. A mother and daughter raise a service dog puppy.

McNamee, G. (2000). *Nothing wrong with a three-legged dog.* New York: Delacorte Press. Ten-year-old Keath learns to deal with bullying and being the only white child in his class with the help of his best friend and her dog, Leftovers.

Okimoto, J. (1993). *A place for Grace.* Seattle, WA: Sasquatch Books. The story of the training of a hearing dog.

Animals As Helpers: Juvenile Nonfiction

Jackson, D. M. (2003). *Hero dogs: Courageous canines in action.* Boston: Little, Brown. A collection of stories about the search and rescue dogs who worked during the 9/11 tragedy at the World Trade Center.

Patent, D. (1994). *Hugger to the rescue.* New York: Penguin. This story describes the life of a member of the Black Paws Search, Rescue and Avalanche Team of Bigfork, Montana.

Paulsen, G. (1998). *My life in dog years.* New York:

Delacorte. The award-winning author relates short biographies of the dogs he's known throughout his life.

Perrow, A. (2000). *Lighthouse dog to the rescue.* Camden: Downeast Books. In this story, set during the 1930s, Spot, a springer spaniel, saves the day during a blizzard at the lighthouse where he lives.

Ring, E. (1994). *Companion dogs: More than best friends.* Brookfield, CT: Millbrook Press. Details the training of service dogs and describes their heroism.

Singer, M. (2000). *A dog's gotta do what a dog's gotta do: Dogs at work.* New York: Henry Holt. A cheerful look at the many abilities of working dogs.

Smith, E. (1988). *A service dog goes to school: The story of a dog trained to help the disabled.* New York: Morrow. This book explains how a service dog is raised, trained, and placed.

Vinocur, T. (1999). *Dogs helping kids with feelings.* New York: Powerkids Press. Two therapy dogs help young people deal with their emotions.

THEME 2: DEATH OR LOSS OF A COMPANION ANIMAL

Death or Loss: Picture Books

Carrick, C. (1976). *The accident.* New York: Seabury Press. A young boy has feelings of sadness and guilt when his dog is hit by a truck and killed.

Cohen, M. (1984). *Jim's dog Muffins.* New York: Greenwillow. Jim is inconsolable when his dog is killed, until a friend helps him find a way to grieve.

Creech, S. (2001). *Love that dog.* New York: Scholastic. In this story, which was inspired by the work of Walter Dean Myers, a preadolescent boy writes in

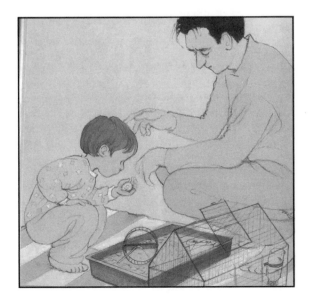

spare, poetic style about the loss of his dog.

Dabcovich, L. (1985). *Mrs. Huggins and her hen Hannah.* New York: Dutton. The loss of a beloved pet leads to sadness and then resolution for Mrs. Huggins.

DiSalvo-Ryan, D. (1999). *A dog like Jack.* New York: Holiday House. A beloved old dog passes away after a long and full life.

Doyle, M. (2002). *Storm cats.* London: Simon & Schuster. A boy and girl who are neighbors, yet unknown to each other, become friends while searching for their cats, who have gone missing during a bad storm. The outcome of the two cats' interaction yields some unexpected and delightful results in this rhyming book.

Graeber, C. (1982). *Mustard.* New York: Macmillan. An 8-year-old boy must deal with the death of his elderly cat.

Harris, R. H. (2001). *Goodbye, Mousie.* New York: Margaret K. McElderry. A very young child comes to terms with the loss of his pet mouse.

Harrison, T. (2002). *Aaron's awful allergies.* New York: Kids Can Press. Young Aaron must find homes for all of his pets when he develops allergies.

Joose, B. (1988). *Better with two.* New York: Harper & Row. A girl tries to cheer up her friend Mrs. Brady when her dog dies.

Keller, H. (1987). *Goodbye, Max.* New York: Greenwillow. A boy refuses to accept the puppy his parents have brought home in the wake of the death of his dog Max.

Kroll, V. (1992). *Helen the fish.* Morton Grove, IL: Albert Whitman. A little girl seeks comfort from her big brother when her pet goldfish dies.

Langenegger, L. (1999). *Blaze, the farm dog.* Herisau, Switzerland: Appenzeller Medienhaus. Heartbroken at the loss of his dog, a young boy finds comfort in adopting one of the puppies sired by his beloved pet.

Schlein, M. (1990). *That's not Goldie!* New York: Simon & Schuster. This story begins as one of loss, but ends happily as a child's dream—in which a goldfish flushed down the toilet reappears at the local park—comes true.

Viorst, J. (1971). *The tenth good thing about Barney.* New York: Atheneum. A boy tries to think of 10 good things to say about his cat for the animal's funeral.

Wilhelm, H. (1985). *I'll always love you.* New York: Crown. A child comforts himself when his dog dies by remembering how often he expressed his affection for it.

Zolotow, C. (1995). *The old dog.* New York: HarperCollins. A boy finds his old dog dead one morning, and spends the day thinking about all the good times they had together.

Death or Loss: Juvenile Fiction

Derwent, L. (1985). *The tale of Greyfriars Bobby.* London: Puffin. An energetic Skye terrier is so devoted to his master that he continues to watch over his grave for 14 years. Based on a true story from Edinburgh.

121

THEME 3: PET CARE

Learning To Care for Pets: The New Pet Picture Books

Abercrombie, B. (2002). *Bad dog, Dodger!* New York: Margaret K. McElderry. Nine-year-old Sam achieves his dream of having a puppy, but must come to terms with the reality of the situation.

Allen, P. (1990). *My cat Maisie.* New York: Viking. Andrew learns that he must be gentle to be friends with his ginger cat.

Anholt, L. (1994). *The new puppy.* New York: Artists & Writers Guild. A little girl learns about how much work and love is required to care for a new puppy.

Banks, L. (1978). *I, Houdini.* London: J.M. Dent & Sons. Told from the pet's point of view, a hamster details his conflict between being a beloved pet and longing to explore the world at large.

Binch, C. (1999). *Christy's dream.* London: Mammoth. A young boy longs desperately for a horse of his own, but has only himself to make his dream come true.

Blades, A. (2001). *Mary of mile 18.* New York: Tundra Books. The touching tale of a young Canadian farm girl, living in the far north, who wants to keep a wolf puppy.

Bridwell, N. (2002). *Clifford goes to dog school.* New York: Cartwheel Books. Emily Elizabeth takes her big red dog to obedience school.

Conlon-McKenna, M. (1999). *Granny MacGinty.* Dublin, Ireland: O'Brien Press. Finding the right pet for Grandma proves impossible until a stray kitten appears.

D'Lacey, C. (1998). *Fly, Cherokee, fly.* London: Corgi Yearling Books. Everyone except 12-year-old Darryl thinks that an injured racing pigeon should be put out of its misery.

Dodds, D. (2001). *Pet wash.* Cambridge, MA: Candlewick Press. Two young entrepreneurs soap up the neighborhood pets in this cheerful rhyming story.

Dorman, N. B. (1993). *Petey and Miss Magic.* Hamden, CT: Linnet Books. A young boy with allergies enters his angleworm in a pet contest.

Fleming, D. (1998). *Mama cat has three kittens.* New York: Holt. In this simple rhyming story for the very young, mother cat has three kittens, two who follow her lead and one who is a rugged individualist.

Herriot, J. (1987). *Bonny's big day.* New York: St. Martin's Press. Farmer Skipton is persuaded to enter his retired carthorse, Bonnie, in the Darrowby Pet Show.

Keller, H. (1992). *Furry.* New York: Greenwillow. Allergies make it tough for a little girl to have a pet, until her brother comes up with a solution.

Langenegger, L. (1999). *Snowflake.* Herisua, Switzerland: Appenzeller Medienhaus. A girl must find a way to keep her pet goat from escaping the farmyard and destroying the village gardens.

Lewis, K. (2000). *Little puppy.* Cambridge, MA: Candlewick Press. A puppy born on her family's farm becomes the beloved pet of a young girl.

MacLeod, E. (1998). *I heard a little baa.* Tonawonda, NY: Kids Can Press. A small lift-the-flap book that can be sung to the tune of "The Farmer in the Dell" invites children to guess which animals will be found on a farm.

Miller, V. (1997). *Be gentle!* Cambridge, MA: Candlewick Press. When Bartholomew gets a small black kitten, he must learn how to handle it properly.

Pearce, P. (1978). *The battle of Bubble and Squeak.* London: Penguin. A family struggles to find a place for the two gerbils that the children adore and the mother detests.

Perkins, L. (2002). *The broken cat.* New York: Greenwillow. Andy's mother tells him the story of how he broke his arm as they wait their turn at the vet's to see what is wrong with their pet.

Reiser, L. (1992). *Any kind of dog.* New York: Greenwillow. Young Richard wants a dog of any kind, no matter what alternative pets his mother suggests.

Reit, S. (1996). *A dog's tale.* New York: Bantam. A puppy finds it has to teach its new girl how to take care of him.

Seeber, D. (2000). *A pup just for me/A boy just for me.* New York: Philomel. A puppy and a boy meet in the middle of these two books in one.

Simont, M. (2001). *The stray dog.* New York: HarperCollins. A scruffy dog appears at a family picnic, and the children want to take him home.

THEME 4: PETS AND THE VERY YOUNG CHILD

Appelt, K. (2002). *Bubba and Beau, best friends.* San Diego, CA: Harcourt. It's a sad day in Bubbaville when their favorite blankie is washed, but Bubba the baby and Beau the pup manage to comfort each other.

Appelt, K. (2003). *Bubba and Beau go night-night.* New York: Harcourt. In this second adventure of the toddler/pup pair, they need a ride in a pickup truck to settle down and fall asleep.

Chapman, N. K. (2000). *Doggie dreams.* New York: Putnam. A humorous look at cartoon-style dogs' wildest dreams.

Church, C. J. (2003). *Pudgy: A puppy to love.* New York: Scholastic/Chicken House. A chance meeting between a lonely pup and a young girl who has no one to play with leads to mutual affection.

Kopper, L. (1999). *Daisy knows best.* New York: Dutton. Everyone needs a bath when the baby tags along with Daisy and her puppies.

Kopper, L. (2000). *Daisy's babies.* New York: Dutton. Daisy the bullterrier has to take care of her puppies and their friend Baby, too!

McCarty, P. (2002). *Hondo and Fabian.* New York: Henry Holt. Hondo the dog and Fabian the cat spend their days differently but happily.

Martin, D. (1993). *Lizzie and her kitty.* Cambridge, MA: Candlewick Press. A cuddle with a kitty lands pudding in Lizzie's hair.

It was a sad day in Bubbaville.

Martin, D. (1993). *Lizzie and her puppy*. Cambridge, MA: Candlewick Press. A box is just right for Lizzie and her puppy to play in.

Noonan, J. (2000). *Going to the corner*. New York: Scholastic. A stroller ride to the store is an adventure for a toddler and puppy.

Ochiltree, D. (2002). *Pillow pup*. New York: Margaret K. McElderry. It's a pillow fight for pup and preschooler!

Voake, C. (1996). *Mr. Davies and the baby*. Cambridge, MA: Candlewick Press. Mr. Davies the dog just LOVES to walk with Mommy and Baby.

THEME 5:
ANIMAL RESCUE

Casey, P. (2001). *One day at Wood Green Animal Shelter*. Cambridge, MA: Candlewick Press. On a busy day at the shelter, workers take care of many different animals in need of help.

Chorao, K. (2002). *Grayboy*. New York: Henry Holt. Two children spend a special summer helping a wounded gull at the seashore.

Goodman, S. (2000). *Animal rescue: The best job there is*. New York: Simon & Schuster. Describes the work of an animal rescue worker.

Graham, B. (2001). *"Let's get a pup!" said Kate*. Cambridge, MA: Candlewick Press. Kate and her parents visit the shelter to select a pup, but decide they absolutely must take home an older dog as well.

Hesse, K. (1993). *Lester's dog*. New York: Crown. A boy overcomes his fear of a ferocious dog in order to rescue an abandoned kitten.

Kehret, P. (1999). *Shelter dogs: Amazing stories of adopted strays*. Morton Grove, IL: Albert Whitman. True stories of eight stray dogs that went on to become outstanding or heroic pets.

Meggs, L. (2000). *Go home! The true story of James the cat*. Morton Grove, IL: Albert Whitman. A family doesn't realize that a cat in their yard is homeless and in need of rescue until he nearly chokes from the constrictive collar he has outgrown.

Parish, P. (1988). *Scruffy*. New York: Harper & Row. The animal shelter provides a young boy with his best birthday present of all: a cat.

Sampson, M., & Martin, B. (2002). *Caddie the golf dog*. New York: Walker & Co. Three different children rescue a stray dog and help to care for the puppies that soon arrive.

Stolz, M. (1983). *Cat walk*. New York: Harper & Row. A young barnyard cat embarks on a quest to find a home of his own, encountering both kind and cruel people along the way.

Thayer, J. (1988). *The puppy who wanted a boy*. New York: Morrow. In this children's literature favorite, reissued with new illustrations by Seymour Fleishman in 1988, a homeless dog who yearns for a boy is adopted by an orphanage and enjoys the affection of not just one boy, but many.

Ure, J. (1999). *Muddy four paws*. Hauppage, NY: Barron's Educational Series. Eleven-year-old Clara rescues a huge, ill-behaved dog, but will her mother permit her to keep it?

Professional Resources in Literature About Children and Animals: A Bibliography of Bibliographies

The preceding list is merely a starting point; there is an almost overwhelming variety of children's materials in print to entertain and delight the reader. Professional educational and library journals are one source of information; your own public or academic libraries are others. The following bibliographies provide valuable subject guides to children's literature.

Coghlan, V., & Keenan, C. (Eds.). (2000). *The big guide 2: Irish children's books*. Dublin, Ireland: Children's Books Ireland.

Gillespie, J. T. (2001). *Best books for children: Preschool through grade six* (7th ed.). New York: Greenwood.

Lima, C. W., & Lima, J. A. (2001). *A to zoo: Subject access to picture books* (6th ed.). New York: Greenwood.

Watson, V. (2001). *The Cambridge guide to children's books in English*. Cambridge, UK: Cambridge University Press.

Yokota, J. (2001). *Kaleidoscope: A multicultural booklist of grades K-8* (3rd ed.). Urbana, IL: National Council of Teachers of English.

Zarnowsky, M., Kerper, R. M., & Jensen, J. M. (2001). *The best in children's nonfiction: Reading, writing, and teaching Orbis Pictus Award books*. Urbana, IL: National Council of Teachers of English.

Recommended Web Sites

Booklists of Children's Literature (sorted by theme)
www.monroe.lib.in.us/childrens/children_booklists.html
Children's Picture Book Database at Miami University
www.lib.muhoio.edu/pictbks/
Fairrosa Cyber Library of Children's Literature
www.fairrosa.info/cl.authors.html
Outstanding Science Trade Books for Students
www.nsta.org/ostbc

Conclusion

Whether in the role of heroes in service to humanity or as victims in urgent need of our assistance, the vital nature of animals as companions has been extensively documented throughout the ages. Children's literature records this in its comprehensive representation of everything from the mythic roots of the human/animal bond to contemporary accounts of children and their beloved pets. When a 21st century child reaches the satisfying conclusion of *Puss in Boots*, it doesn't matter that the story is some 400 years old. Puss, having outwitted an ogre and manipulated a king, gains a castle and the hand of the king's daughter for his master. The clever cat lives the rest of his life in well-deserved peace and luxury. As for the miller's son, a pet keeper, he, of course, lives happily ever after.

References

Alexander, L. (2000). *How the cat swallowed thunder*. New York: Dutton.

Bailey, L. (2003). *Stanley's party*. Tonawonda, NY: Kids Can Press.

Bekoff, M. (2002). *Minding the animals: Awareness, emotions, and heart*. New York: Oxford University Press.

Byars, B. (1993). *Wanted . . . Mud Blossom*. New York: Yearling.

Cleary, B. (2003). *The mouse and the motorcycle*. New York: HarperTrophy.

Coville, B. (Ed.). (1989). *Herds of thunder, manes of gold*. New York: Doubleday.

Florian, D. (2003). *Bow wow meow meow: It's rhyming cats and dogs*. San Diego, CA: Harcourt.

Gardiner, J. R. (1980). *Stone fox*. New York: HarperCollins.

Hearne, B. (2003). *The canine connection: Stories about dogs and people*. New York: McElderry.

Hyland, H. (1999). *The wreck of the Ethie*. Atlanta, GA: Peachtree.

Ichikawa, S. (2003). *My pig Amarillo*. New York: Philomel.

Johnson, N. J., & Giorgis, C. (2001). Children's books. *The Reading Teacher, 55*(2), 204-214.

Kaser, S. (2001). Searching the heavens with children's literature: A design for teaching science. *Language Arts, 78*(4), 348-356.

Katz, J. (2003). *The new work of dogs: Tending to life, love, and family*. New York: Villard Books/Random House.

Katz, J. (2002). *A dog year: Twelve months, four dogs, and me*. New York: Villard Books/Random House.

Lee, H. B. (2003). *While you were out*. New York: Kane/Miller.

Leedy, L. (2000). *Mapping Penny's world*. New York: Holt.

Lowry, L. (1997). *Stay! Keeper's story*. Boston: Houghton-Mifflin.

Lukens, R. (2003). *A critical handbook of children's literature* (7th ed.). Boston: Allyn & Bacon.

Mayer, M. (1990). *Frog goes to dinner*. New York: Puffin.

McFarland, L. R. (2001). *Widget*. New York: Farrar, Straus & Giroux.

McNicoll, S. (2000). *Bringing up Beauty*. Toronto, ON: Stoddart Kids.

Mitchell, D. (2003). *Children's literature: An invitation to the world*. Boston: Allyn & Bacon.

Myers, L. (2002). *Lewis and Clark and me: A dog's tale*. New York: Scholastic.

Nodelman, P., & Reimer, M. (2003). *The pleasures of literature* (3rd ed.). Boston: Allyn & Bacon.

Paulsen, G. (1999). *My life in dog years*. New York: Yearling.

Paulsen, G. (1983). *Dogsong*. New York: Macmillan.

Perkins, L. R. (2003). *The broken cat*. New York: Greenwillow.

Pinkney, J. (2000). *Aesop's fables*. New York: SeaStar.

Rawls, W. (1961). *Where the red fern grows*. New York: Doubleday.

Rosen, M. J. (Ed.). (1993). *Speak! Children's book authors and illustrators brag about their dogs*. San Diego: Harcourt.

Rosen, M. J. (Ed.). (2001). *Dog people: What we love about our dogs—writers and artists on canine companionship*. New York: Artisan Books/Workman.

Rosen, M. J. (Ed.). (2002). *Horse people: Writers and artists on the horses they love*. New York: Artisan Books/Workman.

Rushton, S., & Larkin, E. (2001). Shaping the learning environment: Connecting developmentally appropriate practices to brain research. *Early Childhood Education Journal, 29*(1), 25-34.

Schultz, J. (2003). *Dogs of the Iditarod*. Seattle, WA: Sasquatch Books.

Sewell, A. (2002). *Black Beauty*. (Illustrated Library for Children, L. Kemp-Welch, illustrator). New York: Gramercy.

Sidman, J. (2003). *The world according to dog: Poems and teen voices*. Boston: Houghton-Mifflin.

Sullivan, G. (2000). *Lewis and Clark*. New York: Scholastic.

Ward, C. (1994). *Cookie's week*. New York: Scholastic.

Wilder, L. I. (1932). *The little house in the big woods*. New York: Harper & Row.

Book Illustration Credits for Chapter 8:

p. 116:
From *My Pig Amarillo* by Satomi Ichikawa, copyright © 2002 by Satomi Ichikawa. Used by permission of Philomel Books, A Division of Penguin Young Readers Group, A Member of Penguin Group (USA) Inc., 345 Hudson Street, New York NY 10014. All rights reserved.

p. 121:
Reprinted with the permission of Margaret K. McElderry Books, an imprint of Simon & Schuster Children's Publishing Division from *Goodbye Mousie* by Robie H. Harris, illustrated by Jan Ormerod. Illustration copyright © 2001 Jan Ormerod.

p. 123:
Illustration from *Bubba and Beau* by Kathi Appelt, illustrations copyright © 2002 by Arthur Howard, reproduced by Harcourt, Inc.

Chapter 9

Companion Animals and Technology: Using the Internet, Software, and Electronic Toys To Learn About Pets

Susan W. Haugland,
Elma A. Ruiz, and Yi Gong

S helly's son, 6-year-old Blake, decided he wanted a pet. Shelly's primary concern in selecting a pet was to find a low maintenance pet that would be a hardy animal and did not carry disease. She eliminated a dog because they did not have an adequate yard, and a cat was not an option because of allergies. A friend suggested hermit crabs. Shelly knew nothing about them and so she typed "hermit crab" into the browser on her computer and found "all kinds of Web sites about hermit crabs."

Shelly found these Web sites to be very helpful, providing them diverse information about where to buy a hermit crab, the life span of the animal, how to care for hermit crabs, and what kind of foods are best for the animal. One site even provided a checklist of important things to remember when caring for hermit crabs and when they should be completed, such as changing the rocks, selecting shells, and when to change the shells. Blake has the checklist displayed in his bedroom, a handy reminder of what is important in caring for his pet. Blake has two hermit crabs, because their online

Photo courtesy of Susan Haugland

Blake and his hermit crab.

search uncovered the information that hermit crabs are very social animals and they never reproduce in captivity. After finding the hermit crab Web sites, Shelly went to the local library to find a book on hermit crabs to share with her son. They had no books on the subject! The Internet Web sites provided Shelly and Blake valuable information on selecting and caring for a pet that would have been much more difficult to find in print media.

Using Online Resources To Teach Children About Pets

The above example illustrates some of the valuable online resources available to parents and teachers when helping children learn about pets. There are three types of Web sites useful to teachers and parents: informational sites, communication sites, and teacher resources. Informational sites, such as the sites on hermit crabs, provide information about selecting pets and caring for them. In addition, some sites provide valuable assistance in locating a lost pet. Other informational sites offer real time cam recordings of pets, enabling children to monitor a pet even if they don't have a pet in their own home or classroom. A second type of valuable site is the communication sites. These sites give children opportunities to share information and reflections about their pets with children around the world; they can even upload digital photos. Communication sites provide children an authentic audience for their writing. The third type of site is teacher resources. These Web sites are filled with lesson plans and unit projects designed to teach children about pets. The Web

sites highlighted in this chapter provide detailed guidelines for teaching children about diverse topics related to pets, including learning objectives that help teachers integrate the lessons into their overall curriculum.

All of the Web sites featured in this chapter have been evaluated using the Haugland/Gerzog Scale for Developmental Web Sites (1999). Web sites are scored on a 10 point scale; scores 7.0 and above are developmentally appropriate for children.

Why Use Online Resources?

First of all, home and classroom access to the Internet is increasing (National School Boards Foundation, 2001). For many children it is only a question of if and when parents and teachers will provide children opportunities to use the Internet. For example, the proportion of public schools in the United States connected to the Internet has increased from 35 percent in 1994 to 95 percent in 1999 (U.S. Department of Education, 2000). According to the International Reading Association, "the Internet is rapidly entering nearly every classroom in developed nations around the world, and that equity of access to the Internet and other ICT will ensure literacy opportunities for children around the world" (International Reading Association, 2001, p. 1).

According to a recent report released by the National School Boards Foundation (2001), parents view "the Internet as a powerful tool for education and a positive force in their children's lives" (National School Boards Foundation, 2001, p. 2). In fact, parents are more likely to restrict their children's use of TV and video viewing more than their Internet use. The report emphasizes that Internet use in classrooms "seems to have a strong effect on the school attitudes of low-income children, children from large families and children in single parent households" (National School Boards Foundation, 2001, p. 3). As the National School Boards Foundation emphasizes, it is important to help teachers, parents, and children use the Internet more effectively for learning.

Providing parents and teachers assistance in using the Internet effectively is critical. After using online projects throughout the year, one 1st-grade teacher concluded that "the only limitation to using telecommunications (with young) students are those we impose ourselves by failing to empower them" (Stoicheva, 2000, p. 2). Once adults see the vision of the learning opportunities online resources can provide, children will be ready and able to explore them.

Significant benefits can emerge from children's exploration of online resources. "The Internet leads to student empowerment, increased motivation and interest. It helps at-risk and multilingual students develop literacy skills, and fosters family involvement" (Oakes, 1996, p. 24, 37-9). Teachers also report enriched self-esteem and sense of accomplishment in their students (Medrinos, 1997; Clovis, 1998).

Informational Sites
Focusing on Pets

A wealth of diverse information related to pets and their care is available on the Internet. Informational sites can help individuals, families, or classroom communities select and adopt a pet. This is particularly useful when an unusual type of pet is desired, such as a rare breed of dog or a specific kind of bird. Users can learn about the animal's native environment as well as ideal conditions for maintaining the animal in captivity. They also provide the opportunity to ask questions about a pet or a future pet. Instructions are available for caring for a sick pet should the need arise. Some informational sites feature cam recordings of animals presented in real time. Children or classrooms can observe an animal and then graph behavior patterns. Children who do not have a pet of their own may learn a great deal about pets through such observations. They can also gain valuable information regarding whether a particular pet would match a family or classroom's needs by observing the animal over time. And if a family or classroom pet become lost, Web sites are available that can help connect pets to their owners!

Three informational sites are featured below. The first is an adoption site and the second is designed to provide diverse information about pets, including advice from veterinarians. The third site provides interactive activities to teach children about pets.

Web Site: Pet Finder

Developmental Rating: 8.0
Ages: Teacher Information Site
URL: http://petfinder.com
Description: Petfinder.com is a searchable database of over 60,000 animals that need homes from almost 4,000 animal shelters and adoption organizations across the United States and Canada. Organizations maintain their own home pages and available pet databases. Last year, Petfinder.com was responsible for over a half million adoptions.

Web Site: PetEducation.com

Developmental Rating: 8.0
Ages: Teacher Information Site
URL: www.peteducation.com
Description: PetEducation.com provides excellent information on behaviors, diseases, nutrition, and providing the best environment for pets. The site contains over 2,500 articles written by veterinarians and is an excellent research tool. Searches can be conducted or the directory provides information organized by species (dogs, cats, fish, birds, ferrets, reptiles, and small pets) for easy access.

Virtual Pets: Will Technology Replace Companion Animals?
Yi Gong and Mary Renck Jalongo

What Is a Virtual Pet?

Virtual pets refer collectively to those computerized pets that simulate the life cycle of real animals. Virtual pets may take many different forms, including key chain pets, computer pets, mobile phone pets, robotic pets, Internet pets, and so forth. They are designed to interact with their users through preset computer programs. Among the most popular virtual pets are Furby, Tamagotchi, Gigapet, and Pikachu.

Tamagotchi has the distinction of being the first virtual pet in the world. It was invented in 1996 by a Japanese mother who wanted to simulate the pet-keeping experience for her children. She did not think her family's small apartment could accommodate a real pet, and so designed Tamagotchi, a small, egg-shaped device with a liquid crystal display, tiny control push-buttons, and a miniature speaker as a pet substitute. It was marketed in Japan and quickly became a very popular toy for children (Bloch & Lemish, 1999). The simple and relatively inexpensive components of virtual pets like Tamagotchi (chip, display, speaker, and plastic case) make it easy for toy manufacturers to mass-produce virtual pets at a relatively low cost (Polson, 1997). The reasonable price of most virtual pets, coupled with the appealing animal images they can generate, have made virtual pets popular with children throughout the world.

*How Have Advances in Technology
Affected Virtual Pets?*

Virtual pets could not have been developed without recent advancements in artificial intelligence (AI) research. Before the 1980s, early robots were programmed to deal with only those situations that the designer anticipated. They were not able to handle unpredicted changes. A new concept, articulated by Rodney A. Brooks in 1983 and Marvin Minsky in 1986, changed the total orientation of artificial intelligence development. They posited that AI robots should be able to "learn" from their interactions with the environment and that such types of adaptation would lead to increasingly realistic robot behavior (Pesce, 2000). Virtual pets inherited their primary design principle from AI research and robotics.

The premise of the virtual pet is that it is to function as a "free" creature, following its own agendas rather than existing merely to serve its owners (Kaplan, n.d.). These objectives are best embodied in the virtual pet known as Furby. Besides its reactive and verbal features, the most amazing thing about Furby is that it evolves in response to interactions. For example, a Furby acquires English words through play with children and builds a personal vocabulary. Like a real pet, the Furby remembers its interactions with its owner, especially those activities that amuse its owner. And, also like a real pet, as the Furby spends time with its owner, it takes on certain characteristics that appear similar to those of its owner (Pesce, 2000).

Virtual pets have been proliferating rapidly ever since May 1997 when the first Tamagotchi was introduced into the United States. "Series" pets are available that use similar cases and the same chip and life map, for example, Kitty Pets, Puppy Pets, and Gigapets. New animals (fish, frogs, parrots, lizards, etc.), imaginary creatures (aliens, monsters), and even human pets have been added to the virtual pets line. As with other types of toys, the parents who buy and the children who play with virtual pets expect them to become more interesting, challenging, and visually appealing with each new model. To meet such expectations, the new generation of virtual pets has many more functions (Polson, 1997). For some of the newer virtual pets, the user has to dress the pet appropriately for various weather conditions. Additionally, some of the newer pets participate in more activities and offer more choices in life paths. In response to how the child treats them, some virtual pets can even develop different "personalities" and roles (Oravec, 2001). At the same time, the graphics keep improving, just as they have with video games. Dot Matrix, which provides a better animation view, has replaced the line or segmented display allowing the "body" of virtual pets to evolve from simple dot images to animated 3-D images (Kusahara, 2001; Polson, 1997). The most recent virtual pets even have cuddly, furry bodies, rather than a hard plastic case to better simulate an animal.

How Do Children Play With Virtual Pets?

Frequently, the virtual pet's "life" begins with a birth event. As is often the case with real animals, children usually begin their relationship with their virtual pets by naming them, followed by an interactive process of feeding, cleaning, nursing, communicating, and teaching (Kusahara, 2001). The child's responsibility is to provide virtual care for the pet in order to sustain its life. Such things as food, drink, rest, play, cleaning, and medication are all part of the game. Eventually, the animal will die, electronically speaking; unlike a real animal, however, the life of a virtual pet can be started over by pushing the reset button. Nevertheless, some children have become depressed by the death of their virtual pets; to console these children, a virtual cemetery has been built where owners can "bury" dead virtual pets. Older children who realize that their "pet" is just a machine often lose their enthusiasm for virtual pets (Hafner, 2000; Kusahara, 2001), and so virtual pets typically are marketed to young children.

What Are the Controversies About Virtual Pets?

The emergence of virtual pets changed children's perceptions of "alive" (Turkle, 2000). In her research on children and Furby, Sherry Turkle found that when children play with these electronic toys, they try to develop a relationship with them. The Furby not only asks for nurturance, but also speaks and plays with the child. When asked whether the Furby is alive, the children in Turkle's study tended to focus on their feelings toward their Furbies and how the Furbies might feel about them. In addition to the dichotomous categories of life (i.e., animate vs. inanimate), virtual pets bring up an intermediate, third category: "sort-of-alive" or "Furby kind of alive" (Appel & O'Gara, 2001; Turkle, 2000).

Proponents of virtual pets believe that by taking care of virtual pets children can learn about personal responsibility, develop care-taking skills, and eventually project an emotional response (Bickmore, 1998; Dyrli, n.d.). But it is questionable whether virtual pets can help promote children's creative thought and imaginative growth. Opponents argue that virtual pets might actually inhibit creativity since they have to be played in a game-like, pre-defined way (Mann, n.d.). Experts also caution that too much time spent playing with virtual pets can impede learning about real life (Kulman, 1997; Oravec, 2001).

Clearly, the most controversial issue about virtual pets is their inevitable electronic death (Hafner, 2000). Despite frequent care, the virtual pet will eventually die. Children may become upset or feel guilty about the demise of a virtual pet, even if it can be reversed. There are reports about children who feel a sense of loss even after several weeks have passed, and some children seem to have been traumatized by the deaths of their virtual pets. Such responses from children have led some critics to wonder if the virtual pets really do teach children caregiving behaviors or merely cause undue stress and frustration (Kulman, 1997) as children are needlessly upset by the death of their virtual pet (Dyrli, n.d.). Some experts have argued that virtual pets are not developmentally appropriate for young children—the very group to which the pets are most clearly marketed (Rafferty & Sharma, 1997).

Can these modern marvels of technology take the place of real, live companion animals? Technophiles say yes, arguing that as virtual pets' scripts and interactive systems become more complex, they will become capable of adapting and responding in ways that mimic living creatures (Grand & Cliff, 1998) and their capacity to evoke strong emotional bonds from humans will increase accordingly (Ray, 2001). Skeptics of the virtual pet craze contend, however, that while virtual pets may require attention, the caregiver's role is superficial (Kritt, 2000) and nothing like the commitment that is necessary when one accepts responsibility for a fellow living creature.

References

Appel, A. E., & O'Gara, C. (2001). Technology and young children: A review of literature. *TechKnowLogia, 3*(5), 35-36.

Bickmore, T. (1998). *Friendship and intimacy in the digital age.* Retrieved January 12, 2003, from http://web.media.mit.edu/~bickmore/Mas714/finalReport.html.

Bloch, L. R., & Lemish, D. (1999). Disposable love: The rise and fall of a virtual pet. *New Media & Society, 1*(3), 283-303.

Dyrli, O. E. (n.d.). *New virtual pets are hatching right and left.* Retrieved January 10, 2003, from www.techlearning.com.

Grand, S., & Cliff, D. (1998). Creatures: Entertainment software agents with artificial life. *Autonomous Agents and Multi-agent Systems, 1*(1), 39-45.

Hafner, K. (2000). What do you mean, "It's just like a real dog"? *The New York Times, 149*(51399), G1.

Kaplan, F. (n.d.). *Free creatures: The role of uselessness in the design of artificial pets.* Retrieved January 25, 2003, from www.csl.sony.fr/downloads/papers/2000/kaplaner.pdf.

Kritt, D. W. (2000). Loving a virtual pet: Steps toward the technological erosion of emotion. *Journal of American & Comparative Cultures, 23*(4), 81-87.

Kulman, L. (1997). It's just a toy. *U.S. News & World Report, 122*(25), 13.

Kusahara, M. (2001). The art of creating subjective reality: An analysis of Japanese digital pets. *Leonardo, 34*(4), 299-302.

Mann, D. (n.d.). *The lowdown on hi-tech toys.* Retrieved January 9, 2003, from http://my.webmd.com/content/article/31/1728_77522.htm.

Oravec, J. A. (2001). Interactive toys and children's education: Strategies for educators and parents. *Childhood Education, 77,* 81-85.

Pesce, M. (2000). *Toy stories. The science.* New York: The New York Academy of Science.

Ray, T. S. (2001). Aesthetically evolved virtual pets. *Leonardo, 34*(4), 313-316.

Polson, G. (1997). *Recent developments and trends in keychain virtual pets.* Retrieved January 12, 2003, from www.virtualpet.com/vp/future/trends1a.htm.

Rafferty, F., & Sharma, Y. (1997). Virtual pets prove a real problem. *The Times Educational Supplement, 4225,* 8.

Turkle, S. (2000). *Cuddling up to cyborg babies.* Retrieved January 15, 2003, from www.unesco.org/courier/2000_09/uk/connex.htm.

Web Site: Pet Detective WebQuest

Developmental Rating: 8.5

Ages: 4-9

URL: www.ri.net/schools/Central_Falls/ch/
heazak/petdet.html

Description: In this Webquest, children take on the role of pet detectives in order to find facts about pets and their care. Children gather information from a veterinarian, see photographs of different pets, and even view a mystery pet through the lens of a live cam. The culminating activity supports literacy objectives as children surprise their friend or family with an E-mail pet card.

Communication Web Sites

A tremendous catalyst for children's writing is having an audience and something to share. Often children struggle during journal time if they do not have a specific topic. Communication sites provide children a global community in which to share their thoughts, ideas, pictures, and photographs. Using these sites, classrooms or individual children can connect with pen pals from across the world. Through the process of sharing, children can learn not only about pets, but also about other cultures.

Three communication sites are featured below. The first is a fun site that features a different pet each day. The second and third sites provide children and classrooms opportunities to communicate in an international community.

Web Site: Pet of the Day

Developmental Rating: 7.0

Ages: 7-9

URL: www.petoftheday.com

Description: Pet of the Day aims to bring a few

minutes of joy into each day. On a daily basis, they present a new pet photo and story to try to illustrate how animals enrich the lives of people around the world. The reading level is upper elementary. Providing multiple languages would enhance this site.

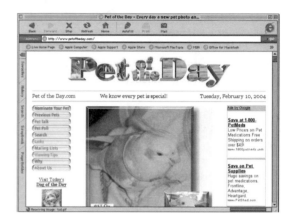

Web Site: ePALS Classroom Exchange

Developmental Rating: 7.5

Ages: 6+

URL: www.epals.com

Description: This site connects classrooms to other classrooms across the globe. Currently, 72,953 classroom profiles are available providing cross-cultural learning from 191 countries. A translator converts text to Spanish, French, German, Japanese, Italian, Portuguese, and English. Classroom projects are featured for children, as are resources for teachers. There is a fee for using the site, which is based upon the classroom or district needs.

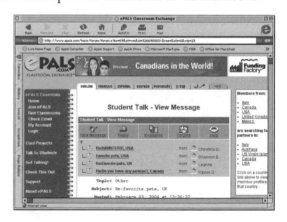

Web Site: International Kids Space

Developmental Rating: 8.5

Ages: 4+

URL: www.kids-space.org/gallery/_animals.html

Description: This site provides an international meeting place for children and teachers from 150 countries. There are two main selections: activities and communication. In communication, individuals or classrooms can be connected to pen pals. In Kids Gallery, children can publish stories and illustrations about their pets.

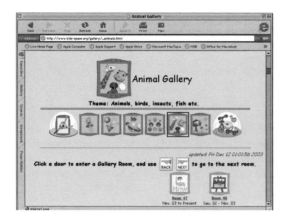

Online Teacher Resources

Many Web sites are designed to assist teachers in curriculum planning. These sites feature not only lesson plans but also learning objectives aligned to state and/or national standards. With these objectives and standards, teachers can integrate units about pets into their overall curriculum. Science, literacy, and math standards are woven seamlessly into classroom activities, maximizing children's learning.

The following two Web sites provide lesson plans for grades 1 through 3. Both are standards-based lesson plans, which teachers can integrate into their curriculum.

Web Site: Units for Grades 2-3: What Are Our Favorite Pets?

Developmental Rating: 8.5
Ages: 7-9
URL: http://ll.terc.edu/toplevel/gr2-3_toc.cfm
Description: Funded in part by the National Science Foundation and the National Geographic Society, this site provides a standards-based pet unit. In Part 1, students develop a class definition of pets, observe pets, and then gather data to be sent to a database. In Part II, analysis of the network data leads to a deeper understanding of

pets. The 31-page teacher's guide provides all the needed resources and alignment documentation to the National Science Education Standards.

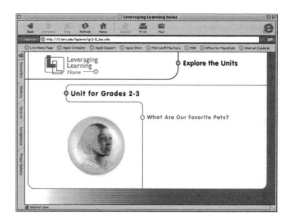

Web Site: Unit Plan for Our Friends— Our Pets, First Grade

Developmental Rating: 8.0
Ages: 6-7
URL: www.michigan.gov/scope/0,1607,7-155-10710_10733_10735-39156—,00.html
Description: This standards-based integrated unit, consisting of 11 lessons, allows children to investigate the needs of pets and learn about owners' responsibility in selecting and caring for pets. Students use the inquiry and research process to produce and present a "How-To" book on the care of a particular pet. Formal and informal performance-based assessments of children's emergent literacy are included.

Safeguards While Providing Online Learning

It is important to remember that the Internet is a non-previewed, uncensored environment. Anyone is allowed to publish information on the Internet. The Web sites that have been featured in this article have been carefully reviewed by professionals. Teachers and parents can review the available Web sites on a certain subject, searching the Internet on a browser and then carefully evaluating the quality of the content within the site. Information regarding Web site evaluation is available on the childrenandcomputers.com Web site.

When children are using online resources, it is important that they remain anonymous. Caution them to use only their first names and not to share details about where they live. Web sites for children to explore can be preloaded or featured on the desktop.

If children are going to be doing their own searches on the Internet for information, a screening device is recommended. Screening devices such as Internet Safari (Heartsoft, 2001) filter out Web sites that have questionable content.

Conclusion

Online resources can be a valuable teaching tool, empowering children and motivating them to learn. As children become engaged in the learning process, information becomes meaningful and powerful. Through the Internet, resources available to parents, teachers, and children expand dramatically.

Three types of online Web sites are available to help children throughout the world learn about their companion animals. Informational sites provide children access to a wealth of knowledge related to the selection, care, and understanding of pets. Communication sites provide children opportunities for authentic writing experiences, which they can share with children from across the globe. Teacher resource sites offer teachers help in planning lessons/units about pets and connecting their activities to the overall curriculum.

After using online resources for a year, a 1st-grade teacher stated that the only limitation was her vision of how to empower children. We hope this chapter and the Web sites listed herein will help you envision how to effectively utilize online resources to empower children's exploration of companion animals.

References

Clovis, D. (1998). Use technology to help multilingual students meet national standards. *Multimedia Schools, 5*(5), 52-4.

Haugland, S. W., & Wright, J. L. (1997). *Young children and technology: A world of discovery.* Needham Heights, MA: Allyn and Bacon.

International Reading Association. (2001). Position statement on integrating literacy and technology in the curriculum. Retrieved December 20, 2002, from www.reading.org/positions/technology.html

Medrinos, R. (1997). *Using educational technology with at-risk students: A guide for library media specialists and teachers.* Oxford, UK: Greenwood Professional Guides in School Librarianship, Greenwood Press.

Oakes, C. (1996). First grade online. *Learning and Leading With Technology, 24*, 37-9.

National School Boards Foundation. (2001). *Research and guidelines for children's use of the internet.* Retrieved January 3, 2003, from www.nsbf.org/safe-smart/full-report.htm

U.S. Department of Education, National Center for Education Statistics. (2000). *Stats in brief: Internet access in U.S. public schools and classrooms: 1994-99.* Retrieved November 20, 2002, from http://nces.ed.gov/pubsearch/pubsinfo.asp?pubid=2000086

Additional Resources

A Frog's Life
www.bgsu.edu/colleges/library/crc/webquest/a_frog.html
This Web site provides well-designed lesson plans for grades 2-3 that include objectives and standards, detailed procedures, and different interesting facts about frogs. Developmental Rating: 7.5

AskERIC Virtual Library
http://askeric.org/Virtual/Lessons
This resource contains hundreds of lesson plans, including, but not limited to, language arts, mathematics, social studies, and science. Developmental Rating: 8.0

Betz's Pet Shop WebQuest
www.geocities.com/mrsevon/webquest.html
Published by Mrs. Evon, a 2nd-grade teacher, the site challenges students to work together to successfully open a new pet shop. Developmental Rating: 7.5

Designing Hermit's New Home
http://projects.edtech.sandi.net/valencia/puppetplay/top.htm
The goal of this lesson is to generate interest in and knowledge about hermit crabs through the introduction of the book *A House for Hermit Crab* by Eric Carle, and then to guide students into researching ocean animals via the Internet. Developmental Rating: 7.5

Filamentality

www.kn.pacbell.com/wired/fil

Filamentality is a fill-in-the-blank interactive Web site that guides teachers and students through picking a topic, searching the Web, gathering good sites, and transforming collected resources into learning activities. Developmental Rating: 7.5

Gateway to Educational Materials (GEM)

www.thegateway.org

A "virtual card catalog," this site connects teachers to lesson plans, activities, projects, and curriculum found all over the Internet. Developmental Rating: 8.0

Homes for Pets

www.michigan.gov/scope/0,1607,7-155-10710_10733_10735-40885—,00.html

In this lesson, children listen as the teacher reads aloud descriptions of homes for various pets and then children do their own research to help them write about the home for their chosen pet. Developmental Rating: 7.5

Kid's Page

www.flbr.org/kidspage.html

This Web site provides a valuable parent guide to facilitate pet safety discussions with children. It also includes pet-related children's books, kid's stories, games, and drawings. Developmental Rating: 7.5

Sounds of the World's Animals

www.georgetown.edu/faculty/ballc/animals/animals.html

This unusual site is the brainchild of Catherine N. Ball, Associate Professor, Department of Linguistics at Georgetown University. It is a collection of animal sounds from around the world, and the ways different languages express these sounds. Developmental Rating: 7.0

Pets at Enchanted Learning

www.enchantedlearning.com/themes/pets.shtml

With an extensive section dedicated to pets, this site features rhymes, crafts, activities, and pet books in English, Spanish, and French. A picture dictionary is available in English, Spanish, Portuguese, Japanese, German, Italian, and French. Developmental Rating: 7.5

Afterword

—Ryan
USA

Mary Renck Jalongo

How do families, educators, and other professionals arrive at the conclusion that companion animals have a rightful place in homes, classrooms, and communities? More often than not, enduring memories from childhood form the foundation for such convictions.

When an apartment building in Nairobi catches fire, residents have just a few seconds to decide what to take with them to safety. A newspaper photographer at the scene captures the image of a young Kenyan boy with a dove nestled against his chest; the bird is irreplaceable to this child. Continents away, in a desperately poor section of New York City, a young girl drops a bag of garbage into a dumpster and hears a sound. She stands on tiptoe to look inside and sees a kitten that is wet, cold, and too weak to stand; someone else's throwaway becomes her treasured pet.

Bring together a group of adults and ask them to describe their most memorable childhood experiences, and bonds with companion animals frequently are mentioned. Adults who are advocates for animals often credit a critical incident in childhood with affecting the course of their lives. Conservationist and animal behavior researcher Jane Goodall (2002) recalls how, when still a toddler, she brought a bunch of earthworms into bed with her. Her mother did not scold or show disgust. Rather, she said with an earnestness that remained with her child forever, "Jane, if you keep them, they'll die. They need the earth" (p. xii).

When adults speak out for animals, they frequently find themselves at odds with their peers and fellow professionals. The struggle described is, in many ways, one of going against the grain of professional training in order to recapture that intense bond of empathy for animals felt during childhood (Schoen, 2001). The conflict is no less keenly felt in education. In the United States, for example, it is common for teachers who want to provide children with a classroom animal companion to do so at their own expense. Furthermore, they often encounter resistance from colleagues and staff. Meanwhile, teachers in the same district who order live animals, such as frogs, for dissection in biology class, have their requests approved, based on past practices. The whole issue of appropriate roles for animals in education needs to be critically re-examined, both in terms of educational value and in terms of ethical treatment (Balcombe, 1999). For example, are there equally effective ways for students to study anatomy (e.g., an interactive computer program) that do not harm animals?

Despite all of the evidence amassed in this book, many adults will no doubt remain unconvinced that companion animals have developmental and educational significance for children. Interestingly, when speaking with such skeptics, their reasons have more to do with the personal absence of childhood bonds with companion animals rather than with the absence of quantitative and qualitative research. Yet close and thoughtful observations of children can soften harsh lines that may have been drawn by adults' lack of opportunity to form positive bonds with companion animals. It is possible to marvel at the sincerity and intensity of a child's response to another species, a response that is less tainted by the customs, routines, and habits that adults may have failed to develop or forgotten to question. If we are sufficiently open-minded, children can take us back not only to old, familiar terrain, but also into uncharted territory. Their reactions often leave an indelible impression, like the one that little Juanita imprinted on me:

A Year of Firsts:
My First Class, Teaching Unit, and Field Trip

My first year as an early childhood educator began by helping to plan and working in a federally funded nursery school in rural Michigan where the sugar beets grow. Many of the families who participated in the program were migrant farm workers or first-generation immigrants from Mexico. Juanita, a 3-year-old, joined our nursery school group reluctantly. She cried frequently when her mother left and could not be coaxed to say much, not even in her first language of Spanish. During our class field trip to a dairy farm, we saw a Holstein calf tied out in the corral. The animal was bawling piteously. The dairy farmer explained that the calf was being weaned and it wanted to stay with its mother in the barn. Suddenly, 3-year-old Juanita crawled through the fence and began speaking to the calf softly in Spanish while gently stroking its neck. Fortunately, the calf was accustomed to being petted because it was a favorite of the farmer's daughter, who had been present when the calf was born. With Juanita's attention, the calf stopped crying immediately, then began to lick her face with its rough tongue. The preschooler was delighted by the calf's response and hugged it around the neck. Although it was difficult to get the pair separated, we finally managed to get Juanita onto the waiting school bus. As the driver pulled away, the calf began to cry again. Tears rolled down Juanita's face as she murmured "pobrecito" ("poor little thing") over and over until, exhausted, she fell asleep in my arms. Why, out of all the animals we saw that day, did Juanita gravitate toward the lonesome little calf? I believe it was because they shared an interspecies bond of empathy. Both young creatures understood what it means to be separated from their loving moms for the first time.

Skeptics might dispute my interpretation of this incident, saying, "You don't have proof that the child connected with the calf." I would argue, however, that my conclusions are based on direct observations of a child's actions (clinging), words ("pobrecito"), and emotional responses (tears).

Children can demonstrate the behaviors of emergent compassion just as surely as they demonstrate the behaviors of emergent literacy. What would our world be like if adults valued those manifestations equally?

From a pedagogical perspective, which lessons about companion animals are most important for children to learn? I would submit that there are at least four. First, children need *to learn tolerance and respect, combined with thoughtfulness and nurturance.* In order to accomplish this, they need adults who reinforce what their children's hearts and fresh perspectives on companion animals tell them: these creatures are sentient beings who experience pleasure and pain, not only physically but also psychologically. In so many subtle and not-so-subtle ways, society tells children this is not so. If a child types a heartfelt story about a companion animal on the computer, the grammar check function will indicate it is incorrect to use "who" in reference to an animal. The personal pronoun is reserved for people; we use "it" to refer to animals, just as we do to inanimate possessions. But children need to get to know companion animals as unique individuals. Two stories by April Boyer, a 1st-grader, illustrate this point. First, she writes a personal narrative about her family's three dogs and her strategy for giving them the attention they crave (see Figure A-1).

Next, April writes a year-long fantasy saga about eight different breeds of dogs—a German shepherd, Labrador retriever, poodle, dachshund, schnauzer, cocker spaniel, collie, and Dalmatian. The dogs are homeless; one is captured by the dog catcher, then rescued by the others (see Figure A-2), then all are put in the pound, where they are miserable. The story has a happy ending as, on the final page of April's book, all of the dogs find a home (see Figure A-3).

Figure A-2

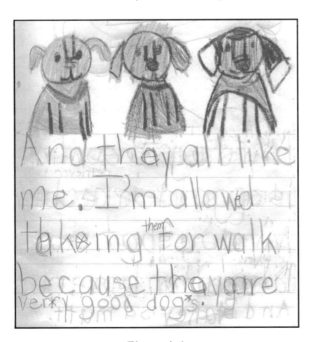

Figure A-1

Figure A-3

A second lesson to be learned through interaction with companion animals is *the importance of acquiring a disposition to seek and apply authoritative information in service to others.* When children conduct research on a companion animal, it is not homework or busy work; rather, it is direct application of research skills to a situation that truly matters. Such investigations yield data that may well determine the quality of the companion animal's life. One 9-year-old yearned to own a bulldog. As she talked with her grandma, the 3rd-grader demonstrated that she had been studying all about the breed on the Internet; she found out, for example, that bulldogs have very sensitive skin. As a result, the folds of a bulldog's skin need to be kept clean, dry, and powdered. The child also reported that bulldogs are not particularly energetic; they can tire easily after a walk and require frequent naps. The grandmother listened attentively, then remarked, "I think a bulldog might be the perfect dog for me—I tire easily, can't walk very far, need my nap, and have to wash and powder my folds, too!" Although the child did not get a bulldog puppy, she eventually did get a dog; she also never forgot that intergenerational meeting of the minds and the sympathetic ally she found in her grandmother. The child who puts an "ethic of caring" (Noddings, 2003) into practice today by researching appropriate care and environments for an animal is more apt tomorrow, as an adult, to have acquired the skills and disposition to locate information that would be of use in other acts of compassion, such as understanding a family member's disease or a neighbor's surgical procedure. Consulting authoritative information in order to understand and help living things is part of the continuum of learning to care.

A third life lesson to be learned through interactions with companion animals is *to appreciate and celebrate human compassion.* Every day, children are barraged by the media with images of excess and greed; of fleeting celebrity and superstardom. Education's role has been, and must continue to be, to stand for something better, to demonstrate that a person's worth and contributions to society are not based purely on physical attractiveness and financial assets. The unsung heroes who care

tenderly for companion animals are an antidote to superficiality. Throughout history, there have been adults among us who have treated all species with care. These individuals often endured the criticism of their contemporaries, who portrayed them as sentimental or unscientific. Yet whether a religious leader such as St. Francis of Assisi, a tribal leader such as Chief Seattle, or a political leader such as Gandhi, the compassion of these individuals prevailed and their kindness became legendary. Their lives demonstrate that abundant kindness transcends the boundaries of the human species to embrace companion animals; children need to know and celebrate the heroism of compassion.

A fourth important lesson for children is *to take positive action on behalf of companion animals.* In education, we are inclined (and increasingly pressured) to set goals and report quantifiable outcomes. Public service can be one of those outcomes. Consider, for example, the experience of a group of middle school students with special needs in an urban school district. Part of the curriculum is a community service project in which the children evaluate and work with homeless animals at the local shelter. The goal is to increase the likelihood of a good match between people and pets. The students' sense of pride in their contributions is reflected in their experience story, which reads:

> *Today we walked one dog. Zach held two cats. The one cat liked Zach. She was purring. She was sitting on Zach's lap. He wanted to hold all three cats, but it was time to go home.*
>
> *Yesterday we walked 3 dogs. They were Honeybun, Angel, and Lightning. They aren't adopted yet. We have worked with 25 dogs. All 25 dogs were adopted. (M. R. Robbins, personal communication, 2003)*

Clearly, this is an important outcome for all concerned—the children and their community, as well as the animals.

Throughout history, many families, educators, and professionals in various fields have believed that companion animals can be a significant force for good in children's lives. Ultimately, adults who welcome a companion animal into their hearts, homes, classrooms, and communities, all the while attending thoughtfully to the animal's needs, are not merely telling children to care; they are demonstrating, by example, a commitment to caring. In a curiously complex and, admittedly, not yet fully understood way, interspecies understanding and compassion is linked to interpersonal understanding. The great humanitarians among us have always known this. Internationally renowned physician Albert Schweitzer once said, "We need a boundless ethic which will include the animals also" (Schoen, 2001, p. 258). It is just such an ethic, an ethic of compassion and generosity, that holds the greatest promise for more responsive parenting, more compassionate teaching, and a more tolerant and just society.

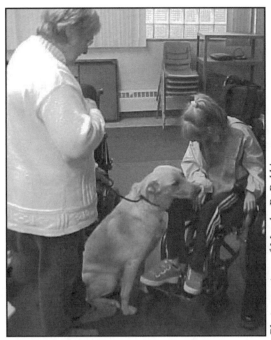

Photo courtesy of Marsha R. Robbins

References

Balcombe, J. (1999). *The use of animals in education: Problems, alternatives, and recommendations.* Washington, DC: Humane Society of the United States.

Goodall, J. (2002). Preface. In M. Bekoff (Ed.), *Minding animals: Awareness, emotions, and heart.* New York: Oxford University Press.

Noddings, N. (2003). *Caring: A feminine approach to ethics and moral education* (2nd ed.). Berkeley, CA: University of California Press.

Schoen, A. M. (2001). *Kindred spirits: How the remarkable bond between humans and animals can change the way we live.* New York: Broadway Books.

About the Authors

Foreword
Michael J. Rosen has created some 25 books for children of all ages, many of them concerned with our relationship to animals. More than a dozen of his books benefit The Company of Animals Fund, a granting program he created in 1990 that supports humane efforts nationwide. Many others support Share Our Strength's (www.strength.org) anti-hunger efforts, a nationwide organization on whose board he has served for a dozen years. He has also created an equal number of books for adults, including the anthologies *Dog People, Horse People,* and the humor biennial, *Mirth of a Nation.* His Web site is www.fidosopher.com.

Editor and Author
Mary Renck Jalongo is the author of over 25 books and Editor in Chief of *Early Childhood Education Journal.* She is a Professor of Education and Coordinator of the Doctoral Program in Curriculum and Instruction at Indiana University of Pennsylvania.

Chapter Authors
Patricia A. Crawford is an Associate Professor in the Department of Teaching and Learning Principles at the University of Central Florida. A former classroom teacher, she now works with graduate and undergraduate students in the areas of language arts, children's literature, and early childhood education.

Anne Drolett Creany teaches undergraduate courses in children's literature and language arts, and she coordinates the Masters in Literacy Program at Indiana University of Pennsylvania, where she is an Associate Professor of Education. She is the author of an ACEI book chapter and article on censorship in children's literature.

Beatrice S. Fennimore is a Professor of Education and Assistant Chairperson of the Professional Studies in the Education Department at Indiana University of Pennsylvania and the author of two books for Teachers College Press.

Yi Gong is a doctoral student in Curriculum and Instruction at Indiana University of Pennsylvania in the Department of Professional Studies in Education. Yi Gong is originally from China and his research interests focus on mathematics and educational technology.

Susan W. Haugland is a Professor of Early Childhood Education in the Department of Teacher Education at Metropolitan State College of Denver. In addition to teaching, she conducts research and provides inservice consulting to schools. She hosts a Web site, childrenandcomputers.com, which provides a variety of resources for effectively utilizing technology with children. Susan Haugland has authored three books and numerous articles focusing on diverse early childhood topics.

Moses M. Mutuku is an Assistant Professor of Early Childhood Education at the Northern Illinois University Department of Teaching and Learning in DeKalb, Illinois. He is originally from Kenya and is the Regional Editor (Africa) for *Early Childhood Education Journal.*

Jyotsna Pattnaik is an Associate Professor of Early Childhood Education at California State University, Long Beach. She teaches graduate-level courses in early childhood education. Her interest and research focus includes multicultural and global education, cross-cultural research, brain research, global child advocacy, technology and pedagogy, and early childhood teacher education. She is editor of the book *Childhood in South Asia: Challenges and Possibilities*, to be published by Information Age Publishing. Jyotsna Pattnaik is originally from India.

Melissa Renck is a children's librarian for the Toledo/Lucas County Public Library system in Ohio. During her career, she has worked with children from urban, suburban, and rural backgrounds. She has also been an assistant editor in young people's literature for Gale Research Company and has co-authored articles in *Childhood Education.*

Marsha R. Robbins is the creator/coordinator of the Pioneer Pet Patrol at the Pioneer Education Center. She has been in Special Education for 30 years, providing services for students with all sorts of challenges across all school age ranges. Animals have always been an important part of the experience that students have in her classrooms. The students who are a part of the Pioneer Pet Patrol learn about different species of companion animals and incorporate the animals into the learning process in school and in the community. The animals have inspired hope in the situations where progress was the most difficult, and enriched the lives of all who chose to participate.

Elma A. Ruiz is currently the Literacy Coordinator, in the Department of Curriculum and Instruction, for the Denver Public Schools. Her areas of expertise include language, literacy, and technology. She has been in the field of education for 19 years and has taught a wide range of levels, spanning from the elementary, secondary, and through the graduate level for teachers seeking to increase their skills in meeting the needs of English language learners.

Marjorie L. Stanek is a graduate student in sociology at Indiana University of Pennsylvania. Her senior year research project in sociology at James Madison University focused on the topic of children and their companion animals. In 2003, she was named outstanding sociology student at JMU.

Chapter Contributors

Jeffrey C. Brewster is a teacher librarian at the International School of Brussels, Regional Editor (Europe) for *Early Childhood Education Journal,* and a doctoral student at the University of Bath in the United Kingdom.

Mark G. Twiest is a science educator in the Department of Professional Studies in Education at Indiana University of Pennsylvania. He has been active in the Pennsylvania Science Teachers Association and the Council for Elementary Science International serving on the Board of Directors for both of these organizations. He has made numerous presentations and authored articles concerning science education for the past 25 years. His experience with animals in both traditional and nontraditional settings is extensive. He is the former Director of Science at the Museum of Arts and Science in Macon, Georgia.

Meghan M. Twiest is a science educator in the Department of Professional Studies in Education at Indiana University of Pennsylvania. She teaches many aspects of animal care and integration into the curriculum in her science methods course. Therapy dogs have been welcome guests in her classroom as she teaches about the advantages of the exposure of young children to animals. She has been an active member and presenter at the National Science Teachers Association, and the Pennsylvania Science Teachers Association for the past 20 years.

Mimi Brodsky Chenfeld is an educational consultant and well-known keynote speaker in the field of early childhood education. She recently published a book, with Heinemann, on children's creativity.

Dana M. Monroe is the Director of Education Services for Autistic Children in Pennsylvania. She runs two programs that focus on changing behaviors and increasing communication for children diagnosed with autism and other related developmental disorders. She oversees a private school for children with autism as well as a behavioral health rehabilitation service.

Nancy Patterson-Uhron is a licensed practical nurse as well as the Community Director of Personal Ponies, Ltd. at Simple Blessings Farm in Shelocta, Pennsylvania. The farm is home to many "child-size" animals—UK Shetland ponies, pygmy goats, a miniature burro, and Shetland sheepdogs.

Contributors of Photographs and Children's Work

Mariah N. Benjamin
Jeffrey Brewster
Darrell Combs
Natalie K. Conrad
Alexandra Creany
Shireen DeSouza
Debra A. Gloster
Xiaoping Li
Amanda Miloser
Colleen Myers
Reade Paterno
Nancy Patterson-Uhron
Jyotsna Pattnaik
Marsha R. Robbins
Sara Rutledge
Mark, Meghan, and Burkely Twiest
Eleanor Winsheimer
Ann Zhang
Ming Zhang